The Key
to Ultimate
Health

RESEARCHERS WORLDWIDE ARE
CONCLUDING THAT A VITAL KEY TO
WELLNESS HAS BEEN OVERLOOKED –
AND IT'S RIGHT UNDER YOUR NOSE!

by
ELLEN HODGSON BROWN, J.D.
and
RICHARD T. HANSEN, D.M.D., F.A.C.A.D.

The Key to Ultimate Health

Researchers worldwide are concluding that a vital key to wellness has been overlooked - and it's right under your nose!

Published by:

Advanced Health Research Publishing
1943 Sunnycrest Drive, Suite 183
Fullerton, CA 92835

ISBN#: 1-879854-25-2

Additional copies of this book may be ordered directly from the publisher, Advanced Health Research Publishing, by calling:

1-888-792-1102

PRINTED IN THE UNITED STATES OF AMERICA

Dedication

To Albert Hodgson, who has Alzheimer's disease, and Genevieve Hodgson, who has devoted herself to his care.

Ellen Hodgson Brown, J.D.

To my parents who guided me by example; taught me to constantly ask questions and desire knowledge and truth; and value the highest standard of moral obligation.

Richard T. Hansen, D.M.D., F.A.C.A.D.

Preface

WARMING UP TO THE SUBJECT

All joys I bless, but I confess
There is one greatest thrill;
What the dentist does when he stops the buzz
And puts away the drill.

— Christopher Morley,
"Song in a Dentist's Chair" (1943)

"We've located the root of your problem," said my health practitioner after doing electro-dermal screening. "You need more dental work!"

Needless to say, I did not consider this good news. The only good news I ever remembered getting about my teeth, in fact, was that I did <u>not</u> need more dental work. Some of my most traumatic experiences had been in the dental chair. I disliked the whole subject, and had managed to avoid it for a number of years. The last time I had done a significant stretch in the chair was about eight years earlier, when in a fit of zeal I had had all my silver/mercury amalgam fillings removed and replaced with composite (plastic) materials. I went through that daunting experience because I had become convinced, after reading the literature, that mercury amalgam is a serious health hazard. Indeed, my health seemed to improve after that. I no longer suffered from the chronic fatigue that had plagued my earlier adulthood. But I couldn't exactly call myself the picture of health. And now I was being advised to get the <u>composites</u> replaced. Supposedly, they were shutting down the critical energetic fields running through my teeth. The recommended replacement material was one said to be so like the natural tooth that it could actually "heal" itself.

I ignored the advice until two of my old crowns broke. There was no alternative but to climb back into the chair. This dental experience wound up including a root canal; yet it was surprisingly pain-free. For several days after that, I actually felt euphoric. Then there was a detox phase, but I had been warned to expect it: my body was dumping toxins. And after about three months, I found I had more vitality than I'd had in years. Bolstered by this experience, I proceeded to have my remaining composites and porcelain crowns replaced with biocompatible materials, with quite remarkable effects on my energy level and overall health.

My attitude toward dentistry has now changed so completely that I feel compelled to write about its virtues. I can write freely about dental issues because I am not a dentist. My professional specialty is the practice of law. Observing cases in court involving alternative medical practices has led me to appreciate the fearless efforts of those dental pioneers who have risked their licenses and their professional standing in the pursuit of excellence in dentistry.

In a survey published in Dentist magazine in 1989, more than a third of dentists said they believed all silver (mercury) alloy fillings should be removed and replaced with alternative materials. But the dentists dared not make that recommendation to their patients, because the American Dental Association's Code of Professional Conduct currently provides that it is improper and unethical for a dentist to recommend the removal of mercury amalgam restorations except for cosmetic reasons.[1]

Professional constraints aside, the materials and procedures discussed in the following chapters have become available so recently that most dentists aren't even aware of them. They aren't taught in dental schools at the undergraduate level; and even if they were, most practicing dentists would have graduated before the new techniques made it onto the curriculum. The dentists' union, the ADA, is also an unreliable source, for political reasons to be discussed hereafter.

My own principal source is Richard Hansen, D.M.D., the dentist who did the dental work that transformed my health. Dr. Hansen teaches continuing education in dentistry at UCLA and has a private practice in Fullerton, California. He was also one of five dentists conducting the research required for FDA approval of the dental use of lasers for removing cavities, which was granted in the summer of 1997. That development is slated to revolutionize dentistry. One of Dr. Hansen's goals has been to educate and change the scope and nature of dental practice — to make dentistry more patient friendly, more sought after, and definitely more healthy. To this end he has appeared on numerous talk shows and news stories showcasing the gentle, advanced, dentistry of the future. His credits include the "Phil Donahue Show," "Southland Today," "NBC Extra," The Discovery Channel's "Next Step," "NBC Evening News" with Tom Brokaw, C/ Net's "The New Edge," NBC's "Dateline," ABC's "Good Morning America," Lifetime's "New Attitudes," and many other national news segments, magazine and newspaper stories.

Although technological advances have diminished my personal fears of dentistry, I remain concerned for my children. One legacy I want to leave them is a mouth free of the toxic materials that impaired their mother's health from early adulthood, and that recent studies suggest may have contributed to their grandfather's Alzheimer's disease. I'm informed that if a tooth makes it through the first 18 or 20 years without cavities, with proper diet and reasonable hygiene it will probably make it for life, since most adult caries are in teeth that have already been weakened with toxic filling materials. But how can kids' teeth be preserved for the first 18 or 20 years? Fluoride, I learned on researching it, not only isn't a foolproof solution but may be highly toxic itself. Sealants, another popular option, aren't ideal solutions either. "Sealed" teeth can decay at their bases and sides; and most sealants leak and fail and like composites block the energetic fields running through the teeth.

Further research revealed that the key to prevention has been known for decades; but the information has been either ignored or suppressed, perhaps because there was no money in it. That key is the subject of the concluding section of this book.

Section I begins with a look at a new paradigm in medicine that recognizes the electromagnetic nature of the body, and at the overlooked but critical role of the teeth in it.

Ellen Hodgson Brown
Guatemala City, Guatemala
December 24, 1997

Table of Contents

Section III. Beyond Dentistry: Perfect Teeth/Perfect Health

Introduction

BY RICHARD T. HANSEN, D.M.D., F.A.C.A.D.

Patients today are increasingly taking more responsibility for their own health care. They tend to be well read, educated by previous health experiences, and much more discriminating in their choice of practitioners and treatment methods. As health practitioners struggling with the complex task of helping these patients achieve optimum wellness, we are constantly searching for the information that best answers their questions and offers solutions to their health concerns.

Our task is complicated by genetics, the environment, nutrition, emotional, and personal habits that compromise and influence our patients' health. These influences include the subtle but powerful adverse effects of dental materials and procedures on the body. If we look at optimum wellness and longevity as a complex picture composed of many puzzle pieces, we find a multitude of influences on our health. Each of these pieces needs to be balanced with the specific needs of the individual in order to ensure as long a life as possible free of disease. We begin our journey in life with certain genetic weaknesses and predispositions toward the breakdown of one biologic system or another. But researchers are coming to appreciate that diseases once attributed to the inevitability of genetics and age can actually be avoided by proper care of the body and the mind. Our bodies have the ability to overcome their inherent system weaknesses if the entire system is maintained at its peak performance level, enabling it to repair itself upon injury and resist the countless negative influences that attack it daily.

In determining the patient's unique needs, it is becoming increasingly important for the dentist to work with other cutting-edge, integrative practitioners to fully assess the individual requirements of the patient before, during and after dental care. We have been fortunate to have worked with many physicians, chiropractors, acupuncturists, nutritionists, ayurvedics and other advanced health care practitioners not only for this purpose but for investigating and developing better methods of delivering advanced dental care — dental care that not only focuses on disease within the mouth but recognizes the integral role optimum oral health plays in the overall long-term health of the body. We are learning how important it is to save as much of the natural tooth structure as possible; and with the materials and procedures now available, much more of it can be preserved than has ever been possible before.

In the past, dentists did not think about dental materials and treatments as they related to the whole body, and they were limited by the materials and techniques available. Today, much more is known about the subtle interactions between the teeth and the whole body system, and the negative effects of many materials, techniques and therapies dental professionals have used for decades without a second thought. We have learned about the systemic effects of localized foci of infection; the fact that placement of metal and alloy fillings can weaken the tooth so that future, more invasive dentistry becomes necessary; the leaking of mercury into body tissues from dental amalgam fillings (now known to occur at the alarming rate of 3 to 17 micrograms per day); the relation of the tooth and jaw position to the natural balance of the human system; and the electric current-generated, corrosive, effects of having mixed metals present in the oral environment. Health practitioners using advanced screening methods have concluded that tooth-colored composite materials containing petroleum products, metal oxides, aluminum, petrochemicals or bis-phenols may be worse for long-term health than the mercury alloys they are replacing.

The traditional style of dentistry has been to treat early, small cavities in children and adults with silver/mercury alloy fillings that necessitated drilling away large amounts of good tooth structure just to wedge the filling in the tooth and make it stay. These fillings profoundly weakened the tooth thereby setting it up for additional decay, fracture, corrosion, and breakage. This invariably leads to much larger fillings, crowns, and in many cases root canals. The new advanced style of dentistry is to preserve as much tooth structure as possible, fill the teeth early with biocompatible materials, and structurally reinforce teeth to prevent further problems.

Until now, most dentists have been reluctant to change materials and techniques because the alternatives to traditional dental therapy were not adequate. But research and development during the last five years have produced dental materials that are not only more biologically compatible than the traditional dental amalgam, but that are stronger and can actually reinforce the tooth internally thereby preventing further damage and need for future dentistry. There are now over one hundred different ceramic, glass-ceramic, and ceramic polymers that are superior to the older restorative materials in terms of both strength and function. In addition, we can now treat small decayed areas with a pin-point laser or air particle beam, inject in a tooth replacement, and fuse the material with a laser to the tooth. These techniques not only preserve the strength and beauty of the tooth, but may keep the tooth from needing future, more destructive dentistry. By using these techniques early on, we may be able to eliminate the need for most root canals and crowns; maybe even eliminate the need for most adult dentistry. After all the best dentistry would be to not need any dentistry at all.

Research has been proceeding so rapidly, however, that most dental practitioners, — even those who practice more biologically-oriented dentistry — do not understand the properties and proper placement techniques required for using these more advanced materials. There is no widely available educational source where dental practitioners can learn the precise indications for materials selection and the technique-sensitive restorative methods unique to each patient's needs. The Pacific Institute for Advanced Dental Studies was created to respond to this problem. With the help of the Advanced Health Research Foundation, we are compiling research, educational materials and faculty to provide practitioners in all fields of health care with the most up-to-date information necessary to better serve patients. The Pacific Institute will also provide a program to help educate and train dental professionals, their staff, and interested health care professionals on advanced dentistry as it relates to total patient care. Professionals who have completed advanced training become members of the American College For Advancement In Dentistry. This provides a vehicle for continuing the process of education, keeping up with future advances, and to contribute ideas, thoughts, and research, toward advanced, future dentistry so that all may benefit.

We are propelled by a strong sense of urgency and mission in publicizing both the new methods and techniques, and the little-appreciated hazards of the conventional alternatives. Dentists are still grinding perfectly viable teeth down to 'pegs' and placing potentially toxic metal crowns on them, when techniques are now available for repairing the damaged part of the tooth with wholly biocompatible materials, leaving the bulk of the natural tooth intact. Dentists are still placing huge amalgam "plugs" in the center of viable teeth, wedging the cusps apart and leading to inevitable leakage and breakage, when techniques are now available for placing materials that not only don't force the cusps apart but help "weld" them together, strengthening rather than weakening the tooth.

Besides researching the latest in dental materials and techniques to provide viable alternatives to traditional dental care, one of the primary goals of our facility is advancement of our profession through education. Our center also provides information on advanced dentistry to interested professionals and others on request. If you have any questions regarding any of these topics or wish a referral to an advanced, integrative health practitioner, you may call our facility at 1-800-9-LASER-0 or the Advanced Health Research Foundation at 1-888-792-1102.

Richard E. Hansen, D.M.D., F.A.C.A.D.
Director, Center for Advanced Dentistry
Fullerton, California

SECTION I

THE MISSING LINK:
THE MIND/BODY/MOUTH CONNECTION

Chapter 1

The Millennial Paradigm

Aging is a mistake.

—Deepak Chopra, M.D.

An exciting new paradigm is emerging in medicine. The goal until now has been merely damage control — patching up holes in a leaking boat. The old paradigm involved cutting out disease with surgery or poisoning it with toxic chemicals and radiation, in the hope that the disease would succumb before the patient did; or masking symptoms with drugs that turned off the pain that constituted the body's alarm system, leaving the fire to rage until it finally consumed the patient. The new paradigm sees the body as self-healing — and as capable, at least in theory, of eternal youth and eternal life.

Dr. Julian Whitaker, an author and physician in Newport Beach, California, writes in his book 'Guide To Natural Healing' "One problem with our current health care system is its focus on treating disease rather than promoting wellness. The majority of our health care dollars — over $700 billion — is going towards the treatment of conditions that are largely preventative.

Geneticists are now mapping the genes that direct us to get old. Anti-aging researchers, studying an area at the tip of the chromosome that appears to shorten with age, are theorizing that if the chemical fire that shortens this tip can be extinguished, so can aging itself. Other scientists are studying how cells can be cleaned of waste products, extending their viability. And scientists who believe in nanotechnology — technology that operates at the molecular level — predict that we will one day be able to build microscopic robots that will fight disease, excise tumors and clean clogged arteries at the cellular level.[1]

Cutting-edge medical doctors are also maintaining that aging is reversible. Deepak Chopra, M.D., a popular author and founder of the Chopra Center for Well Being in La Jolla, Ca., writes, "If DNA can manage to make perfect arteries for five hundred centuries, each one containing millions of perfectly operating cells, there is no intrinsic reason why *your* DNA should botch the job after sixty years." According to the Indian Ayurvedic philosophy Dr. Chopra espouses, aging is a mistake of thinking. In 1978, he observes, a team of researchers made the remarkable discovery that transcendental meditation could retard or even reverse the aging process.[2] Other researchers are discovering that this process can be reversed with certain natural substances, including antioxidants, hormone replacement therapy, melatonin, and the hormone precursors DHEA and pregnenolone.

Andrew Weil, M.D., a professor at the University of Arizona College of Medicine and another very popular M.D./ author, attributes the current revolution in medical thinking to the health care crisis. "The ship is sinking," he asserts. "Conventional medicine is going down the tubes." Hospitals are going bankrupt. The insurance system is breaking down. There is real desperation in the system and a corresponding willingness to look at alternatives. This does not mean that alternative care will replace conventional medical care. If you have an acute health need, then acute care medicine will always be the best option. Rather, alternative care may well be the best option for early, interceptive, preventive medicine — an option for working with the mind/body's natural energy and immune system to prevent disease and illness. Dr. Weil believes that the future of our health care system depends on the integration of alternative therapies with current accepted medical practices.

The alternative therapy that is currently most well-accepted among doctors, says Dr. Weil, is acupuncture. Acupuncture treatment is popular in hospitals for pain relief, and training programs are widely available for M.D.'s. Yet Chinese acupuncture is based on a totally different paradigm from Western medicine. It is a functional rather than a structural system, aimed at correcting imbalances in an energy field that Western medicine doesn't even recognize. Acknowledging that acupuncture works means accepting that the body is criss-crossed with a system of energy meridians that can be stimulated with tiny needles. This notion, says Dr. Weil, was akin to Voodoo when he was at Harvard Medical School in the sixties. Acupuncture is a form of energy medicine that has become accepted remarkably quickly.[3]

The Ayurvedic medicine taught by Dr. Chopra is another functional system that works with subtle energies. Ayurvedic doctors consider disease to be an imbalance of "dosha" (the flow of energy). They practice a form of preventive medicine based on detoxification and cleansing of the mind as well as the body. Effects may take longer than in Western medicine, but the result is said to be permanent, since it reaches the actual cause of disease.

Can alternative therapies really reverse disease, prevent illness, and delay aging? Is the answer to our deteriorating health care system the integration of complimentary treatment options that focus on wellness rather than illness — as well as focusing on the whole individual not just the disease? According to James Gordon, M.D., author of 'Manifesto For A New Medicine' and director of The Center For Mind-Body Medicine in Washington, D.C., "Large numbers of Americans have already decided to find the answers. A definitive survey of 'Unconventional Medicine in the United States' published in the New England Journal of Medicine in 1993 indicated that more than one third of the adult population was, in 1990, making 425 million visits to practitioners of alternative therapies — a number of visits that exceeds those made to all primary care physicians."

Heal the Mind — Heal the Body

Over the last two hundred years, the direction and focus of conventional or allopathic medicine has been based on scientific and technological advances. Along with the rise and influence of the pharmaceutical industry on medical education and practice, modern, science-based medicine has primarily focused on three treatment modalities — drugs, surgery, and radiation. In the case of acute care medical need or trauma, no other form of medicine can perform such heroic feats or obtain such miraculous results as scientific medicine. However, along the way conventional, scientific medicine has narrowed its focus to the disease and not on the patient as a whole. Patients often comment that they feel they are being looked at as walking stomachs, gall bladders, hearts, or whatever is the source of their disease. Perhaps that is one reason that alternative, integrative care is rising so rapidly in popularity. The focus of alternative care is centered around the patient as a whole — physical, biochemical, emotional, and spiritual.

More and more advanced health-care practitioners have recognized that optimal healing and wellness cannot take place unless the mind is treated along with the body. Christiane Northrup, M.D. writes in 'Women's Bodies, Women's Wisdom' "Healing occurs when you align with the pure, positive energy that created the planet — and that keeps your heart beating and your blood chemistry normal. Healing occurs when you release all yourself to be well. Healing occurs when you're in harmony with your life's purpose and those who are meant to accompany you on this path. Healing occurs when you've created a sense of safety and security in your life. Healing is a major leap of faith in this culture." The energy of the mind may well be one of the most powerful of influences on our total health puzzle. Without a powerful belief system composed of both faith and hope our immune system will not function at peak performance. Likewise if our mind is clouded with negativity and hostile feelings optimal health cannot be achieved and our bodies are hindered in their ability to fight disease and illness. At a recent seminar, Ellen Kamhi, Ph.D., R.N., presented a dramatic video tape taken of a patient's white blood cells under a microscope. As irritating vibrational sound energy was directed at the patient, his white blood cells became inactive. As pleasant sounds and meditation influenced the patient the white blood cells once again became active able to defend the body. Remember, this was under a microscope outside the patient's body, indicating an energy that connected the cells to the body.

Another video tape demonstrated that this unseen energy can transcend distance to influence biologic activity. The patient's cells were again observed in the laboratory with an accurate recording of the time of cellular activity. This time the patient traveled some distance on a trip. An observer accompanied him and recorded the daily events as well as the precise time of these events. When the results were correlated, the stressful activity in the patient's daily life corresponded to the exact time of decreased immune potential of the cells; while the peaceful, relaxed state of the patient correlated to enhanced potential.

Group prayer and devout belief in God have also been shown to repeatedly increase one's ability to recover from disease and speed healing. Neale Donald Walsch in his moving book 'Conversations With God' describes the human body that God has given us as miraculously perfect in it's capacity to repair and heal itself. By combining the energies of the spiritual with the psycho-physical energy of ones own body, anything is possible or as Bernie Siegel, M.D. says "Miracles can happen." Neale Walsch writes that "You can solve your health problems by solving the problems in your thinking. Yes, you can heal some of the conditions you have already acquired (given yourself), as well as prevent major new problems from developing. And you can do this all by changing your thinking." In other words disease can be either created or corrected by our thinking. We literally make ourselves sick! He also writes "Worry is just about the worst form of mental activity there is — next to hate, which is deeply self destructive. Worry is pointless. It is wasted mental energy. It also creates bio-chemical reactions which harm the body, producing everything from indigestion to coronary arrest, and a multitude of things in between."

This can be illustrated by the example of a patient that was recently referred to my office to evaluate the biocompatibility of recent dental work and potential areas of bone necrosis. She was gravely ill having suffered with a degenerative disease for over five years which had been getting progressively worse. She had been treated by nearly every conventional medical specialty with little or no results except for temporary relief of some symptoms. For the past two years she had sought hope in alternative therapies and received much greater improvement through nutritional support, acupuncture, and chelation therapy. She also had all her dental work redone with what she thought were biocompatible materials and had several root canaled teeth pulled along with very aggressive, destructive cavitational surgery that left little bone to replace the missing teeth. However, her condition had begun to deteriorate and she had become quite angry and depressed. During her new patient interview, she was blaming everyone and everything for her lack of wellness and her inability to recover from her disease. She was actually blaming her family for causing her diseased state in the first place. In addition she was accusing all her practitioners, conventional and alternative, of a lack of skill, knowledge, and ability to heal. She called her last dentist a "butcher" for destroying so much of her face from the cavitational surgeries. As I listened patiently to her entire history, it seemed obvious to me that she had not accepted the fact that this is her disease and it is her responsibility for healing and wellness — not her doctors. I recognized that unless she accepted this and forgave all those who had 'wronged' her and stopped being angry at everyone including God for 'giving' her this disease, she would not have a chance at wellness. I also recognized that I would be the next 'victim' of her wrath and could not possibly achieve any success in treating her.

Understanding that this woman needed help, I asked myself 'What can I possibly do for her?' And 'How can I begin to help her?' without hurting myself in the process. The first step was to tell her that I would not treat her, unless she would agree to read a book that I gave her on mind/body medicine and consult with a practitioner that I use frequently on this subject. Fortunately for both of us she had a strong desire to get well and was open to these suggestions. She did as requested and instantly her attitude toward herself, her body, and her disease improved. After I felt that her mind was allowing her body to start down the road to wellness, I replaced some obvious materials that were energy blockades and performed a minor surgical procedure to remove some residual necrotic bone from a previous cavitational surgery. She continued to receive nutritional therapy, acupuncture, chelation and perform daily meditation. It has been a year since her last dental treatment and she has continued to make dramatic improvements in her health. She says she feels better than she has in fifteen years. With many patients we find the dental care is of primary importance, however in her case I believed it to be a minor influencer. I believe her spiritual and emotional states may have actually been the major contribution to her disease, and that no healing could take place until her mind would free the natural immune response and allow the other alternative therapies to benefit.

Joan Borysenko, Ph.D. writes in her book 'Minding the Body, Mending the Mind' that each of us is inherently created perfect with both good and bad emotions. Emotions are human and natural. Each of us also has emotional mind traps, such as denial, overexpression, and repression, that can lead to anger, rage, conflict, and hostility all of which have been linked to psychosomatic illness and a depressed immune system. Each of us must learn how to handle our good and bad feelings and develop a healthy attitude toward our emotions and our bodies. She writes "There are three attitudes toward the emotions that lead to their constructive use. 1. It's natural and human to experience emotions. 2. You are entitled to feel however you are feeling whether or not the emotion is 'justified.' And 3. Negative emotions are a real opportunity to enhance self-understanding." Our goal is to first recognize and understand our emotional style and restore balance to the emotions. When we achieve this balance we can begin to utilize the positive emotions to enhance our immune system and anything becomes possible. Bernie Siegel, M.D. writes in his book 'Love, Medicine and

Miracles' that "Unconditional love is the most powerful stimulant of the immune system. The truth is: love heals. Miracles happen to exceptional patients every day — patients who have the courage to love, those who have the courage to work with their doctors to participate in and influence their own recovery."

Self-healing

Dr. Herbert Benson, author of 'The Relaxation Response' and 'Timeless Healing', is founder and director of the Mind/Body Medical Institute in Massachusetts. He feels that the medicine of the future will be like a "three-legged stool" composed of self-care, medications (pharmaceutical and botanical), and procedures. There are substantial economic incentives and enormous cost savings that can be achieved by incorporating these mind/body influences and recognizing the value of self-care. The ability of the body to heal, repair, and eliminate disease by using the inherent energy of the mind is actually not a new concept. A flow of healing energy that allows the body to self-correct was actually recognized by Hippocrates, the father of modern Western medicine. His two most widely-quoted maxims are "first do no harm" and "honor the healing power of nature." Hippocrates called this healing energy "physis." Chinese acupuncturists call it "ch'i." Indian yogis call it "prana." Naturopathic doctors refer to "vis medicatrix naturae" (Latin for "the healing power of nature"). Homeopathic doctors call it the "vital force." Alternative medical systems see disease as a cleansing process, the attempt of a body out of balance to right itself. The appropriate treatment, from this perspective, is whatever it takes to put the system back into balance so the natural recuperative powers of the body can function unimpaired. How the therapist stimulates and balances the body's natural forces varies with the system, but in all of them the underlying principle is the same. In acupuncture, it means stimulating the "meridians," or lines of energy, that run through the affected areas. In Ayurveda, it means treating the patient not the disease through a complete system of health for mind, body and spirit. In chiropractic, it means adjusting vertebrae that may be affecting the nervous system and the body's natural defense mechanisms. In nutritional therapy, it means balancing the body's chemistry through diet and nutritional supplements to augment what foods may be lacking. In homeopathy, it means administering substances which, in healthy people in larger doses, produce the very symptoms of the patient; but in the patient in minute doses, they stimulate the natural defenses and recuperative powers of the body.

Under the homeopathic principle of "vitalism" or "vital force," humans have an innate energy that promotes life and encourages homeostasis (balance). Treatments that are effective over the long-term stimulate this life force. Treatments that block the life force may effectively suppress symptoms, but they are counter-productive for long-term recovery.

Unblocking the Life Force

The phenomena known as "spontaneous remission" and "the placebo effect" attest to the power of the body to heal itself under certain optimum conditions. But what are those conditions? Obvious factors include diet, appropriate nutritional support, exercise, fresh air, sufficient sleep, and stress-free thinking. Beyond that, obstructions to healing need to be removed. Cure depends on an immune system and bodily organs that are intact and functioning normally. Healing requires not only feeding and stimulating the life force but clearing a path so this force can get through. Factors that act to suppress the body's natural healing ability need to be avoided or eliminated.

Homeopaths list among those life-force suppressing factors various conventional medical treatments, including cancer chemotherapy and radiation, surgery that produces dead scar tissue, steroids, painkillers, drugs that suppress fever (a natural healing reaction that "cooks out" germs), and antibiotics (which kill germs, but do it without stimulating the body's own immune system. Many feel that the waste products of this 'antibiotic kill' may be quite damaging to our long term health). Other factors considered to suppress the body's healing power include previous surgeries, missing organs, a previous history of drug-taking (legal or illegal), smoking, alcohol, poor nutrition, stress, hereditary conditions including birth defects and obstructions, and dental fillings of non-biocompatible materials.[4]

New evidence suggests that removing this last obstruction is particularly critical for many people and that without it other therapies may not be effective. If the body is criss-crossed with energy meridians, the mouth is a switchboard through which virtually all of them pass. German research indicates that the majority of the "interference fields" blocking the body's energy meridians arise in the teeth. Once thought to be isolated structures that could be altered without affecting the rest of the body, the teeth are now recognized as integral parts of a living system, interacting chemically and electromagnetically with the whole. The mouth may indeed be the missing link in our total health puzzle and many advanced, integrative health practitioners are beginning to appreciate the 'Mind-Body-Mouth' connection.

Chapter 2

Reversing Disease:
The Critical Role of the Teeth

> The body has an amazing ability to heal itself. Only a few things impede that process: environmental chemicals, viruses, and heavy metals.
> —Stephen Edelson, M.D.,
> Director of the Environmental and
> Preventive Health Center in Atlanta, Georgia[1]

In 1988, notes Dr. Chopra, the notion that heart disease might be reversible was a revolutionary one. That was the year that Dr. Dean Ornish, a San Francisco cardiologist, proved that the fatty plaque deposits blocking the coronary arteries of advanced heart patients could be made to shrink using natural therapies alone. The therapies used in his study were a strict low-cholesterol diet, meditation and yoga. The official position of conventional medicine before that was that heart disease progressed inexorably to the patient's death, no matter what he ate, did or believed.[2]

Since then, evidence has been accumulating that many chronic degenerative diseases previously blamed on irreversibly defective genes are actually diseases of civilization, which can be reversed by lifestyle changes, detoxification, and the removal of blocks to strategic energy meridians.

In 1997, W. John Diamond, M.D., and W. Lee Cowden, M.D., in collaboration with Burton Goldberg and a long list of M.D. contributors, published the 1,120-page Alternative Medicine Definitive Guide to Cancer. Its authors boldly assert that "cancer can be successfully reversed using alternative medicine." They ascribe the disease to multiple factors impinging on the body.

Factors cited as contributing not only to cancer but to other chronic degenerative diseases include energy blockages and toxicity from mercury amalgam dental fillings. Symptoms ascribed to mercury toxicity include fatigue, depression, anorexia, insomnia, arthritis, moodiness, irritability, memory loss, nausea, diarrhea, gum disease, swollen glands, and headaches, among others. The authors note that methylmercury (to which elemental mercury is converted by bacteria in the mouth) easily crosses the blood-brain barrier, where it has been linked to various chronic neurodegenerative diseases.[3]

Reversing Disease: The Dental Connection

Dental factors have been associated not only with the cause but also with the cure of chronic disease. A number of cases are on record in which "incurable" conditions have been reversed following dental overhaul. They include the following published examples:

Alzheimer's Disease Reversed

Tom Warren, in a book called Beating Alzheimer's, attests that his own diagnosed case of Alzheimer's disease was reversed after he had all of his teeth pulled and replaced with dentures. His teeth had harbored 28 amalgam fillings. He also had chelation treatments and took homeopathic remedies to remove heavy metals from his tissues, changed his diet, took heavy doses of nutritional supplements, and eliminated environmental toxins and allergens from his surroundings. He maintains that his is the first case on record in which Alzheimer's disease has been reversed. Other cases he cites for this remarkable phenomenon include that of a physician who recovered from the disease in a stunning two hours, after the removal of 13 teeth containing root canals.[4]

Multiple Sclerosis Reversed

In December of 1990, "Sixty Minutes" featured the amalgam issue. Among other testimonials, a woman on the segment asserted that she had had multiple sclerosis so severe that she was unable to walk unassisted, could not hold a pencil, and could not speak properly. The day after she had five mercury amalgam dental fillings removed, her voice returned and she went out dancing: "It was that quick," she said.

Parkinson's Disease Alleviated

Thomas Levy, M.D., a doctor in Colorado Springs, Colorado, describes this memorable case:

> One of my own patients had such an advanced neurological syndrome, previously diagnosed as Parkinsonism, that he literally resembled a piece of wood in my office, unable even to bend and conform appropriately to his wheelchair. He could neither move his head, make facial expressions, nor talk. The extent of his contact with the world was limited to squeezing his sister's hand with his right hand. In less than two weeks, after total dental revision, he was moving his head, smiling, moving all of his limbs, crying for joy, and forming his first simple words in a long time. No amount of cynicism from any of my medical or dental colleagues will convince me that my trained medical eyes didn't see what they saw . . . I saw life return.[5]

Arthritis Reversed

Weston Price, D.D.S., M.S., F.A.C.D., president and first director of the American Dental Association Research Institute, reported the case of a woman patient who had arthritis so severe she was confined to a wheelchair. Medical science could find no cause or cure for her condition. Dr. Price extracted a tooth with a root canal from her mouth, then planted the tooth under the skin of a rabbit. Within two days, the rabbit had developed the same debilitating arthritis as the patient. The woman, meanwhile, began to improve. She eventually recovered from her disease and was able to walk.

Dr. Price was so impressed with this case that he continued a further 25 years of research in the field, involving hundreds of patients and thousands of rabbits. Being nothing if not thorough, he used the same tooth or shavings from it in a minimum of thirty rabbits (an affront to the species for which he apologized profusely). He found that the diseases of his patients could consistently be duplicated in the test animals, not only by implanting them with root-filled teeth, but simply by injecting them with a sterilized powder made from the teeth. Evidently, this powder contained the disease-producing toxins created by the tooth's bacteria. When Dr. Price implanted healthy teeth or sterilized coins in the rabbits, by contrast, nothing detrimental happened to the animals.

Diseases that were linked in this way to infected root canals included heart and circulatory problems (heart blocks, angina, arteriosclerosis, anemia, myocarditis, endocarditis, high and low blood pressure, etc.); kidney, liver and gallbladder problems; back, neck and shoulder pains; neuritis; neuralgia; appendicitis; pneumonia; rheumatism; shingles; arthritis; eye, ear and skin conditions; stomach ulcers; ovarian cysts; and intestinal disturbances. Dr. Price observed that angina pectoris, phlebitis, hypertension, heart block, anemia, and inflammation of the heart muscle were often side effects of root canal therapy in humans. Remarkably, these symptoms resolved when the offending teeth were removed.[6] Many dental practitioners state that while his research in the 1920's and 30's was extensive, his results have not been duplicated except for subjective anecdotal reports.

Cancer and Other Chronic Conditions Reversed

The medical specialty of Mulhim Hassan, M.D., was actually diseases of the eye. He was prompted to study the link between dental infection and other bodily disease by his personal experience. His right foot had been painful and swollen for eight months. He had chest pain in his heart, a recurrent fibrillation (muscle contraction) in his left shoulder muscles, a thirteen-year-old claudication (limp) in his right knee, and a ten-year-old disc problem in his back that was torturously painful. All of these problems were completely and permanently cured when, against the advice of dentists, he had all of his pyorrhetic (infected) teeth removed.

Dr. Hassan followed up on this enlightening discovery by studying his patients. "By 1970," he wrote, "I had enough cases to prove that all body diseases I met, treated, and cured were caused by foci of infection in the mouth or were related to them . . . . Many cases, considered hopeless, were completely cured, sometimes in a short time."

His cases included cancer, prompting him to write a book called The Prevention and Cure of Cancer. He observed that cancer is almost always preceded by inflammation; and that in his experience, the inflammation could always be traced to an acute apical abscess (inflammation in the root of a tooth). Diseases he cured in his patients by treating these focal infections included not only eye conditions (cataracts, glaucoma, iritis, retinal detachment, and styes), but tumors and cancers of all types, migraine headaches, sinusitis, hemiplegia, obsession, insanity, cardiac disease, hypertension, diabetes, hepatitis, nephritis and prostatitis. While his cases are considered anecdotal, they further illustrate the often unsuspected link between dental problems and other bodily ills. Here are some examples:

Tumors Eliminated

Two tumors in the retina and skin of the left lower eyelid of a patient were eliminated by removing a focal infection in the mouth. The carcinoma returned a year and a half later, precipitated by a new acute abscess in a tooth. When the abscessed tooth was extracted, the carcinoma disappeared permanently.

Kidney Stone Spontaneously Eliminated

A 31-year-old patient complained of pain in his right kidney caused by a kidney stone. Examination revealed an infection in his right lower wisdom tooth. After the tooth was removed, the stone was spontaneously eliminated.

25-year History Of Migraine Headaches Reversed

A 69-year-old man had suffered with migraine headaches on the left side of his head for 25 years. He had seen many specialists and was taking eight different types of medication, but still the problem persisted. After his infected teeth were extracted, his headaches disappeared. His migraines did not return until thirteen years later, when Dr. Hassan examined the man's mouth and found that ill-fitting dentures were causing inflammation on the left side of his palate. After the patient's dentures were corrected, his migraines again disappeared.[7]

Systemic Infection Arising in the Teeth

These cases illustrate the critical but often overlooked connection between the teeth and the rest of the body. The solid and impenetrable-looking teeth turn out to be living systems, which are ready marks for infection. The impervious-looking enamel may actually be a semi-permeable surface through which fluids and nutrients pass back and forth from the saliva outside to the dentin inside especially through micro cracking within the crystalline enamel prisms. Blood carrying oxygen and nutrients comes up through a main canal at the root of the tooth and proceeds from the pulp through the dentin to the hard enamel surface. (See Figure 1 and 1A.)

The dentin, which makes up most of the tooth's inner structure, is also less solid than it looks, being composed of millions of small hollow tubules. The pulp at its center is like a large cave, with only one small opening into it. Through this opening must go the artery carrying blood in, the vein carrying blood out, the nerve, and the lymph system. Typically this opening is very small and is at the bottom end of each root. Some teeth have one root, some have two, three, or occasionally four or more. Problems arise because the passageways that transport blood and nutrients can also carry bacteria and parasites.

If an infection gets in the pulp from a cavity or fracture, or if the pulp is exposed to the environment of the mouth in any way, the blood supply may need to be substantially increased to combat the infection. This swelling often produces a more sensitive tooth. When infections occur in other parts of the body, new blood vessels can rapidly be created to bring in more blood to fight the infection and carry away the debris. But in the pulp, there is only a very small opening where it enters the tooth through the root tip. When sufficient blood can't be brought in to carry away the debris, the pulp tissue dies. This dead, gangrene like tissue forms a breeding medium for bacteria and other harmful organisms, which slowly trickle out through the tip of the roots and into the jawbone. As it continues, the bone itself around the tooth may die and then spread toxins to the rest of the body through the blood and lymphatic systems, possibly affecting many other sites throughout the body.

To counter this dire threat of infection, the procedure popularly called a root canal is performed. (The term is actually a misnomer: the "root canal" is the interior portion of the tooth.) The procedure involves removing the diseased pulp tissue from inside the tooth; sterilizing the hole by mechanically filing or scraping the inside of the tooth and applying medication, and filling the pulp chamber with a commercial root canal filling material. Infection is thus blocked from seeping either into or out of the tooth — or so the theory goes. But Dr. Price's research indicated that root-filled teeth could actually harbor and perpetuate infection in the body. This problem is discussed more fully in Chapter 8.

The Critical Role of the Bite

Disturbances in the health of the body can arise in the tooth and jaw area in another way. Lost teeth, malalignment and aggressive dental work can impair the bite, throwing off functions far distant from it.

The functions of the jaw joint (the temporomandibular joint or TMJ) are extremely complicated. It moves the lower jaw up and down, side to side, forward and backward, and in the complex maneuvers involved in speaking, biting, chewing, swallowing, smiling, and laughing. Six of the twelve cranial nerves are devoted to serving the mouth complex, and so is a large percentage of the brain. More than half the nervous system serving this complex is involved with the movement of the lower jaw, including the tongue, lips, cheek, soft palate and throat. Forty-four sets of muscles, including those of the neck, upper back, and upper chest, are involved with chewing, speaking, swallowing, facial expressions, and other motions of the jaw. When the jaw is in the correct position, these muscles function normally. But when teeth are lost and the bite becomes "overclosed" due to insufficient back molar support, the geometry of this entire set of muscles is disturbed, making their function far more complicated and stressful for the nervous system.[8]

Harold Gelb, D.M.D., a professor of dentistry and founder of the Gelb Craniomandibular Pain Center at Tufts University School of Dental Medicine, has spent most of his career studying the jaw joint and its effects and disorders. In his writings, he lists symptoms associated with TMJ dysfunction that go on for two pages. They include arthritis, chronic jaw and facial pain, headaches, ear aches, ear noises, clicking sounds in the jaw, restricted jaw movement, hearing loss, aches and tiredness in neck and shoulders, and pain in the teeth that mimics toothache. Symptoms can also include such apparently unrelated complaints as postnasal drip, chronic sore throat, asthma, blurred vision, acne, hair loss, constipation, upset stomach, diarrhea, bladder and kidney infections, premenstrual tension, excessive or irregular menstrual flow, miscarriage, nervous tension, cold hands and feet, back and leg aches, lowered thyroid activity, depression, irritability, forgetfulness, uneven leg length, and curvature of the spine.[9] Dr. Gelb found that many complaints that are recalcitrant to other therapy, including cardiovascular, gynecological, digestive, and back problems, can be relieved merely by correcting the position of the bite. For this purpose, he designed acrylic splints that fill in for too-short teeth or otherwise mechanically realign the jaw. Worn like a football player's mouth guard, they help align the jaws and chewing muscles.[10]

Dr. Larry Lytle, D.D.S., Ph.D., a dentist practicing in Rapid City, South Dakota, has been doing extensive research linking a closed vertical dimension of the face to major illness such as multiple sclerosis. He has observed remarkable reversal of disease by re-establishing normal tooth height and vertical dimension. He feels that overclosure disturbs the delicate balance and sends proprioceptive signals to the Thalamus (the adrenal meridian that passes through the center of the front teeth) altering normal neurotransmitter release. Dr. Lytle has shown that diseases such as multiple sclerosis can be reversed by re-establishing normal biologic vertical dimension to the face.

The Electromagnetic Connection

The featured roles of the teeth and the jaws in the structure and functions of the body make them prime suspects when the system breaks down. New research shows that the teeth are integrally linked to the body not only systemically but electromagnetically; and that many diseases once thought to be irreversible may be alleviated by eliminating energetic blocks, toxins, and "focal infections" arising in the mouth.

Chapter 3

Electromagnetics and the Battery Effect

> Today, the magnetic field (called the magnetoencephalo-gram, or MEG) produced by the brain is easily detected using the SQUID magnetometer (a device based upon the fact that a superconducting current is extremely sensitive to very small magnetic fields).
>
> Dr. Robert O. Becker,
> Cross Currents[1]

Recent research indicating that the body and the brain generate electromagnetic fields reflects another scientific revolution: that from Newtonian to quantum relativistic physics.

Newtonian physics saw nature as consisting of many related physical objects in motion. It emphasized entities rather than organization, and local systems rather than their relation to the total field. Conventional medicine is modeled after Newtonian physics: it sees different diseases as isolated entities, and predicates treatment on the removal of isolated symptoms. Disease is viewed as an enemy to be attacked with scalpels and poisoned with toxic chemicals. The limitation of this approach is that the "enemy" is in the body; is the body that feels the knife and is drugged with the chemicals.

Newtonian physics was modified by Einstein's theory of relativity, which showed that the behavior of a particle is not independent of the field but is conditioned and determined by it. Field physics recognizes the existence of many fields containing particles that interact with each other, ranging from the tiny gravitational fields within atoms to the vast ones of planetary systems. According to quantum field theory, particles cannot be separated from the space that surrounds them. They are nothing but condensations of a continuous field that includes all of material existence.

Scientists have now applied the principles of field physics to develop an "electrodynamic theory of life." This concept has grown out of research showing that living matter is surrounded and controlled by electrodynamic fields; that electrical forces are inherent in all living systems and are important determinants of their organization; and that disease states are accompanied by consistent changes in the electrical conductivity of individual tissue cells.[2] The medical corollary of this theory is a new field approach to healing. Dr. Chopra calls it "quantum healing." All forms of matter are composed of atoms with electrons moving around the central nucleus. This pattern of movement is unique to each atomic particle. Robert O. Becker, M.D., writes in his book 'The Book Electric,' that these electrons move from one particle of matter to the next, forming interlinking compounds and molecules. "Any flow of electrons sets up a combined electric and magnetic field around the current, which in turn affects other electrons nearby." He has measured different electromagnetic patterns around healthy tissue, diseased tissue, and tissue that is repairing and regenerating.

At the University of California at Los Angeles, Professor Emeritus Dr. Valerie Hunt has spent 25 years probing the human energy field, using Kirlian photography, computers, oscilloscopes, and "chaos theory." She has found that all living things have a "chaos pattern," and that "anti-coherency patterns" result in various physical disabilities. She observes that the body has the capacity to regenerate itself if the field is strong and coherent. Using fractal geometry and a chaos graphics pattern in a computer, Dr. Hunt is currently mapping and comparing the patterns of healthy and diseased bodies. Her goal is to be able to diagnose and treat future disease electromagnetically before the body shows symptoms.[3]

Dr. Julian Whitaker, in his new book, "The Pain Relief Breakthrough," describes how he has been using magnets to eliminate patient's pain and help treat disease. He says that magnets have been used as therapy for thousands of years and that stimulating the electromagnetic fields of the body have been shown to dramatically increase blood flow and speed healing of bone and soft tissue injuries.

The Battery Effect

Competing and interfering with the natural electromagnetic field generated by the brain is that generated by dental metals. Recent evidence links neurological and other degenerative disorders, including Alzheimer's disease, multiple sclerosis, and Parkinson's disease, to distortions in the brain's field caused by the "battery effect" arising between dissimilar metals in the teeth. The standard "silver" amalgam that composes 75 percent of all dental fillings is actually a collection of metals — silver, copper, tin and zinc dissolved in a solution of 50% mercury. A galvanic flow of electrical current results when electrons move from one metal with a high electrical potential to another metal with a low electrical potential. When two or more dissimilar metals are placed together in the mouth, the metals interact with the liquid medium of the saliva — an alkaline electrolytic fluid — to form an alkaline battery that produces a small electrical current.

Dentists and the public have periodically reported unusual reactions to dental fillings, including picking up radio transmissions and getting electric shocks whenever the teeth bite down. These reactions have been the subject not only of humor on TV and in the movies, but of serious study by researchers.[4] The first report of "oral galvanism" appeared as far back as 1754. In the 1870s, dental amalgam was labeled "the new health hazard" because it caused "oral electricity."[5] The Journal of the American Medical Association reported in 1933 that "within every oral cavity containing dissimilar metallic dentures there is a complete galvanic battery."[6]

Usually, the dissimilar metals creating electrical currents are silver dental amalgam and cast gold, since a large electrochemical potential difference exists between these two metals. However, a galvanized current has also been reported between a single amalgam and saliva, between amalgam and the metal frame of a partial denture, and between two gold restorations. The restorations act as electrodes, and the saliva or other oral fluids act as electrolytes. Once an electrical potential is created, the "oral electric cell" short circuits, sending a stimulus to the tooth that the patient can feel as a shock, tooth pain, or metallic taste.[7] The phenomenon underscores the hidden hazards not just of mercury amalgam but of gold and other metals in the mouth. As one dental researcher wrote:

> Often, the DC current levels in the mouth of a patient with both silver-mercury and gold materials exceed that of the 60 mvolt firing threshold for single nerve fibers. These constant levels of DC current in excess of the normal energies of the nervous system must produce a severe distortion of the electromagnetic fields of the brain, especially since the trigeminal nerve is in direct communication with dental materials.[8]

Author Tom Warren observes:

> [E]lectrolysis in the oral environment of the mouth can produce galvanic electrical current in the brain 10^3 times greater than the miliamperage of the brain's own circuitry. Galvanic current can interrupt and distort signals to the brain and other biological structures, causing premature ventricular contractions (PVCs), tachycardia, epilepsy and other imbalances throughout the body. A beehive of electrical energy surges from the teeth and through the jawbone to every major organ in the body. When we stick metal into the electrical circuit within the teeth and jawbone, it is the same as throwing a penny into a computer terminal.[9]

The problem of galvanic current and electrolysis generated by the use of mixed metals, such as silver and gold, has come to the attention of the manufacturers selling the material.

Dentsply/Caulk, one of the largest manufacturers of dental silver amalgam recently began placing a warning label on their metals saying that the use of amalgam is contraindicated:

- In proximal or occlusal contact to dissimilar restorations
- In patients with severe renal deficiency
- In patients with know allergies to amalgam
- For a retrograde or endodontic filling in root canals
- In children 6 and under
- In expectant mothers

Side Effects/Warnings

Prior to use, read the MSDS information and product instructions for this item.

- Exposure to mercury may cause irritation to skin, eyes, respiratory tract and mucous membrane. In individual cases, hypersensitivity reactions, allergies, or electrochemically caused local reactions have been observed. Due to electrochemical processes, the lichen planus of the mucosa may develop.

- Mercury may also be a skin sensitizer, pulmonary sensitizer, nephrotoxin, and neurotoxin.

- After placement or removal of amalgam restorations, there is a temporary increase of the mercury concentration in the blood and urine.

- Mercury expressed during condensation and unset amalgam may cause amalgamation or galvanic effect if in contact with other metal restorations. If symptoms persist, the amalgam should be replaced by a different material.

- Removal of clinically acceptable amalgam restorations should be avoided to minimize mercury exposure, especially in expectant mothers.

Precautions

- The number of amalgam restorations for one patient should be kept to a minimum.

- Inhalation of mercury vapor by dental staff may be avoided by proper handling of the amalgam, the use of masks, along with adequate ventilation.

- Avoid contact with skin and wear safety glasses and gloves.

- Store amalgam scrap in well sealed containers. Regulations for disposal must be observed.

Angina Reversed

Fuller Royal, M.D., H.M.D., of the Nevada Clinic in Las Vegas, illustrates this effect with the case of "H.R." A 66-year-old man with severe angina pectoris, H.R. was facing his third coronary bypass surgery. Dr. Royal diagnosed his problem using a simple galvanometer, a device that measures electrical current. The reading on the patient's left lower wisdom tooth proved to be an alarming -35.9 microamps. The tooth was pulled, and the man was treated with homeopathic remedies.

"Immediately following the extraction," says Dr. Royal, "H.R. experienced a dramatic improvement, stating that 'It felt like an elephant jumped off my chest!'" H.R.'s previously abnormal EKG readings then returned to normal. Within six months he was walking 4-1/2 miles a day, without angina and without surgery.[10]

Visual Disturbances Cleared

Everett Payne, D.D.S., professor of dental anatomy at the University of Southern California and then at Baylor School of Dentistry in Dallas, cites another remarkable case. The patient was a man who had for several years had double vision so severe that he was forced to drive with one eye closed in order to avoid seeing two layers of street. The problem disappeared immediately after he had a wisdom tooth removed. The wisdom tooth, it turned out, was covered by a gold crown; and under the gold crown was a silver amalgam filling.[11]

Electromagnetic Interference Fields: The Innovative Research of Dr. Voll

Dr. Royal, H.R.'s astute physician, was introduced to the electrical problems that could arise from metals in the teeth when he visited Reinhard Voll, M.D., in Germany in 1979. Dr. Royal was impressed when Dr. Voll pinpointed Mrs. Royal's past and present physical problems using a diagnostic device called a Voll machine. Dr. Royal was even more impressed when, based on these readings, Dr. Voll recommended homeopathic remedies that caused Mrs. Royal to completely recover from recurring arthritis.[12]

Dr. Voll was a former professor of neuroanatomy who developed EAV (Electro-Acupuncture according to Voll) in the 1950s to test the different electrical points of the body. Like the later EEG, ECG and EMG, his EAV machine measured electrical skin resistance. In his research with it,

Dr. Voll observed that as little as two or three microamps of electrical current could create health disturbances. (A microamp is one millionth of an ampere of electricity.) In later research conducted at the National Institute of Dental Research in Bethesda, Maryland, currents of around 17 microamps have been reported in many people with dental problems.[13]

Acupuncture Meridians Confirmed by Electrical Skin Resistance Testing

Using EAV, Dr. Voll also confirmed the existence and location of acupuncture meridians, or patterns of energy flow, mapped in the body by the Chinese thousands of years ago. The teeth were found to be a central transmitting station through which the meridians of all the major organ systems passed.

Dr. Voll and a dentist colleague, Dr. J. Thomsen, proceeded to locate and map an electromagnetic connection between specific organs, muscles, joints and tissues and every tooth in the mouth.[14] Figures 2 and 3 chart these connections. They show, for example, that the top incisor teeth are connected energetically to the urogenital area; the bottom incisor teeth are connected to the bladder; and the wisdom teeth are connected to the nervous system and heart.[15] Dr. Voll estimated that 80 percent of the body's energy blockages arise in the teeth and jaw. These "interference fields" impair the functioning of other parts of the body by preventing the necessary electromagnetic signals from getting through.

Graphic anecdotal evidence of this connection was reported in the April 1997 Townsend Letter for Doctors. A woman with a breast tumor was asked by her doctor to have an abscessed tooth treated before her surgery. After this dental work, while lidocaine was still in her system, she had a thermographic x-ray taken. It revealed a white line extending from her tooth down her neck through the tumor on her breast and on into her stomach. Struck by this remarkable data, her physicians decided not to operate. Four months later, the tumor disappeared. The incident is considered the first on record evidencing a direct connection from a diseased tooth following an acupuncture meridian to a distant diseased area.[16]

Electro-dermal Screening Devices

Later modifications of the Voll machine are becoming popular diagnostic tools in various health fields, including dentistry. Called electro-dermal screening devices, these machines are used for determining what remedies the patient needs and what materials are compatible with the body. Like the Voll machine and the EEG, the machines measure electrical skin resistance. According to Richard Gerber, M.D., in his paradigm-shattering book Vibrational Medicine, the devices can also tell the type and degree of dysfunction in particular organs, along with causes and potential cures. How they do this is a function of biological resonance, the same principle underlying the later imaging systems of MRI and EMR scanning.[17]

Many researchers have verified that the skin electrical potential is more positive at acupuncture points than for the surrounding tissue.[18] The conductivity of acupuncture points on the heart meridian increases as heart rate is increased by biofeedback, while the conductivity of normal skin nearby does not change.[19] Electro-dermal screening devices measure the energy flowing through particular acupuncture points, which are connected to acupuncture meridians running to various organs of the body. When the meridians are in balance, the needle registers somewhere around 50 on a scale of 0 to 100. When the needle drops too low or soars too high, the meridian is out of balance. The correct remedy, placed on a plate attached electronically to the indicator touching the acupuncture points, will bring the needle back to 50.

Proponents contend that the accuracy of these devices is equal to or better than that of the various orthodox tests of Western medicine, without their risk of dangerous side effects. Disease processes have been shown to begin with a change in the electrical potential of the skin. Practitioners say this change can be identified by electro-dermal screening in the disease's initial stages, when the patient is still unaware of any sensations and conventional diagnosis produces no definitive results. Electro-dermal screening can establish an immediate case report, without a prior patient history, based entirely on measurement readings. The machines can also tell what remedies will resonate harmonically to correct electromagnetic imbalances in the body.

Electro-dermal screening devices do not yet have the approval of the FDA, but case studies have shown them to be effective.[20] Obtaining FDA approval may take awhile, since for a single drug or device this process now requires an average of more than 100 million dollars and ten years of rigorous research.[21] However, several of these devices currently have investigational device status; and practitioners interested in getting them approved have banded together to share experiences and join forces in satisfying legal requirements.[22]

The Role of Electro-dermal Screening in Dentistry

In the field of dentistry, electro-dermal screening devices are being used to indicate chronic low-level sensitivities to dental materials, both locally in the mouth and systemically in the rest of the body. The devices are also used to measure patients' possible reactions to particular dental materials before placing them in the mouth, and to study the local and systemic effects of electrical current produced by dissimilar and toxic metals.

David Eggleston, D.D.S., who taught at the University of Southern California and has a private dental practice in Newport Beach, observed of his experience:

> Before I got involved with [electro-dermal screening], I was using amalgam and nickel based alloys rather extensively. Once you start using electro-acupuncture and start measuring some people, you won't use these materials. We saw major changes in electrical conductivity when we used these particular materials, mainly nickel based alloys. . . . I would categorically state that no one should have nickel in the mouth.[23]

And yet nickel containing metals are very common in crowns that are covered with porcelain.

Other researchers using electro-dermal screening have confirmed the central importance of the teeth to the overall health. Dr. Robert Marshall, a clinical nutritionist, uses an EAV device called a Computron, which graphically projects its results onto a computer screen. He states that he has tested thousands of patients on it; and that in the vast majority of them, energy meridians have been impinged at the site of the teeth and jaw.

Forbidden Dentistry

For all that, the American Dental Association (ADA) continues to look askance at the removal of dental metals for reasons of health rather than mere aesthetics. The saga of the rise of the ADA and its professional commitment to silver/mercury amalgam restorative materials is discussed in Chapter 4, along with the history of dentistry in general.

Chapter 4

Yesterday's Quackery

All great truths begin as blasphemies.

— George Bernard Shaw

Today, the dental profession is so thoroughly separated from medicine that for a dentist to recommend dental work for health reasons is considered unethical and a violation of their state license. Yet for 2,000 years after Hippocrates separated medicine from magic, medicine and dentistry were joined. Care of the teeth, at least for the well-to-do, was the province of doctors and surgeons; while the poorer masses took their toothaches to tooth-drawers, barbers, charlatans, and "quacks."

More than two thousand years ago, the Etruscans were already replacing missing teeth with wholly biocompatible materials. They used human or oxen teeth for this purpose. The problem was getting the borrowed teeth to stay put. For that, gold bands were required, soldered together and placed on either side of the replacement tooth for support.[1] Repair of the teeth with wholly biocompatible materials without metal reinforcement was not accomplished for another 2,500 years. In the meantime, dentists were simply struggling with the mechanics of developing materials that would stay in place and ways of placing them that wouldn't unduly torture the patient.

Edicts providing for the separate licensing of dental practitioners made dentistry an autonomous specialty only in the eighteenth century. This specialty was fully developed by the nineteenth century, but access to it continued to be limited to the rich. The treatment for caries (cavities) favored by the new dental profession was to remove visible decay, drill the cavities into funnel shapes with hand drills and other devices, and pack them with gold foil. Hammer blows were then used to weld the gold foil in place. The procedure left much to be desired. It was expensive, tedious, and required a high degree of technical skill, and since it was before the development of anesthesia, it could be excruciatingly painful. The patient sometimes had to be tied down to keep him from bolting from the dental chair. It is no wonder, with that kind of history, people learned from early on to hate a visit to the dentist and went only when it was absolutely necessary.

Anesthesia with nitrous oxide (laughing gas) was not used successfully for painless tooth extraction until 1842, and another half century passed before it caught on. Like with many medical innovations, it met with stiff resistance by conventional interests. One of its developers, a Connecticut dentist named Horace Wells, wound up addicted to laughing gas and committing suicide under its influence. His work was carried on by a student and former associate named W. G. T. Morton, who died a poor man after his dental colleagues opposed both the principle of anesthesia and him personally. He was damned even from the pulpit, for daring to eliminate "the pain ordained by God."

The pain and expense of the prevailing dental treatments in the first half of the nineteenth century laid the stage for the popularity of the new "silver" amalgam filling. Consisting of filings from silver coins softened with mercury, it was cheap, relatively painless, and took virtually no training. Originally called "Bell's putty," the material was simply pressed into the dental cavity with the thumb like silly putty. It required no drilling or pounding and could be done by barbers and blacksmiths, the dentists of the poor. Many mercury filling placers traveled town to town by wagon filling as many teeth as they could before moving on to the next town.

The Amalgam War

Silver/mercury amalgam was introduced to American dentistry in the 1830s by the Cracour brothers, two dental charlatans from London who fraudulently claimed to be dentists to the courts of Austria, France, Russia and Prussia. The Cracours made a fortune in a short time selling their mercury rich amalgam, paving the way for the "amalgam war" that split dentistry for half a century and inspired such passion that it resembled a religious conflict.

Pretentiously calling their mercury amalgam "Royal Mineral Succedaneum," the Cracour brothers advertised that it could be used to fill teeth "in two minutes without any pain, inconvenience or pressure." The material was simply pressed into the open cavity of the tooth. The cavities were not excavated and the teeth were not prepared, so many of the fillings fell out; and those that stayed in tended to crack the teeth when the material expanded as it hardened. At best, the fillings merely concealed the decay that proceeded unabated underneath. Yet the new material enjoyed great economic success, mainly because it was cheaper, quicker and more painless than the available alternatives.

The secret to the new amalgam's malleability was the semi-liquid metal mercury, which today composes more than 50 percent of the standard "silver" filling. Mercury is now recognized as one of the most toxic nonradioactive inorganic heavy metals known to man, outranking even lead, cadmium and arsenic. But to people in the nineteenth century who couldn't afford either gold or a professionally-trained dentist, it seemed a reasonable solution to their dental problems.

The American Society of Dental Surgeons, however, was fanatically opposed to the new trend. This society was the original dental association founded in the United States to develop and foster the skilled, artistic craft of treating dental disease. It's members underwent years of apprenticeship to learn the intricate skills necessary to become a practicing dentist. They supported gold fillings and banned anyone espousing the cheaper but more toxic amalgam. This organization required its members to sign an agreement that they would never, under any circumstances, use amalgam, on penalty of expulsion. A Dr. Payne proclaimed in the <u>Chicago Medical Journal</u> in 1873 that "neither Asiatic cholera, nor smallpox, nor any malarious disease, is doing half the mischief in the world that is done by this poisoning." Dentists who used mercury were called "quacks," a defamatory epithet actually derived from "quicksilver," or mercury (in German called, "quackenslaver"). First used during the Renaissance, the term was applied to wandering peddlers who sold mercury concoctions for curing syphilis and virtually all other illnesses, who were known as "quacksalvers" or "quacks." Yet inspite of the criticism by the reputable dental community, the number of mercury placers flourished largely because this technique required virtually no training and was cheap, quick and easy to place. Quite a contrast to the exacting techniques and training required of the skilled artisans who used gold.

The Rise of the American Dental Association

Mercury amalgam nevertheless retained its appeal, particularly among the working classes. A rival organization called the American Dental Association was formed to promote its use. Eventually the ADA came to dominate the profession, largely because of the market appeal of the cheap and pliable material it endorsed and the large number of individuals who placed it. inevitably the original dental society of the skilled craftsman ceased to exist leaving only the American Dental Association to represent American dental interests.

Amalgam became the industry-wide standard late in the nineteenth century, when a dentist named G. V. Black developed a better product and procedures for cavity preparation. Black was a reputable dentist who was so idealistic that he gave his achievements away for free. In 1896, he succeeded in developing a formula for producing an amalgam that did not expand or contract appreciably. This material, and Black's rules for preparing the tooth before placing it in the mouth, remained in use without change for the next century. His techniques are still taught in all U.S.

dental schools and are considered to be the standard for American dental practice.

In his protocol for tooth preparation, Black introduced the principle of "extension for prevention." It involved drilling out the tooth's small natural indentations along with any areas that were actually decayed, on the theory that this would keep the indentations from turning into cavities later. The protocol required the invention of a usable dental drill, which was accomplished in 1871. Due to the efforts of Black and of Adolph Witzel, who published a carefully researched book in German in 1899 called <u>The Filling of Teeth with Amalgam</u>, by the turn of the century amalgam had become established around the world, particularly as a material suitable for less well-to-do patients.[2]

By the late nineteenth century, anesthesia had also become widely accepted for both dental and medical practice. It transformed both, allowing the development of new methods of treatment that had the potential for reaping huge profits. Without anesthetics, doctors had to work gently in harmony with the body. Anesthesia made invasive, tissue-destroying procedures like surgery and radiation feasible approaches to attacking disease. Doctors began recommending major operations that required the development of expensive and lucrative hospital systems.

At the same time, the thriving patent medicine business had developed into the synthetic drug industry. Patentable synthetic drugs provided an economic incentive that was lacking in the "common weed" (natural herb) business. Advertising the new pharmaceuticals became the chief source of revenue for the new American Medical Association. By promoting the new treatments, the AMA not only helped transform medicine into an industry but gained political power. Soon, it was in a position to change the licensing regulations to exclude other medical schools and any competing thought. Likewise as most medical research was now performed or supported by the financially rich drug companies, most current medical training and technique revolved around use of their products. This gave rise to the growth of the hospital industry which greatly influenced the fundamental content of medical knowledge and practice. Traditionally, the medical profession of the West has concentrated on diagnosis and treatment of illness, rather than on the promotion of health and prevention of disease. Modern western scientific medicine is often criticized for dehumanizing and overlooking the whole patient while concentrating on just the disease. The focus of western medicine seems to revolve around drugs, surgery, and radiation. If the ailment cannot be treated by one of these three, medicine has few answers. There is a lot of money to be made in illness, drugs, and surgery — very little by comparison to be made with maintaining wellness. As the politically correct, institutionalized western medical system, and the AMA, controls the accepted knowledge and training of doctors, we may be headed for, as Dr. Julian Whitaker says, "the allopathic dark ages in which information not even remotely related to fact is 'generated' to serve allopathic medical dogma."

The American Dental Association achieved similar power and position in the dental field. Concerns about the safety of mercury amalgam periodically continued to be voiced, as when a German chemist published The Dangers of Mercury Fumes in 1926, creating a stir of uneasiness that took years to be allayed. But by the end of the twentieth century, seventy percent of all dental fillings consisted of silver/mercury amalgam. By the 1980s, mercury amalgam was so well accepted that an article in the American Dental Association Journal could categorize "removing serviceable dental amalgam from nonallergic patients because it is a toxic substance" as "dental quackery."[3] Ironically, the word originally applied to practitioners who promoted mercury's use had now come to be applied to those who opposed it.

As an example of the fanaticism supporting mercury amalgam, Dr. Terry Donovan, chairman of the Department of Restorative Dentistry at USC Dental School, threatens his class, "If I hear of anyone in this class who removes metals and tells their patients they are bad for them, I will come after you."

Dr. John Dodes and Dr. Marvin Schissel, who both practice in New York, have set themselves up as crusaders against, what they call, the incompetents, the quacks and the frauds. They interpret these dentists to be those who "do not practice the 'right' way." They continue to say that "there was a right way to do dentistry and dental school had taught us the right way." In other words, anyone who practices other than the way they were taught some 20 years prior, which was based on teachings from some one hundred years prior, was "an incompetent, a quack or a fraud." In addition they write that "hypnotism, acupuncture, TENS, other electronic contraptions, herbs — none of these has been proved effective." Concerning TMJ syndrome they assert "Most of the information foisted on the public about this condition has at best been anecdotal speculation and at worst the self-serving lies of quacks." This attitude, which is prevalent in mainstream dentistry, guarantees that <u>nothing</u> will ever change or progress.

It seems that the traditionally trained dentist, who does not know how to practice other than the way they were taught, is determined to preserve their old way of practice. And so they brand all others as quacks, frauds, and incompetents. Whereas in reality they simply have not kept up with current research and science and choose to ignore anything new. Even the faculties of dental schools, who have become proficient and expert at the old style of dentistry, would have to become students to learn the new style. Further, they would have to admit that they did not know something; that what they had been teaching their students may be wrong; and at worst the style of dentistry they had taught and practiced for years may have been harming their patients. This is too difficult for these practitioners to face and so it becomes easy to accept the old way as gospel truth and condemn and criticize others who practice differently.

Chapter 5

Mercurial Maladies

"In that direction," the Cat said, waving its right paw around, "lives a Hatter: and in that direction," waving the other paw, "lives a March Hare. Visit either you like: they're both mad."

—Lewis Carroll,
Through the Looking Glass

The toxicity of mercury has long been known. Lewis Carroll alluded to it in his nineteenth century character the Mad Hatter. Felt hat workers exposed to mercuric nitrate were observed to exhibit emotional symptoms including sudden anger, depression, loss of memory, timidity, insomnia, irritability, hallucinations, delusions, and mania, a condition referred to as "the mad hatter syndrome."[1] But for over a century, the ADA has continued to maintain that when mercury is combined with other metals and allowed to harden in the teeth, it becomes a stable compound that will not leak into the body. The ADA has continued to insist that mercury amalgam is safe, and that it is a tightly bound chemical complex that does not permit any leakage or release of mercury into the body, based simply on its 150 years of continuous use. (Both lead and asbestos were also used for over 150 years before they were banned.) Clinical studies were never done, since FDA testing for chronic toxicity was bypassed under a grandfather clause. It wasn't until 1990 that the toxicity of mercury amalgam became a media event. The furor began with two new animal studies reported in the Chicago Tribune in August of that year.

Mercury Does Indeed Leak from the Teeth into Body Tissues

In one of these studies, conducted by Drs. Lorscheider and Vimy of the University of Calgary in Alberta, twelve radioactive mercury amalgam fillings (a typical number for a human adult) were placed in the mouths of each of six sheep. A control group received fillings made of an inert material. Within thirty days, the sheep that got the amalgam had lost half their kidney function.[2] The study showed that mercury in amalgam fillings is not locked in the teeth but spreads through the body to the organs.

The ADA's rebuttal to the Canadian study was that sheep, unlike humans, are constantly chewing. The response of Dr. Lorscheider was that the sheep were fed only twice a day and chewed no more than gum-chewing humans; and that similar data have been reported for monkeys, which do chew like humans. Both sheep and monkeys with amalgam fillings show poisoning of the internal organs and the brain with the isotope labeled mercury.[3]

This study was dramatic, and it made headlines. But earlier research had already shown that mercury vapor escapes from amalgam fillings in humans, particularly with chewing; and that this vapor is inhaled and enters the bloodstream. After five years, only about half the mercury used in a filling has been found to remain on the chewing surface of the tooth; and after twenty years, little of it may remain on the surface.[4]

The other study reported in August of 1990 involved monkeys given amalgam fillings. The researchers found that normal bacteria in the guts of these monkeys were replaced by mercury-resistant bacteria that were able to assimilate the metal. The new bacteria recycled mercury in the body rather than letting the monkey excrete it. According to researcher Anne Summers, "It proves that mercury is 'bioavailable' — something that dentists have been denying for years." She added, "This may . . . explain why not all mercury entering the body is excreted and high levels are found in certain organs."[5] The World Health Organization states that between 3-17 micrograms are released into the body each day by chewing while fish and all other environmental sources combined only releases 2-5 micrograms.

Mercury and Alzheimer's Disease

More disturbing news came on October 17, 1990, when the Lexington Herald-Leader reported the findings of a University of Kentucky study involving humans. Significant elevations of mercury were found in the brains of 180 Kentucky residents who were autopsied after dying of Alzheimer's disease. When concentrations of trace elements were analyzed, the most important imbalance found was an elevation in mercury.[6]

The researchers observed that Alzheimer's disease is characterized by groups of twisted filaments in the cells of the parts of the brain called the neocortex and hippocampus. These "neurofibrillary tangles" result from insufficient synthesis of a protein substance called tubulin. Mercury was found to alter tubulin in rat brain tissue in a way that mimics its alteration in the brains of human Alzheimer's patients.[7]

These findings meshed with earlier studies demonstrating a direct correlation between the amount of mercury in the brain and the amount in mercury dental fillings. In studies of the cadavers of accident victims, those with a mere five amalgams had three times the amount of mercury in their brain tissues as cadavers without amalgams.[8]

On October 18, 1990, the New England Journal of Medicine published an editorial calling mercury fillings "possibly the chief source of exposure [to mercury] of a large segment of the U.S. population."[9]

A later autopsy study done by the Mayo Heavy Metals Lab on an 82-year-old decedent with confirmed Alzheimer's disease and multiple amalgams in her teeth showed 53 times the normal level of mercury in the brain. The "neurofibrillary tangle" characteristic of Alzheimer's disease was also found.[10]

Alzheimer's disease now affects an estimated four million Americans and is on the rise. Nearly twenty times as many deaths were reported from it in 1993 as in 1979. Conventional research has focused on genetics, but the cause remains elusive; and even people with a genetic predisposition to a disease may not develop it unless they are pushed over the edge by toxic environmental factors. Mounting evidence points to accumulation in the brain of heavy metals, including not only mercury but aluminum and lead. The blood/brain barrier is intended to keep toxins out of the brain, but those that do get in are prevented by it from getting back out. They continue to build up over the years, progressively blocking brain and nerve function.[11]

The ADA Responds

The 1990 media event culminated when CBS's "Sixty Minutes" featured the amalgam issue in December of that year. The segment generated so much interest that many in the "biological" dental community expected a change in the official stance. Instead, the ADA and its allied government agencies launched a huge campaign to counter the evidence. Press releases discrediting the information were sent to all the major media, and letters were sent to every dentist in the United States. The press releases continued to insist that amalgam is safe, based solely on its 150 years of use[12] even though both lead and asbestos were used for over 150 years before they were discovered to be hazardous.

The few studies that defenders of mercury amalgam have come up with since have failed to withstand careful scientific scrutiny. In frequently-cited study, for example, nuns with amalgams were compared to nuns without amalgams. No correlation was found with cognitive dysfunction, a symptom considered to be a forerunner of Alzheimer's disease.[13] Critics observed, however, that the "control" group all had dentures. They may have had no mercury left in their teeth, but they had obviously had significant dental work at some time in their lives, presumably including heavy doses of mercury amalgam. Removing all the teeth won't eliminate the mercury that has accumulated in body tissues. To run an accurate test, the researchers should have compared nuns with amalgams to nuns who had never had dental work.

European Reactions

While U.S. authorities were busy trying to discredit the evidence, European governments were taking steps to ban amalgam's use. In February of 1994, Sweden announced a total ban on it in fillings in children and young adults, effective June of 1995; and all use of it in Swedish citizens, effective January of 1997. This step was based on evidence that amalgam triggers autoimmune disorders.

Denmark, Germany and Austria followed suit, banning amalgams and phasing them out. Degussa, Germany's largest producer of amalgam and the world's largest producer of metals for dentistry, completely shut down its amalgam production, following a federal court ruling that dentists who use it face legal liability.[14] In Switzerland and Japan the dental schools no longer teach amalgam use as the primary source of dental care.

The State of California Inquires

The U.S. government so far has not taken any action, preferring to defer to ADA guidelines and policy. However, in 1993, the California State legislature passed a law mandating that the Board of Dental Examiners develop a fact sheet describing and comparing the risks and effectiveness of various dental restorative materials.[15] Under political duress, the California State Dental Board then released a document titled "Dental Materials Fact Sheet," discussing various dental restorative materials including silver amalgam dental fillings, gold, porcelain, and tooth-colored filling materials (cements, composites, and plastics). The Fact Sheet admitted that the mercury found in the standard "silver" filling is a known toxin, and that it has now been shown to escape into and be absorbed by the body. The Fact Sheet also admitted that composite fillings, the most popular alternatives to amalgam, contain elements that have been determined to be cytotoxic and carcinogenic (cell-killing and cancer-producing). The Fact Sheet conceded that every restorative material carries risks, and that patients and dentists alike need to be made aware of them.[16]

In 1994, California passed a proposition requiring that a warning be posted in dental offices using mercury amalgam, stating that "the people of the state of California have determined that the use of mercury in dental amalgam causes birth defects and other health problems." The proposition also required the dentist to obtain the patient's informed consent before placing hazardous material in the patient's mouth. The new law is currently tied up in federal court, after being contested by the ADA and the California Dental Association.[17]

Mercury, MS, Depression, Anxiety and Insomnia

Meanwhile, the evidence against mercury amalgam has continued to mount. One link for which there is mounting evidence is with multiple sclerosis. In a study reported by Colorado State University researcher Robert Siblerud in 1992, MS patients having amalgams were compared to MS patients whose amalgams had been removed. The former group was found to have significantly lower levels of red blood cells, hemoglobin, hematocrit, T-Lymphocytes, and T-8 suppressor cells (indicating lowered immunity). They also had 33 percent more flareups of their symptoms during the previous year.[18]

Again, these findings weren't new. Siblerud observes that MS was first described by a French doctor in the mid-1830s, less than a decade after silver/mercury fillings were first promoted in Paris.[19] In the late 1940s, "acrodynia," a childhood version of multiple sclerosis, was traced to poisoning from the mercury in teething powder and laxatives; but no one seems to have linked the adult form of the disease to the amalgam fillings that were the most widespread source of mercury in adults. It wasn't until 1966 that a Swiss neurologist recognized the possibility that amalgam fillings could be such a source.[20]

In 1978, in the United States and 45 other countries, a direct epidemiological link was established between the incidence of MS and dental caries.[21] In 1983, a researcher named Ingalls also suggested a link after observing his own case. He had MS on only one side of his body — the side on which all his dental caries were located.[22] A 1987 study then showed that mercury levels in the cerebrospinal fluid of MS patients were eight times higher than in controls.[23] The researchers also found that inorganic mercury is capable of producing symptoms that are indistinguishable from those of multiple sclerosis.[24]

A series of French studies found that autoimmune diseases like MS and chronic polyarthritis are triggered by silver amalgams. A British study also correlated MS incidence with the incidence of cavities and dental fillings.[25]

The relationship between mercury amalgam and autoimmune disorders like MS has been explained by mercury's high affinity for the sulfhydryl groups in the molecules composing collagen and other tissues. When mercury alters these groups, "self" molecules appear as "non-self" and become targets for autoimmune recognition.[26]

MS and mercury poisoning are both associated with depression and a general deterioration in mental health. Other mental symptoms attributed to mercury poisoning include lack of interest, poor concentration, forgetfulness, headaches, fear, excitability, indecisiveness, hopelessness, insomnia, delusions and mania.[27]

Mercury Impairs Fetal Development

A study reported in 1994 showed that methylmercury (the organic mercury that forms after mercury is eaten) crosses the barrier to the placenta. Earlier studies with pregnant sheep and monkeys had found elevated levels of mercury in the animals' fetuses within two weeks of placing amalgam fillings in the mothers.[28] Similar findings were now being reported for humans. Mercury concentrations in the kidneys, liver, and cerebral cortex of fetuses and infants were found to correlate significantly with the number of dental amalgam fillings in the mother.[29] That means children can become mercury-toxic although they have never had cavities, by absorbing mercury leached from their mothers' mouths. Fetuses are eight times as sensitive to mercury exposure as their mothers, and methylmercury is 100 times more toxic than elemental mercury. Methylmercury has been shown to cause damage to children ranging from stillbirth to mental retardation to psychomotor and behavioral disturbances in the growing child.[30]

Mercury and High Blood Pressure

Robert Siblerud's research also linked mercury amalgam to high blood pressure. When fifty 22-year-olds who had amalgams were compared to an equivalent number of 22-year-olds who did not have them, blood pressures in the former group averaged six systolic points higher than in the latter group. The amalgamated subjects also had a greater incidence of chest pains, tachycardia (racing heart beat), anemia, fatigue, and loss of memory — and these were young adults. The difference undoubtedly gets greater over the half-century it takes to develop "essential hypertension."[31]

Mercury has been shown in autopsy studies to accumulate with age in the kidneys not only of sheep but of humans. The kidneys, in turn, play a key role in controlling blood pressure. Nine out of ten people with high blood pressure have what is called "essential hypertension." Essentially, that means hypertension for which doctors don't know the cause.

Other researchers have observed that when the removal of mercury from the teeth is followed by its removal from the body by chelation, blood pressure goes down.[32] (Chelation is discussed in Chapter 14.)

Mercury Amalgam and Smoking

Siblerud found another interesting association with mercury. Women were 2-1/2 times more likely to smoke if they had mercury amalgam fillings than if they didn't.[33] Why? He suggested that the desire to smoke is a subconscious physiological response to the effects of mercury on the neurotransmitters of the brain. Mercury depresses the neurotransmitters' uptake of dopamine, serotonin, acetylcholine, and norepinephrine, while nicotine has the opposite effect. He observed:

[N]icotine has highly desirable effects upon the brain, and this is one reason people like to smoke. One might postulate that, if the amalgam mercury reduces the function of neurotransmitters and results in anxiety and if nicotine increases neurotransmitter functioning, people with amalgams would perhaps smoke more to relieve their anxious feelings.[34]

In what promises to be the nation's largest class action, a coalition of sixty personal injury attorneys filed suit in March of 1994 against the tobacco industry for concealing information concerning the addictiveness of their products. In March of 1996, the Liggett Group became the first tobacco company to negotiate a multimillion dollar settlement with the plaintiffs.

Meanwhile, the dental industry managed to escape liability. Hungry lawyers might argue that the ADA, which has endorsed the universal use of a substance that makes people crave cigarettes, should have been among the defendants.

The Hazards of Chewing Gum

As an aside, if you have mercury amalgam fillings and are trying to quit smoking, medicinal chewing gums marketed for this purpose are a dangerous solution. Mercury vapor release when you're chewing gum has been shown to be 40 to 200 times as great as when you're not chewing.

The potential hazards were illustrated in the case of a close friend of the author's, who gave up smoking for health reasons. To allay her cravings for cigarettes, she began chewing a popular medicinal gum practically continually during her waking hours. She couldn't understand why she felt worse instead of better. Two months later, she was diagnosed with colon cancer. Living in Guatemala, she had been troubled for years with parasites, which have been linked to colon cancer. Arguably, the mercury released from her many amalgam fillings during her excessive gum chewing aggravated a precancerous parasitic condition in her colon, producing full-blown cancer. Japanese researchers have found mercury at the center of cancer and pre-cancer cell nuclei.[35]

Chapter 6

Exceptions That Prove the Rule

[M]ercury poisoning is most often not diagnosed in patients because of the insidious onset of the affliction, vagueness of early clinical signs, and the medical profession's unfamiliarity with the disease.

— Goodman and Gilman,
Pharmacological Basis of Therapeutics
(8th edition, 1990)

Opponents of the theory that mercury amalgam is toxic point to the fact that most people with amalgam fillings suffer no obvious ill effects. They also argue that for every case in which "total dental revision" has led to dramatic improvements in health, another case can be found in which it either has had no effect or has actually made the patient worse.

Critics of amalgam counter that even people with no obvious symptoms may be suffering from the toxic effects of dental materials. Symptoms of mercury poisoning are the vague, hard-to-trace kind, including depression, low stomach acid, candida, belching, gas, infection (parasitic, fungal, etc.), chronic fatigue, leaky gut syndrome, food allergies, chemical sensitivities, obesity, liver toxicity, dry flaky skin, abnormal white blood cell count, and discolored genitals.[1]

Amalgam critics also observe that cases in which a treatment has failed don't disprove those in which it has worked. The failures may attest only to flaws in procedure. If removing mercury amalgam from the teeth of just a few patients reverses the symptoms of "irreversible" diseases like

Alzheimer's, Parkinson's disease, and MS, the data are remarkable and need to be investigated. A number of possible complicating factors could explain the treatment failures. They include:

(1) The replacement dental material (gold, composites, nickel or aluminum reinforced porcelain) may have been as toxic to the patient as the material that was removed.

(2) Proper safety precautions may not have been taken during removal. Mercury vapor is highly toxic. Indiscriminate drilling out of the mercury without adequate precautions can be very dangerous, increasing mercury vapor by up to 1000 times the release by chewing. If substantial amounts of it are inhaled during the removal procedure, the patient could well get worse instead of better.

(3) The patient's symptoms may have been due, not to mercury in the teeth, but to mercury that had already leached from the teeth into other body tissues. Symptoms could then be eliminated only with the removal of heavy metals from those tissues.

(4) Damage to the organs may have been too extensive to be repaired. The condition may simply have been "too far gone."

The Question of Biocompatible Replacement Materials

Improvements in health won't result if the replacement material is as toxic to the patient as the amalgam being replaced. The usual replacement material is some form of plastic composite. Hal Huggins, D.D.S., observed that in a test of three of the more popular plastic composites, 97 percent of the 800 patients tested reacted with an immune response to the materials. To avoid what he called the "frying pan into the fire" syndrome, Dr. Huggins recommended blood serum compatibility testing (a blood test that indicates allergic response) to determine which of the more than 750 dental materials available at his office was most compatible with the patient's own body.[2]

That was a step, but the reliability of blood serum compatibility testing has also been questioned. According to Sam Ziff, president of the Foundation for Toxic-Free

Dentistry, "Unless a patient is extremely allergic, such as a universal reactor, dental materials reactivity testing may or may not be of benefit."[3]

Dr. Robert Marshall, the nutritionist cited earlier who tests with an electro-dermal screening device called a Computron, puts the percentage of patients who react poorly to composite materials at nearly 100 percent. Blood serum compatibility testing, he observes, involves exposure to dental materials for only a few seconds. Dr. Marshall has found that composites that initially passed that test do not test well if taped to the body and tested on the Computron after a period of time — five or ten minutes, or overnight. The Computron tests effects not only on immunological function (allergic response) but on neurological function. Composites might or might not impair immunological function; but Dr. Marshall feels that all of the hundreds of composite materials he has tested shut down the body's neurological functions. Other practitioners also using electrodermal screening, disagree and have found that for some of their patients certain ceramic based composite polymers have tested very strong on not only the Computron, but the Listen and Vegetest as well.

Then What Material is Biocompatible?

After testing hundreds of materials on more than 300 patients, Dr. Marshall found one dental filling material that he prefers 100 percent of the time. So much so that he no longer routinely tests all his patients for specific biocompatibility. That material is called Degussa low-fusing ceramic, or "Degussa porcelain." However, it isn't a true porcelain. It is composed of substances approximating those of natural teeth. Degussa porcelain is discussed at length in Chapters 9 and 10.

"It's brought just marvelous improvements for so many of our patients," says Dr. Marshall. "We've worked on hundreds of people who got their mercury amalgam fillings replaced with composites, by dentists with the best of intentions, and terrible problems resulted. We've seen migraine after migraine, and people who have wound up losing their teeth because their composites leaked. I've had 20 or 25 migraine patients who would say things like, 'I never knew why anyone would want to commit suicide until now. When I get up, it's the first thought I have.' In case after case, replacing their composite fillings with Degussa porcelain has eliminated their headaches." Other practitioners, however, have found some of their patients not well suited to Degussa porcelains. Since each patient has individual needs, it is recommended that before considering dental treatment, they be evaluated by their own primary health practitioner to determine optimum biocompatibility of any material selected.

Migraine Headaches Relieved

A typical case was that of a nurse who was having weekly migraines so severe she couldn't work. Dr. Marshall tested her on the Computron and determined that her energetic fields were blocked in the tooth area. On questioning, she then recalled that she had never had a migraine until her mercury fillings had been replaced with composites by a well-meaning dentist known for this type of work. When the last two of her composites were replaced with Degussa porcelain, her migraines disappeared as suddenly as they had begun.

Another case involved a 28-year-old missionary who had never had dental work before he was sent to Mexico. When he came back he had four cavities, for which he got composite fillings. He then began suffering from severe migraine headaches, which became so bad that he entertained thoughts of suicide. When the composites were replaced with Degussa porcelain, his migraines, too, completely cleared.

Dental revision, which should have made these patients' symptoms better, had made them worse. The symptoms resolved only when the composites were replaced. This does not mean that Degussa may be compatible with everyone. Many other health practitioners have found a few of their patients that do not respond well to Degussa LFC. It should be noted that since each of us is an individual, your health practitioner should perform extensive tests to determine exactly which dental materials are ideally suited to your specific needs.

The Compounding Effect

The fact that not everyone with toxic teeth gets crippled by disease has been explained by the "compounding effect." Mary Buckley, a nutritionist formerly employed by Dr. Hal Huggins, D.D.S., observes that the immune system is normally capable of handling dental metals, until some other stressor comes along and tips the scales.

She illustrates with the case of a 27-year-old female MS victim who came into the office in great pain and weighing only 76 pounds. The woman said her problems had begun when she was fourteen, when she got several root canals and amalgam fillings. Metal posts had also been inserted to hold her teeth together. These posts, Mary maintains, are among the worst offenders in impairing the immune system. But what seems to have precipitated this patient's immunity crisis was the fact that her childhood playground was a nearby golf course that had been heavily sprayed with pesticides to keep it artificially green. The combination of the two stressors, one internal and one external, was evidently more than the woman's immune system could ward off.

The compounding effect was also demonstrated in a recent study prompted by the mysterious Gulf War Syndrome. When chickens were exposed to toxic chemicals, those exposed to only one chemical showed no outward signs of illness or debilitation. But chickens exposed to any two chemicals exhibited varying degrees of weight loss, diarrhea, shortness of breath, decreased activity, stumbling, leg weakness and tremors. Chickens exposed to three chemicals showed the most severe symptoms, including total paralysis and death in some cases. This was true although the total amount of chemicals to which the chickens were exposed was the same in each group. It was the combination that evidently tipped the scales.[4]

The compounding effect may also explain why some but not all mercury-toxic patients get Alzheimer's disease. Dr. H. Richard Casdorph and Dr. Morton Walker, in their book Toxic Metal Syndrome, state that there is a threshold level beyond which toxic metals accumulate in the body. They cite a study involving aluminum-containing antacids. Patients ingesting less than five milligrams per day of aluminum remained in negative aluminum balance. But when the patients' diets were supplemented with antacids, the scales tipped the other way and aluminum was retained in their bodies. Other studies show that the neurotoxicity of aluminum is increased by exposure to mercury and other toxic metals.[5] Abnormal accumulations both of mercury and of aluminum have been found in the brains of Alzheimer's patients. It follows that people absorbing heavy doses of mercury from their teeth <u>and</u> ingesting heavy doses of antacids would be more likely to develop symptoms than people exposed to only one of these heavy metal sources.

Elusive Side Effects

Although most people with amalgam fillings escape Alzheimer's disease and MS, they may be subject to more subtle adverse effects. If your teeth don't hurt, you aren't likely to link them to remote bodily ills; but research shows that that is just where such reactions tend to show up — systemically in the rest of the body. In a study reported in several dental journals including <u>The Journal of the American Dental Association</u>, eight out of ten patients implanted with dental nickel alloys showed systemic reactions, although they had no oral symptoms.[6]

The hazards of mercury in large doses are well known. Mercury disrupts most biological systems as a result of its affinity for sulfhydryl groups, which are essential constituents of most enzymes and hormones. Cats fed fish containing methyl mercury show Alzheimer's-like brain lesions; and humans who eat mercury-laden fish exhibit neurological symptoms including memory loss, tremors, irritability, insomnia, numbness, and visual disturbances.[7] What are harder to establish are mercury's effects in small doses. But according to researcher Robert Siblerud:

> Even small amounts of mercury exposure over a long period can produce the same devastating effects as a large dose in a short time. Insidious long-term

exposure to mercury can produce damage after many years <u>with no trace of the etiology of the problem</u>.[8]

Unsuspected Immuno-suppression

David Eggleston, D.D.S., observes that to definitively demonstrate amalgam sensitivity, the patient should be tested before, during and after insertion. Then the amalgam should be removed and the patient should be re-tested. Few people are willing to volunteer for these harrowing procedures, but Dr. Eggleston managed to find one. His dental assistant was in her twenties, in good physical condition, on a soccer team, and without evident symptoms; yet blood tests revealed that her "T" cell count was very low. "T" cells, the white blood cells essential for the proper functioning of the immune system, are measured conventionally to determine the immuno-suppressive effect of cancer chemotherapy. The average range is 50 to 80, and an ideal count is in the 70s. Dr. Eggleston's dental assistant had a "T" cell level that was a low 47.

When he removed her dental amalgams and replaced them with temporary restorations, her "T" cell level rose dramatically — to an ideal count of 73. This result, noted Dr. Eggleston, represented a larger immune system boost than drug companies are getting with drugs. To clinch his results, he did the procedure in reverse. When he drilled some "pits" in his assistant's temporary fillings and plugged them with amalgam, her "T" cell level went back down to a low 55.[9]

Mysterious Headaches Eliminated

Dr. Marshall cites another example of amalgam toxicity that was unsuspected by either the patient or the dentist. The patient was a woman in her late fifties with devastating migraine headaches, whose problem was traced by electro-dermal screening to two crowns. The dentist Dr. Marshall referred her to, however, said there was certainly no problem visible from the outside. The dental work was beautifully done, and the woman wasn't experiencing pain in those teeth.

He wouldn't have touched them without Dr. Marshall's insistence.

When the crowns came off, the dentist was shocked to find that they had been electroplated together. The battery effect between a stainless steel crown and a gold alloy (palladium) crown had turned the concealed adjoining area into a green and brown mess of corrosion. When the steel crown was replaced with a gold one, the woman's migraine headaches disappeared — but only for about three weeks. When she finally had both crowns replaced with unreinforced Degussa porcelain, her regular weekly migraines abated for good.

Chapter 7

Science and the Law:
The Dentist's Dilemma

The ADA has covered up its culpability in the same way
breast implant and cigarette manufacturers deny disease
connection to those products. . . [F]rom a legal
standpoint, the most logical way for the ADA to avoid
the largest class action lawsuit ever brought before the
courts and its consequences, is to stop using amalgam,
tomorrow.

— Tom Warren, author of
Beating Alzheimer's

To date, the only materials found by electro-dermal
screening to be wholly biocompatible long-term are those
found naturally in the body: calcium, phosphorus,
magnesium, etc. But until recently, no material composed
solely of these natural components was strong enough to
withstand the daily stresses of chewing. New fusion
techniques using lasers or high intensity light of specific
wavelengths have finally made this feat possible, allowing
biocompatible materials to be laminated to the tooth in a
way that duplicates the strength of the tooth itself.
Disinfection with lasers, has also insured the safety of root
canals filled with biocompatible materials. The field is
extremely new, but hundreds of cases already demonstrate
the reversal of chronic symptoms when dental metals, plastic
composites, and non-biocompatible root canal fillings have
all been replaced in the mouth with wholly biocompatible
materials.

That's the latest on the dental front, but you aren't likely to hear about it from your dentist. When a new material promises to revolutionize computers or cars or toothpastes, manufacturers are swift to tout the news. If millions of mercury amalgam fillings are now obsolete, why aren't dentists rushing to tell their patients? The market potential for dental revision, after all, is enormous.

The Threat of Litigation

One deterrent is the threat of lawsuits. Like the cigarette industry, which is currently facing a huge legal liability in the wake of research linking its products to thousands of cancer deaths, the American Dental Association could face an ominous liability for its support of dental materials in the face of research showing their toxicity. Small wonder, then, that the ADA has not been eager to embrace data incriminating the materials used conventionally in dentistry.

For the individual dentist, there is also the threat to his license. State licensing laws require practitioners to follow standard practice in the medical or dental community. These laws essentially make innovation illegal, since anything "new" cannot yet be "standard practice" in the community.

The problem was illustrated in a 1990 case involving a North Carolina family physician named Charles Guess, M.D. Revocation of Dr. Guess' medical license was confirmed by a federal district court on the ground that he had used homeopathic remedies in his practice. The remedies were not only legal but were available without a prescription, and Dr. Guess testified that he had found them to be more effective on his patients than pharmaceuticals. The only thing wrong with them was that no other M.D. was using them in North Carolina. Dr. Guess was therefore held guilty of not conforming to "prevailing medical practice" as required by statute.[1]

Imposition of legal liability on the dental profession for endorsing toxic materials is actually unlikely, since until now the technology wasn't available to make a filling material that was functionally superior to the conventional options. But a conspiracy of silence has nevertheless prevailed. Except for a very limited use of composites, the more advanced technologies aren't taught in dental schools, where the "gold standard" remains mercury amalgam. Dental schools are geared toward graduating students to pass state dental board exams, which test applicants only on their knowledge and use of the conventional amalgam. The school's administration states that if they don't teach the old techniques and materials, their students won't pass the state board exams whose tests are based on these subjects. If students do not pass the exams, the schools say they will lose their accreditation. The state boards, however, state that they test on these subjects because the schools teach them. Therefore, they assume, these subjects are current thought. Each entity uses the other to justify continuing old-style dentistry and neither one is willing to change. Practitioners who have become comfortable and proficient with the traditional way are understandably leery of venturing into trickier, more controversial waters. The new materials also require new equipment, which is expensive, and requires training that isn't offered in dental school.

The standard of practice will no doubt change with the introduction of the laser into dentistry, just as it did in medicine. When delicate eye surgeries became possible with a beam of light, there was no longer any justification for cutting into that area with a knife. But impeding this sort of rational evolution of the health sciences are licensing laws that penalize innovation and the dissemination of information. As noted in the Preface, the ADA's Code of Conduct currently provides that it is improper and unethical for a dentist to recommend the removal of mercury amalgam restorations except for cosmetic reasons. Hal Huggins, D.D.S., the Colorado Springs dentist who pioneered mercury amalgam removal for health reasons, recently had his dental license revoked; and other practitioners have found themselves in similar litigation over their licenses.[2]

The Case Against Dr. Huggins

Dr. Huggins deserves a great deal of credit for his groundbreaking work in removing mercury amalgam fillings.

But as with all pioneers, his trial-and-error protocol evidently had flaws. Many of his hopeful patients did not get well, and some actually got worse. Perhaps this was because their mercury fillings were replaced with plastic composite materials that also blocked the body's energetic pathways. Or perhaps it was because the drastic alternative of extracting root-filled teeth and drilling out cavitations gave rise to new problems. (These bone-destroying approaches to hidden infection have now been obviated by the laser and micro-surgery within the bone. See Chapter 13.) For whatever reasons, Dr. Huggins had enough dissatisfied patients that the Colorado state dental board was able to build a case against him, resulting in the revocation of his dental license in the spring of 1996.

Regardless of the merits of the case, there is reason to suspect a political agenda. Dr. Huggins had been a lone voice speaking out on the amalgam issue for the previous twenty years. Suspicion is aroused by the nature of the charges and the magnitude of the offense mounted by the attorney general's office. The allegations began with the charge that Dr. Huggins' publications were "misleading, deceptive, and false because they suggest that a wide range of medical problems are caused by amalgam fillings." Some 23 members of the attorney general's office busily prosecuted the case at taxpayers' expense, including an estimated two million dollars' worth of investigations over the last two decades. How was that price tag justified? Perhaps it was considered cheap compared to the worst case-scenario: if Dr. Huggins and his supporters were to succeed in proving mercury amalgam constitutes a consumer hazard, an estimated two billion mercury amalgam fillings might arguably have to be replaced at practitioners' expense.

The complaint branded Dr. Huggins' unconventional treatments "sham, illusory and without scientific basis." He countered that his claims of immune reactivity to toxic dental materials were supported by the records of about 10,000 patients, on whom he had the results of about 80 or 90 tests each. He also had data on approximately 3,000 patients showing changes in lymphocyte viability induced by dental materials in the oral cavity.

"Lymphocytes," he notes, "are the primary white blood cells in the immune system . . . One thing that's rather interesting is that you get a certain compromise from adding mercury, a certain compromise from adding nickel and a certain compromise from copper. But if you add them together, one plus one plus one does not equal three. There is a compounding effect here that I think is quite serious and should be addressed by dentistry, but honestly dentistry is not interested in this for some reason or another."[3] Dr. Huggins suggested the reason might be the enormous potential liability facing the profession.

A letter to the editor in the April 1996 Townsend Letter for Doctors concluded:

> The investigation and prosecution of Dr. Huggins is driven by more than a concern for the public interest. It is built on government careers, agency funding, sales profits and a fear of the truth. The interests allied against Dr. Huggins . . . share one commonality: they all have something to gain by eliminating the debate on the safety of amalgam.[4]

Caught Between the American Dental Association and the American Bar Association

Meanwhile, a growing group of dental practitioners has become uneasy with the ADA's official stance. These "biological" dentists are acutely aware of the health hazards of poorly done dental work, and of the toxicity of many of the materials commonly used in dentistry. They have even taken their grievances to court, suing the ADA for nondisclosure of information critical to the proper treatment of their patients. The suit, however, was unsuccessful.

If lawsuits by concerned dentists won't prompt a change in recommended materials and dental training, consumer lawsuits soon may. Paralleling the revolution in medical thinking is one in consumer awareness. Patients are demanding a voice and choice in their own medical treatments. Under the legal doctrine of "informed consent," a doctor or dentist is required to inform his patient not only of the patient's condition and prognosis, but of the benefits, risks, and costs of <u>all</u> the available alternatives. That means not only the dentist who does <u>not</u> use mercury amalgam but the dentist who <u>does</u> use it must now be prepared to defend his practices in court. Worse, he must be prepared to undertake that battle alone. He can no longer rely on his dental association to come to his rescue.

This was illustrated in a lawsuit filed recently in Santa Clara, California, for damage incurred when mercury amalgam was placed by a dentist without first obtaining the plaintiff's informed consent. The ADA was joined as a defendant along with the dentist, on the ground that it officially endorses dental amalgam. But it moved to be dismissed from the lawsuit, stating, "The ADA (as a trade association) owes no legal duty of care to protect the public . . . ." The ADA contended that while it supports the individual components of amalgam, it cannot stand behind the dentist's mixture of the final product, over which the ADA has no control. Based on this argument, the dental union was dismissed from the case.[5] This argument seems ridiculous as today's amalgam come in a pre-sealed capsule and the dentist has little or no means of altering its components prior to automated mixing. Yet inspite of this the judge dismissed the ADA from the suit.

It isn't hard to envision what looms on the horizon. Hungry attorneys need only hang around the doorsteps of managed care dental facilities, in which patients are almost certainly not being advised of their dental options, to find themselves wading in work. Mercury has now been shown to be released from dental amalgam at the rate of 3 to 17 micrograms per day, and mercury is classified as a drug. The astute hungry lawyer can argue that the dentist is, in effect, implanting a time-released drug into his client's body, an act requiring the patient's prior informed consent. The patient is also entitled to be informed that amalgam weakens the tooth, potentially leading to breakage; and that there are other materials that not only don't fracture teeth but can reinforce them, preventing future dental problems; and that the largest dental manufacturer now has a warning label on its usage.

That puts the dentist who uses mercury amalgam in an awkward position. He is caught between the legal sharks who are waiting for him <u>not</u> to warn his patients of amalgam's hazards, and the ADA's Code of Conduct, under which he is liable to lose his dental license if he <u>does</u> issue these warnings.

Solving the Dentist's Dilemma

While training in the newer, safer dental materials is not currently available to dental undergraduates, it is offered to practicing dentists in continuing education courses and advanced professional seminars. Dr. Richard Hansen, who teaches such a course at the University of California at Los Angeles, and at his training facility, the Pacific Institute for Advanced Dental Studies in Fullerton, Ca., concedes that the toxicity of mercury amalgam is a controversial issue in the dental industry. But he observes that the ADA's proscription is against advising patients of mercury's toxicity. Removing amalgam on structural grounds remains within the dentist's scope of practice even by ADA standards. The prudent dentist needs to learn the newer options if only to avoid malpractice charges arising from the structural damage amalgam fillings can cause.

"When I recommend having amalgam fillings replaced," says Dr. Hansen, "I recommend it for a dental reason. Almost all silver fillings cause leakage, cracking and structural problems. I recommend changing them when we see obvious damage to the tooth; and we see breakdown, deterioration, leakage and decay under almost every amalgam filling. Of course we are always able to remove them upon a patient's request or prescription from their primary health care provider."

If amalgam's toxicity remains controversial, its structural limitations can hardly be disputed. Charges that it is a structurally inferior material date back 150 years. "Amalgam is inferior because it leads to more dental work," asserts Dr. Hansen. "Most adult dental work is done around fillings that have leaked or teeth that have been cracked by amalgam fillings. It's only because of failing materials that more dental work is usually required. We've seen in videotaped camera exams on several thousand patients that the need for new adult dental work is nearly always required only on teeth that have already been 'restored' by a dentist. Virgin teeth right next to them remain cavity and fracture free." It seems that most adult dentistry is necessitated by previous dentistry.

Amalgam Leads to Root Canals and Crowns

Root canals and crowns are virtually always preceded by mercury/amalgam fillings. The non re-enforcing mercury/amalgam acts like a wedge that forces the cusps of the teeth apart. Eventually, part of the tooth breaks off and a crown is required; or bacteria penetrate to the nerve, and a root canal is required.

Root canal therapy involves removing the nerve and other infected or dead material, then packing the canal and sealing it. The procedure is necessitated by exposure of the nerve, even when that result comes about from excessive drilling by the dentist himself. The procedure is done to eliminate pain and counter the imminent threat of infection; but whether it achieves this result is hotly debated, as we have seen.

A crown, also called a cap or jacket, is an artificial tooth-shaped fabrication put over the natural crown (the part of the tooth above the gum line) after a major portion of the tooth has been ground away to make space for the cap. Crowns made of conventional materials are reinforced with metals that may be toxic to the body and that can give rise to the battery effect.

Newer filling materials discussed in Section II can be bonded in a way that avoids these dire results. Not only are the cusps not forced apart when the new materials and procedures are used; they are actually fused together and reinforced.

Trading Convenience for Strength

Amalgam's major advantage is that it is pliable and easy to insert. Where hard restorative materials have to be sent out to a lab for precision manufacture to the shape of the tooth, amalgam can be pressed like bubble gum into the decayed area on the spot.

"There's a joke going around," says Dr. Hansen, "that the only reason we don't see thumb prints on amalgams anymore is that dentists now wear gloves. But it's true. I have seen thumb prints in some old amalgams."

The downside of amalgam is that it doesn't naturally stick, bond, or re-enforce the tooth. In addition, a large amount of the inside of the tooth must be carved into the shape of a wedge to prevent the filling from falling out after it dries. With "extension for prevention," the top of the wedge winds up being quite large; and the bottom has to be even larger.

"Dentists have to do 'extension for prevention' because amalgam leaks like a sieve," says Dr. Hansen. "It doesn't seal, it's non-adhesive, so you have to extend it to where nothing can get trapped under it and cause new decay. Another reason dentists placing amalgam remove a larger than necessary amount of good tooth structure is that they don't know exactly where the decay is, and they want to make sure they get it all. Small conservative preparations and fillings can also fall out or break. What remains of the natural tooth is a mere hollow shell filled with a large ugly plug of mercury amalgam. A small cavity can end up with a filling that drills out three-quarters of the tooth. But studies have now shown that if even thirty percent of the intercuspal width of the tooth is removed, the tooth loses as much as eighty percent of its structural strength." It is no wonder all dentists tell their patients not to eat hard substances and not to chew on ice. Whereas healthy, unrestored, non-dentist treated teeth are quite strong and resistant to fracture, mercury/amalgam treated teeth are quite weak.

The hard outer enamel is just the structural protective shell of the tooth. If the enamel were removed from the tooth, it too would be brittle and weak. It becomes strong when it is laminated to the inner dentin, with very high bond strength, making the normal tooth structurally sound, quite strong, and resistant to fracture. Inside is dentin, which has tubules that go directly to the nerve. When alloys are put in, the whole structure gets ripped apart; and with repetitive stress, it gets fractures. The sides of the teeth break away, fractures run through the root, and bacteria get into these areas. Long-term infiltration of bacteria causes progressive degeneration in nerve health. The dentin eventually cracks through and fractures, and a root canal is required. The tooth is an engineered object that is structurally reinforced and interconnected inside. Amalgam shatters the reinforcements, contributes to fracturing and allows bacteria to invade.

"We've been taught in dentistry," says Dr. Hansen, "that there is a central pit in the teeth, but researchers studying the teeth with an electron microscope have now shown that this may not be true. We've been taught that all the ridges and grooves on a tooth are 'sluiceways' for funneling food off the tooth, but teeth chew whether they are flat, grooved, or any other shape. If you were an engineer designing structural reinforcement, you'd put in T-members, structural ridges and reinforcements, and that's what we have in the tooth — structural reinforcements and connections designed so that as you bite down, the whole tooth absorbs the force and dissipates it. We set up self-destruction by removing these structural reinforcements and by jamming amalgam into this engineered structure at an early age. Tiny fracture lines can be seen in the teeth around virtually all amalgams."

Visual Evidence

As evidence for his contentions, Dr. Hansen has provided the photographs in Figures 4 through 17.

Figure 4 shows a normal chewing surface of a back tooth. Note the reinforced ridges of enamel that give the outer part of the tooth the strength to absorb and withstand the heavy forces of chewing. In the deep grooves of the tooth, cavities begin and process into the inner portion of the tooth (dentin). Note the dark holes of small beginning cavities (dental disease). The normal treatment of small cavities has been to drill open a large amount of tooth structure just to wedge in the silver/mercury filling.

Figure 5 is a photo of an entire lower jaw with standard traditional dentistry. We can see several large mercury fillings that are fractured and leaking decay; large gold crowns that have been placed over previous large mercury filled teeth that had decayed, fractured and failed; and also a missing space where a prior mercury filling had fractured the tooth down the middle and required an extraction.

Figure 6 shows a tooth that has a small cavity in its surface. Figure 7 shows the cavity being vaporized with pin-point precision by the laser. Note that the structural reinforcements in the tooth are preserved keeping the tooth strong. Figure 8 shows the tooth being filled with an injectable, glass-filled, biocompatible tooth replacement material. The tooth and the filling are fused together with the argon laser light.

Figure 9 shows two teeth. One filled with a silver mercury filling (note cracking inside of tooth, leaky margins around filling, and corrosion). The other is filled and fused with the laser (note the tooth remains structurally strong and resistant to future problems). Which one would you rather have done?

Figure 10 and 11 show teeth that have had similar mercury fillings placed and over time these fracture lines, and the lack of structural support for the teeth, have led to portions of the teeth breaking completely off. The normal dental treatment now would be to grin down the rest of the good outer tooth and place a crown. Many times a root canal would also be necessary.

Figure 12 shows a photo of mercury fillings before they are removed from the teeth. These teeth looked normal to the eye of the dentist, since they are used to seeing the fracture lines and corrosion around most alloys. The x-rays did not reveal any decay or other problems. However when these fillings were removed, figure 13 shows the black corrosion and large decay that was present under the mercury fillings. Also note that only a hollow shell of the tooth was left after the teeth were prepared for amalgam insertion. The teeth had deteriorated under the amalgam and decay and bacteria have leaked inside under the teeth. Because the amalgams do not hold the teeth together and are non-adhesive, they also contribute to the cracking and fracturing of filled teeth. It is no wonder dentists tell us not to bite on hard things like ice. Rarely do unfilled, non dentist treated teeth break, even when chewing something hard.

Figure 14 shows gold crowns that have been used to restore broken or fractured teeth as in the previous photos. On x-rays and during examination these crowns appeared normal and no problems were detected. Figure 15 shows what the inside of the teeth looked like when these crowns were removed. The black is the metallic, oxidative, corrosion byproducts of the gold and other metals from the years of the cement dissolving and leaking. The subsequent bacterial invasion accelerates the corrosion and leaking, as does the presence of other materials nearby.

Figure 16 shows a section of the mouth filled with the mercury amalgams that are leaking, decaying and fracturing the teeth. Figure 17 shows the same section of the same mouth restored with strong, biocompatible, tooth-like ceramics that have been fused into the teeth. With these materials and techniques the teeth have been restored back to the original strength that God had made the tooth. Because they are now structurally strong again, perhaps these teeth may not need any other dental treatment for the rest of the patient's life. Wouldn't that be a great benefit to the patient and save countless hours of retreatment, expense, and inconvenience?

Ironic, Isn't It?

Tooth decay is considered a serious liability because it may lead, successively, to loss of part or all of the crown, infection of the dental pulp, infection of the structures at the end of the root, loss of the tooth, and infection of the whole body through the bloodstream.[6] To prevent this dire progression, cavities in the tooth are drilled and filled with mercury amalgam. Mercury amalgam and high-speed drilling, in turn, can result in structural damage to the tooth, which leads to dental infection, root canals, crowns, extractions, and systemic infections — the very consequences cavities are filled to avoid. Yet inspite of this, the average, traditional dentist continues to tell their patient that amalgam is the strongest, best, longest lasting filling that they can use. The fact that these metal fillings last for quite some time has more to do with the remarkable strength of our God given teeth, even when destroyed by drilling and filled with amalgam. When they do finally break, larger more invasive, expensive dentistry is needed.

The conventional techniques may have been acceptable when there was nothing better, but now there is. Consumers themselves can solve the dentist's dilemma, by demanding the best.

Chapter 8

The Problem of Hidden Infection

First, one makes fun of such hypotheses. Later, one becomes silent. Finally, one exclaims, 'That's what I've always said.'
— Ernesto Adler, M.D., D.D.S.[1]

What's wrong with the occasional root canal? Like with amalgam, dentists are split into two camps on this issue. The furor began in 1992, when George Meinig, D.D.S., a founding member of the American Association of Endodontists, published his controversial book Root Canal Cover-up Exposed! Dr. Meinig's book was based on the work of Weston Price, D.D.S., M.S., F.A.C.D., the president and first director of the American Dental Association Research Institute, whose extensive research during the 1920's and 30's was discussed in Chapter 2. Dr. Price found that:

(1) No medication tested could sterilize the root canal cavity sufficiently to kill all the bacteria inside.

(2) The packing material (usually gutta percha) shrank when it dried, leaving spaces around it where bacteria could multiply and spread.

(3) The cementum (the hard outer protective coating of the root of the tooth) was not the impenetrable barrier it was assumed to be. Bacteria could not pass through it, but the toxins they created could.[2]

Later studies have verified some of Dr. Price's findings. A 1987 study demonstrated that anaerobic bacteria (bacteria not requiring oxygen to live) could survive and breed in the lesions in non-vital teeth. In a 1990 follow-up study, microorganisms were recovered from these lesions in every endodontically-treated tooth examined.[3] Recent research conducted by Dr. Boyd Haley of the University of Kentucky showed that the strains of bacteria found in these covert breeding grounds are more toxic than botulism. In fact, they are some of the most toxic substances known to man.[4]

Dr. Meinig raises the ominous specter that possibly a third of the diseases in the United States are traceable directly or indirectly to dental infections. About one billion teeth are now root-filled, and 24 million new root canals are performed yearly in the United States. Gutta percha, one of the filling materials he tested extensively, remains the most widely used filling material today.[5]

When Theory Lags Behind Facts

Dr. Price published a monumental two-volume, 1,170-page work summarizing his experiments and revealing the root canal's hazards in 1923.[6] He also published 220 papers on dental subjects and conducted research so extensive he was called "the world's greatest dentist." He remains well-known today, but it isn't for his work on root canals. It is for another monumental work, <u>Nutrition and Physical Degeneration</u>, which links the modern commercial diet to degenerative diseases. (See Chapter 17.) His work linking root canals to these same diseases was challenged and then suppressed by the dental profession of his day, and it had no significant impact on subsequent procedure.

Dr. Meinig was particularly well qualified to review Dr. Price's work. Besides specializing in root canal therapy, he was for twenty years the director of the Price Pottenger Nutritional Foundation, an organization whose purpose is to maintain and publicize the work of Dr. Price and Francis Pottenger Jr., M.D., on degenerative diseases. Despite this extensive background, Dr. Meinig had not heard of Dr. Price's root canal research until Hal Huggins, D.D.S., alerted him to it. How, wondered Dr. Meinig, was that possible? How and why had these exhaustive studies been so long buried?

He attributed the "coverup" to theoretical disputes. Dr. Price's discoveries relied on several theories that conventional medicine rejected in his day. Ironically, says Dr. Meinig, these same concepts are now accepted virtually without comment.

From Fringe to Mainstream

One of these controversial concepts was that bacteria are polymorphic: they can mutate into other, hardier, more toxic forms. When Dr. Price publicized his observation that the bacteria in root-filled teeth are more virulent and resistant to disinfectants than their forebears, he was not merely ridiculed but was accused of fabricating the data. Yet today, it is well known that bacteria can mutate into strains that can survive in autoclaves or resist antibiotics that would have annihilated their progenitors.[7] The concept of dangerous mutant bacteria has even invaded Hollywood. Dr. Price's controversial assertion that the infection-causing bacteria are anaerobic (thrive in the absence of oxygen) has also now been amply demonstrated.[8]

Another disputed concept he relied on was that of the "focal infection" or "interference field" — the idea that a localized disease-producing process can cause disorders somewhere else in the body. Dr. Price maintained that the vast majority of focal infections originate in the teeth. Bacteria gain an easy entry from there into the bloodstream, bypassing the body's usual defense systems and hitching a ride to any organ in which they choose to take up residence. Usually, he found, that organ was the heart. Acceptance of this once-controversial theory today, says Dr. Meinig, is evidenced by the fact that patients with heart problems are routinely given antibiotics before tooth cleanings and other dental work. However, this only applies to those patients who have a know history of heart damage, transplants, hip or joint replacements or other high risk conditions. The drugs are intended to circumvent the well known possibility that bacteria in the mouth can travel to the heart and precipitate a dangerous infection there.

Dr. Meinig adds as a cautionary aside that antibiotics may not be sufficient to prevent such infections. In September of 1996, the ADA's Council on Scientific Affairs (SCA) concurred, issuing a warning about the alarming rate at which microbial resistance to antibiotics is increasing. The Council blamed the trend on antibiotic misuse and overuse.[9] Ironically, new research also links the trend to the mercury amalgam used in dentistry, which seems to spur resistance to antibiotics.[10]

(Women are liable to dread getting these prophylactic drugs for another reason: the heavy dose of antibiotics they are routinely given wipes out their friendly flora, resulting in vaginal yeast infections and many may interfere with oral contraceptives.)

Neural Therapy

The interference field theory was verified independently by German dentists in the 1920s. The "Huneke phenomenon" was the experimental finding that injection of a local anesthetic (procaine or lidocaine) at the base of a suspect tooth could make distant pains and symptoms go away. The procedure was called neural therapy. Ernesto Adler, M.D., D.D.S., an early pioneer of the technique, described many cases in which it was used to pinpoint the hidden source of focal infection. The interference field itself (usually an infected or impacted tooth) was then removed.

One case involved a 21-year-old woman whose teeth appeared to be perfect — she had no cavities or fillings — but she complained of intense migraine headaches and of neck and back pains. X-ray revealed a wisdom tooth under the gum that was causing pressure from lack of space. When neural therapy was done over the wisdom tooth, the procedure resulted within seconds in a 100 percent complete Huneke phenomenon: her migraines disappeared for several days. This test was repeated several times, always with the same result. Her wisdom tooth was then removed, and with it went her migraines.[11]

Today, neural therapy is used not merely for diagnosis but for treatment. Researchers have discovered that the injection of local anesthetics to carefully-selected points on the body can often cure or ameliorate a variety of conditions, usually of the chronic type. Visible scar tissue is a common focal interference. The scar evidently blocks the energetic field running through it. Injection of the scar is reported to bring immediate pain relief at points far distant from it. The injected anesthetic apparently induces changes in the function of the nerves and of the cells and tissues they serve. The effect continues for days, weeks or months — significantly longer than can be attributed to the anesthetic alone. Repeated injections last for progressively longer periods until the effect becomes permanent.[12] Neural therapy has been extensively researched and is the subject of many publications, mainly by physicians in Europe and South America. The definitive text is the Dosch Manual of Neural Therapy.[13]

The Cavitation Problem

In the 1990s, Hal Huggins, D.D.S., added further fuel to the dental interference field theory with the discovery of the "cavitation" as a major source of focal infection.

After reading Dr. Price's studies, Dr. Huggins added the removal of root-filled teeth to his protocol. At first, he says, there was a dramatic increase in patient response. But later, some patients would backslide. Apparently, the focal infections had not all been removed. But if not, where were they hiding? He suspected they were buried in the periodontal ligament — the "hammock" in which the tooth sits. This ligament is routinely left behind after an extraction. If it isn't removed with the tooth, the cells filling in the hole with new bone will come up against it. These cells are programmed to make bone only next to bone. When they come up against the soft tissue of the ligament, they stop rebuilding. A hole is left, over which the skin re-grows. This hidden cavern then becomes a haven for bacteria and other mutant organisms.

Dr. Huggins postulated that most jaws never completely fill in with bone, even after years-old extractions. When he explored these old sites, he confirmed that they usually contained a hole or cavitation under the skin where the tooth had been pulled. After the drill had broken through the skin and bone a couple of millimeters, he could feel it drop down into the invisible hole below. He estimated that such cavitations were left after extractions in 95 percent of cases, whether or not the holes showed up on x-ray.

To counter this problem, he began drilling old extraction sites as a matter of routine, including those done on wisdom teeth and for orthodontia. He routed out the ligament and about one millimeter of surrounding jawbone, and supplemented the patient with extra calcium. He maintains that this modification significantly improved his success rate with multiple sclerosis.

A major problem with the procedure was persuading patients of the necessity for it. In addition the bone for the jaw resorbed following surgery and many cavitational surgeries became infected or had to be redone. There is also no guarantee that the bone will completely fill in a treated site. However, inspite of the complications and risks, he felt compelling evidence for the necessity of cavitational surgery finally came from an unfortunate patient who, after suffering with overwhelming problems with his teeth, committed suicide after donating his remains to dental science. Figure 18 is an actual cross-section cut from the jawbone of this patient. The unretouched photo, which was done at autopsy after the jaw was sliced down the middle, exposes a cavitation of alarming proportions.[14]

Weighing the Risks

Drilling out cavitations traumatizes the jaw and weakens the bone, so you don't want to do it unnecessarily. But whether you have an infected cavitation under an old extraction isn't easy to ascertain. Sixty percent of the bone's density must be lost before a lesion will show up on x-ray. Also, the traditional means of diagnosing a cavitation, a panorex, is actually the poorest method. It is largely guesswork. A panoramic x-ray, panorex, is considered a non-diagnostic screening tool not capable of even diagnosing cavities in teeth because of it's high distortion factor.

The problem of diagnosis has now been solved by a test to verify the toxic potential of non-vital teeth and bone cavitations. Developed by experts at the University of Kentucky, it is currently available to dentists. (See Resources.)

In addition new computer enhanced x-rays may now be used. These actually can reduce the radiation by up to 90% as well as enhance the image to provide greater resolution of bone density patterns. Ultrasound and thermal mapping are being developed to determine density patterns as well as hot and cold areas of bone. This will be useful in determining which areas of bone may be infected or inflamed and which areas of bone may be dead or necrotic.

Even if toxicity is found, however, the question remains whether invasive procedures are the best solution. A physician at a lecture recently given by Dr. Hansen reported that at least half the patients he has seen who have had cavitational surgery have wound up with large infections and cavitations caused by the surgery itself. Dr. Hansen observes that routing out the bone doesn't guarantee that bone will grow back. The patient may simply be left with a damaged jaw. Also, the traditional method of removing cavitation, grinding out bone with a large round drill, just pulverizes the toxic products and inoculates the patient by mixing them up to be absorbed into the blood stream.

Drs. Price, Huggins and Meinig are pioneers who have led the way; but besides the obvious discomfort of their protocol, extracting teeth and routing out bone are destructive procedures with their own hazards. They destabilize the bite, weaken the jaw, and can lead to dentures, partials and bridges. These devices may be made of non-biocompatible materials, creating additional interference fields in the body. Extracting the teeth can also disturb the body's energetic patterns. Scar tissue is produced that may also be an energetic blockage. Other symptoms may result from overly aggressive manipulation of the jaw and TMJ complex during the oral surgical extraction procedure. Many physicians point out that grinding out the jaw bone and the cavitation does not automatically regrow new bone. Many of these aggressive procedures may actually produce a cavitation or void where new bone does not grow back.

Figure 19 is a photo of a patient treated with an extraction and aggressive cavitational surgery. Note the residual hole left into her exposed sinus cavity that never healed. This patient experienced continual pain and many other symptoms created by the cavitational surgery. Additional surgery with the laser, new bone regeneration techniques, and microcrystalline bone replacement material, was required to help fill in and rebuild the damaged bone. Even in the best of cases the bone shrinks and causes collapse of the surrounding tissue and facial dimensions.

In addition, drastic surgical procedures can damage the jaw so much that in later years, not even dentures can be worn. Many people become so disfigured by the excessive bone removal that they become clinically depressed, just at a time when they need the optimum of positive mental energy to fight off illness.

The Hazards of Extraction and Dentures

The real teeth keep the alveolar bone around the roots intact. Removing the teeth can cause continual erosion of the bony ridge, which consists of tissue combined with spongy bone. This erosion soon causes the dentures to no longer fit properly. Dentures may also contain hazardous materials. The white portion of normal dentures is a composite or acrylic material, while the pink may contain cadmium and mercury. All of these materials can produce toxic reactions in the patient.[15] Although chrome-cobalt and nickel containing alloys have been used for many years in removable partial dentures and seems to have been well-tolerated in them, the dentures were traditionally only from 5 percent to 30 percent nickel. The newer alloys may contain 60 to 80 percent nickel, or up to 15 times as much as earlier versions. Some also contain up to 1.8 percent beryllium. Beryllium is used because it allows the material to be cast in a more fluid state, but it is one of the most toxic metals known.[16] Bridges and dentures can also throw off the bite, resulting in interference fields that are responsible for unsuspected ills in distant parts of the body.

Another risk of extraction, ironically, is infection, the very thing it may have been done to avoid. If all of the infection in the tooth socket is not removed along with the tooth, the site can be a hideaway for bacteria that can then impact the rest of the body. Infected roots can lead to serious health problems, including a condition called neuralgia inducing cavitational osteonecrosis (NICO). The patient winds up harboring a little festering bone that never gets well, and that can produce chronic, disabling pain in the jaw. Estimates are that 70 percent of atypical facial neuralgias, 10 percent of trigeminal neuralgias, and 23 percent of phantom pain and headaches are due to NICO lesions from cavitations.[17]

Meanwhile, this focal infection can be responsible for referred pain in distant parts of the body, even when the patient experiences no pain or tenderness in the mouth. The connection is established only when this pain — which no amount of local treatment has eliminated — resolves after the dental infection is cleared. A chronic painful hip joint, for example, may resolve only after a back molar socket has been cleaned out; or recurrent blinding headaches may go away only after an infected upper bicuspid tooth has been cleaned out.

We'll look at a more tooth-friendly solution to the problems of infected cavitations and infected root canals in Section II.

Chapter 9

In Search of an Ideal Dental Material

All that glistens is not gold.

— Shakespeare

Silver/mercury amalgam isn't the only hazardous dental material. Concerns have also been raised about gold, nickel, porcelain, composites, and other materials commonly placed in the mouth.

Fool's Gold

David Eggleston, D.D.S., notes that insurance companies are troubled because eighty percent of all crowns now being manufactured contain nickel-based alloys; yet the majority of insurance claims describe the covered crowns as porcelain fused to gold. Either widespread fraud is occurring, he says, or dentists themselves don't know what they are putting in their patients' mouths.[1]

Gold has been the preferred filling material for centuries for people who could afford it, but pure gold is too soft to use for most dental purposes. Pure gold foil can be used, but only in non-chewing areas. For other areas, gold castings (inlays, onlays and crowns or caps) must be used. Gold castings consist of gold alloyed with other metals to increase its strength.[2]

The more durable "gold" or "silver" fillings or crowns may now contain up to 78.5 percent palladium, a heavy metal referred to as the "fool's gold of dentistry." Like mercury, palladium is methylated or synthesized in the digestive tract; and in its methylated form, it is even more toxic than in its inorganic form. Methylated palladium is thought by some experts to be more toxic than methylated mercury, and it seems to induce symptoms of toxicity much sooner than mercury does. Metallic silver, another metal compound that may be present in "gold" dental materials, has been reported to be a solid state carcinogen.[3]

Other experts are concerned not only about the alloys in gold crowns but the gold itself. Even if pure gold were strong enough for use in dentistry without mixing it with other metals, it would still not be the ideal dental restorative material, because it is highly susceptible to the battery effect and blockage of energy meridians.

The "Porcelain" Crown

Another popular dental material is porcelain. Dental porcelains consist of crystalline minerals (feldspar, silica, alumina) in a matrix of finely ground glass particles that fuse together at high temperature to form an enamel-like material.[4] Like with gold, most "porcelain" crowns are reinforced with metal; and usually it's the non-precious variety. Introduced when the cost of gold became prohibitive in the seventies, the non-precious metal alloys contain high levels of base metals which corrode readily, release metallic components into the saliva, and are potentially quite toxic.

The Hazards of Nickel

Nickel, the most popular of these reinforcing alloys, is commonly used not only in orthodontic wire and braces for children, but in a large percentage of the bridges, partials and crowns made in the United States. Yet nickel has been known for many years to be toxic to the nervous system, and its continuous release from alloys in the mouth has now been well documented. Like mercury, it seems to affect the auto-immune system, making it particularly hazardous for people with auto-immune diseases like arthritis and some forms of cancer. Nickel compounds cause upper respiratory and lung cancers. Anecdotal evidence also links them to breast cancer. Nickel implanted in laboratory animals produces sarcomas and carcinomas, while similar metals used as controls do not. In fact, nickel is routinely used to <u>induce</u> cancer experimentally in laboratory animals. The nickel alloys used in these experiments are disturbingly similar to those used by 80 percent of the dental community as bases for "porcelain" crowns. Nickel is also the most allergenic metal known. Typically 15 to 20 percent of the population tests positive to it in skin tests. Substantially more women than men are allergic to it, apparently because women have been sensitized by wearing nickel-based jewelry. Men who pierce their ears have 33 times the incidence of nickel sensitivity as men who don't.[5]

Composites

Some of the drawbacks of metals were overcome with the development of plastic resin (composite) restorative materials. Although composites have been on the market for more than half a century, many dentists still feel they are not strong enough to be relied on. Dr. Hansen agrees they aren't the ideal filling material when used in large cavities. However, in very small cavities, especially with the pin point precision of the laser or air particle beam abrasive, where they can be injected within the structurally intact tooth the structure of the tooth itself provides the strength. In these instances, when the material is tested for compatibility on the individual patient, he considers them to be an ideal filling choice and durability to be one of their major strengths, thanks to the development of new laser fusing techniques.

"Dentists have formed the opinion that tooth-colored restorations aren't durable," he explains, "because they did break in the '70s and '80s, when they were treated like gold and were cemented rather than fused into the teeth. If you took a chunk of tooth enamel and cemented it on, it would fail. Enamel by itself is rather weak. It becomes strong only when it is laminated with high strength to the inner dentin. Your own tooth would break if it weren't fused to the inner core of the dentin. Glue merely sticks things together. To fix teeth so that the repair materials won't break off, you need to laminate them together the way beams of ceilings are laminated together and the way the enamel is laminated to the dentin. There are now ways to literally fuse the parts together, interlocking them like fingers meshing. These materials actually penetrate down into the tooth and hook or bind into the tooth itself. They aren't fused with heat but with chemicals — adhesion agents that go into the tooth, dissolve water molecules out of the dentin tubules, and carry the resin binder in. Then the solvent or carrier is evaporated out, leaving behind the resins that interlock within the tubules of the dentin. Then additional glass filled resins are placed along with the tooth replacement restoration and it's all fused together with the laser." For larger restorations, lab manufactured or computer manufactured high strength ceramics and ceramic polymers, when fused correctly, can provide not only the original strength of the tooth but may actually surpass it.

New Resins and Fusion Techniques

The original composite materials were acrylic based, which were weak; and the lack of adhesive materials to make a proper seal allowed bacteria to find their way in and cause decay. Then in the 1960s, the BIS-GMA composite resins were developed. They are interlinking polymers, a highly developed form of plastic that is harder than the acrylics and can be bonded better to the tooth structure because of another new development — micro etching of the teeth. This process dissolves the debris filled layer covering the dentin tubules thus preparing the tooth for the bonding and fusion process.

Acid etching was originally thought to be injurious to the nerve, so it wasn't done inside the tooth; but later research showed that nerve damage was the result, not of the etching acid, but of (1) bacteria that had leaked in due to an improper seal, and (2) the use of eugenol, a cyto toxic material found in many temporary cements composed of an oil extracted from cloves. When these two problems were corrected, bonding became possible to the inner core of the tooth.

"That's the foundation for most of our fusion techniques," Dr. Hansen observes. "Now we can bond to the dentin and tubules of the tooth itself. Fusion and bonding agents have been developed that approximate and in many cases surpass the strength of the natural tooth. That's a real key — fusing materials into the tooth that are stronger than the tooth itself. The technique was developed in Japan in the early '70s, but it wasn't accepted in the U.S. until 1990. That's why many dentists still don't buy into it. It's relatively new, and the exacting protocols necessary for proper placement are not yet taught in dental schools. But it's been shown over and over again that the basis of high quality dentistry is adhesion — sticking things together in a way that is bacteria-free, with materials tested for compatibility, and in a manner similar to the way the tooth is held together."

Pros and Cons of Composites

The real advance was in the bonding techniques. The composite materials themselves, unfortunately, still left something to be desired. That was the conclusion at least, of Dr. Robert Marshall after extensive testing on the Computron.

Dr. Marshall says he became interested in dental materials for personal reasons. In 1990, he had a personal brush with death as a result of poisoning from a tainted batch of the amino acid tryptophan. On the road to recovery, he set out to remove every possible source of toxicity from his body; and chief among these were the metals in his teeth. He was then faced with the problem of finding an appropriate replacement material.

He had become familiar with electro-dermal screening devices while visiting various clinics in Europe, where they were state-of-the-art. Though still considered investigational in the United States, the devices have the status in Germany, Austria and Switzerland of conventional medical procedures. Dr. Marshall purchased a computerized version called a Computron and proceeded to test not only himself but hundreds of patients with it, to determine what dental materials were compatible with their bodies. He tested materials on more than 300 patients. Disturbingly, the composite and conventional porcelain materials proved in long-term tests to impair the body's energy fields. He was quite relieved when he finally found one material that he felt was nearly universally biocompatible. This was low-fusing Degussa ceramic, or "Degussa porcelain." The rare cases in which he found it was not compatible involved patients whose immune systems were so impaired that they reacted adversely to this material. Other practitioners have also found some patients who do not test well with Degussa but have found other materials with which these patients have been compatible.

Blocking the Electromagnetic Flow

After reviewing the results of extensive testing on the Computron, Dr. Marshall and Dr. Forbes have concluded that composites may actually be <u>more</u> hazardous than amalgams.

"With composites," explains Dr. Forbes, "there is a partial blocking or abnormal conductance of the meridian, so the normal electromagnetic flow is disturbed. Amalgam works the other way; it's more highly electrical, causing a battery effect. It shorts out some other meridian, giving you headaches, etc. It can poison you, and so can other heavy metals. The high-copper silver fillings that came in in the 1980s are highly linked to neurological damage. But you can live for a number of years before you actually get symptoms. Composites, on the other hand, will sometimes make you symptomatic immediately, because they disrupt the meridian associated with that tooth. The link hasn't been proved, but there have been suspicious cases where this disruption has been followed by a sudden stroke or heart attack or hemorrhage."

Dr. Forbes adds that it's hard to tell what is actually in your composites. If you buy a can of soup, you can read a detailed breakdown of its contents on the label. But no such breakdown is required for the materials that are intimately and permanently implanted in the teeth. Many composites, however, are known to contain bis-phenol A, one of the xeno-estrogens that mimic true estrogen. Bis-phenol A has been shown to be a promoter of cancer. It can be harmful for men or women, because it sits on the hormone receptor sites and can disrupt the endocrine system.

Sexual Exhaustion And Genito-urinary Symptoms Reversed

The hormonal effects of toxic dental work were illustrated in the case of a tall, virile-looking man of about 40, who had rippling muscles and obviously worked out. Not the type normally seen in a doctor's office, he confided to Dr. Marshall that he was sexually exhausted. His sex life was virtually nil — something Dr. Marshall found hard to believe to look at him. The man also complained of serious gastrointestinal problems: burning urethra, kidney infections, frequent fevers, hormonal problems, "urine you could cut with a knife and fork." Testing on the Computron confirmed that he had chronic bladder and kidney problems; but his teeth looked great. There wasn't a cavity in his mouth. Then the man revealed that when he was twelve or thirteen, both his front teeth had been knocked out. They now consisted of porcelain crowns: porcelain jackets over stainless steel.

Dr. Marshall recommended that he have these steel-backed crowns replaced with unreinforced Degussa low-fusing ceramic, and the man agreed. This dental work was followed by a heavy detoxification for about three weeks, during which he experienced fatigue and fitful sleep. But the transformation after that, says Dr. Marshall, was remarkable. The man's symptoms completely disappeared. (The detox phase of dental work is discussed more fully in Chapter 15.)

The Ideal Solution

After exhaustively testing a broad range of dental materials, Dr. Marshall has concluded that neither metal nor composites belong in the mouth. Composites are petrochemical products, which are quite foreign to the body. They also contain metal oxides. Aluminum dioxide, particularly, has been found to be a significant blocking factor (unlike aluminum silicate, the virtually harmless form found in food). Both composites and metals obstruct the body's electromagnetic pathways.

Dr. Marshall observes that stainless steel is typically used in the bases of porcelain crowns because it's cheap; but it contains nickel, which has been shown to be carcinogenic. It's also an exquisite receiver, so it blocks and distorts the normal electromagnetic fields of the brain. If metal must be used to stabilize the lateral parts of the tooth, he says, only a very thin ring of it should be used. Metal should not cover the center of the tooth, where the energetics are flowing through to the rest of the body. The best alternative, however, is to use no metal at all. Then you will have no metallic energetic interference fields in your teeth.

"Basically," he observes, "we can't fool around with materials on the body that don't naturally occur there. The reason hydro thermal low fusing ceramics are so good is that it's made of the same materials as those found in the body. We have aluminum in our body, for example, but it's usually aluminum tri-oxide. The aluminum in composites is aluminum dioxide. It's missing a charge; it's a totally different substance." Composites with aluminum dioxide seem to be kidney-toxic."

Patients can be tested to determine toxicity, but the tests can run into hundreds of dollars; and not all practitioners are proficient at them or agree on the reliability of the results. The safer course, Dr. Marshall maintains, is to use a material that logic dictates is biocompatible, since it contains the same elements, in the same configurations, as those found naturally in the body.

"When you laser bond hydro thermal ceramic," he observes, "it's stronger than the original tooth bond; and it's the same material and hardness as the normal tooth. It's the best of the ceramics. Other ceramics are more abrasive on the opposing teeth, and they can shatter; whereas hydro thermal low fusing ceramic will 'heal' itself if there's a crack."

Besides composite filling materials, other dental products found by electro-dermal screening to test in the hazardous range include most crown, bridge and denture materials; many of the cements, binders and temporary materials; and all conventional root canal filling materials. But what are the alternatives? In Section II, we'll look at high-tech solutions to that and other challenges facing contemporary dentistry.

SECTION II
SPACE AGE DENTISTRY

Chapter 10

True Biocompatibility: Dental Materials That Mimic Nature

> After 17 years of work, scientists at the University of Southern California's dentistry school have finally. . . identified and cloned the protein that catalyzes enamel's growth. The researchers hope to harness this breakthrough to produce a putty of 'real' enamel for tomorrow's bioceramic fillings within two years.
>
> — Business Week, September 1996[1]

In February of 1997, the successful cloning of a sheep was featured in the news. If you can clone a sheep, you can clone a tooth. Researchers are now actually cloning enamel and dentin.

"This is where we'll see the more biocompatible materials of the future," Dr. Hansen maintains. "As you clone more enamel and dentin products, or get closer to the organic and inorganic components of the body, you're going to get more and more beneficial effects. If we can put those products into an injectable material, we can remineralize the teeth just by pinpointing the decayed area with a laser and injecting it. Those materials are still in research and development, but they will be totally biocompatible."

Attacking decay with a laser rather than with a drill reflects another dental milestone: the FDA approved the use of lasers on the teeth in the summer of 1997. Dr. Hansen, who was one of five dentists conducting the clinical research necessary for its approval, feels the development will help revolutionize dentistry. Lasers are replacing high-speed drills that traumatize the teeth and can lead to fractures, crowns and root canals. Laser fillings tend to be painless, eliminating the need for anesthesia. Lasers can thoroughly disinfect root canals, painlessly treat gum disease, and streamline cosmetic procedures. Lasers are also being developed that may alter the tooth structure to make it more resistant to decay and disease — a form of natural immunity to dental problems. Lasers have also made feasible what could not be consistently and reliably done before: reconstruction of damaged teeth with wholly biocompatible materials, without the use of either metals or plastics.

While we're waiting for enamel and dentin to be cloned, dental materials are available that approximate those of natural teeth.

Hydro Thermal Low Fusing Ceramics — Degussa Porcelain

Degussa porcelain isn't actually porcelain, and it isn't actually new. What is new are bonding techniques that allow it to be bonded to the tooth in a way that duplicates the strength of the tooth itself — and the discovery that it, apparently alone among available restorative materials, is wholly compatible with the body.

These new hydro thermals may actually get stronger as time goes on. Degussa porcelain takes moisture in and internally strengthens. It's more like the natural tooth than anything else.

Dr. Marshall explains, "It's like the ground substance of a tooth. It's basically calcium hydroxide, magnesium hydroxide, sodium hydroxide, and aluminum silicates. Bone is usually made of microcrystalline hydroxyapatite — calcium hydroxide, magnesium hydroxide, etc. — bound into a crystalline structure with a number of other minor elements. Degussa looks like regular porcelain, but small cracks that might occur in it will actually heal like a living substance will. In normal porcelain, the cracks will propagate and the porcelain will simply shatter. Degussa porcelain also has an abrasion coefficient that is much closer to the natural tooth than conventional porcelain. Ordinary porcelain is harder and more abrasive than natural teeth and can wear out the opposing teeth with chewing."

As Good As Gold?

Degussa porcelain works for fillings, but more strength is needed for making crowns. Many biological dentists recommend reinforcing Degussa porcelain with a higher noble content of gold called Golden Gate Gold, which tests well in short-term blood serum compatibility tests, such as the Clifford or Huggins diagnostic tests. That means the gold is less likely to provoke an immunological (allergic) reaction in the body. But this form of gold is still a metal and it is always alloyed with other metals, which is subject to the battery effect. In addition, it doesn't seem to test well in long-term biocompatibility tests on the Computron.

"Besides testing allergic response," Dr. Hansen observes, "the electro-dermal screening tests the electrical meridians of the body: is the material blocking the electromagnetic energy that the brain and nerves produce? Metals — even pure gold — are by their very nature blocking the flow of energy through the meridians running through the teeth, thus interfering with the body's immuno-responses and neurologic transmitters. If we use materials that don't block the meridians and electromagnetic potentials, we have a better chance of allowing a free flow of energy to achieve balance and wellness."

The question remains, can crowns be made with unreinforced Degussa porcelain? Dr. Hansen maintains that they can. Like with composites, the secret is in the preparation, the attention to detail, and meticulous fusing techniques.

Laser Fusion

The potential for duplicating the strength and biocompatibility of natural teeth, as noted earlier, has been accepted and used in the United States only since 1990. This achievement was the result of two developments: (1) the increased strength of the material itself, and (2) fusion techniques that allow stronger bonding directly to the tooth itself.

"In the past," explains Dr. Hansen, "crowns were merely glued or cemented to the base of the tooth. Cement was always the weak link in the gold crown system: it can dissolve or wash away. Saliva, along with the multitude of chemical reactions taking place daily in the mouth, has potent acid and enzyme activity that can break down lots of materials. Even composites can be dissolved out by saliva over time." The cement that is used for most metal and porcelain covered metal crowns has approximately 0.25 to 0.5 megapascals of strength. The strength of the enamel-dentin bond within the tooth is approximately 25.0 megapascals. The newer fusion materials have a fusion strength to the tooth of 25-30 megapascals. Therefore cement has roughly 50 to 100 times less strength to the tooth structure than either the enamel to dentin bond or the ceramic to enamel bond. Whereas the newer fusible ceramics can equal or surpass the bond strength of the natural tooth.

The reason most teeth had to be ground down to a 'peg' to construct a crown when the structure of a tooth could no longer be filled, was because of the cement. The cement held the tooth replacement so poorly to the tooth that the dentist had to grind the tooth down just to obtain a larger surface area than was necessary so that the poor adhesion of the cement would hold. This always seemed to be so destructive since most of the inner part of the tooth was usually already gone because of the large filling that was placed inside of the tooth. The dentist would then grind away the only good part of the tooth, the exterior, just to get a crown to stay and not fall out.

Now, crowns can be bonded in a way that duplicates the strength of the bond between enamel and dentin. With these newer techniques, less of the tooth needs to be ground away. In fact, very little if any, of the good, sound tooth structure needs to be removed. Just the old, broken filling and any new decay, corrosion, or disease is replaced — all of the good tooth remains. This helps insure the structural integrity of the tooth and help eliminate future problems.

To join the remaining tooth with the replacement restoration, adhesives are used that harden with the help of light. The adhesives aren't glues but are glass-filled resin bonding agents. Although they're called composite resins, they aren't the composites we normally think of — the hydrocarbon-based plastic products like the methyl methacrylates traditionally used in dentures. Rather, they're composed of 70-80% glass and other crystal-like materials, and are "plastic" only in the sense that they are pliable due to the resin matrix that holds the glass filler particles.

Like with composite fillings, acid together with laser etching is used to prepare the surface of the tooth for these materials. Then the composite resin is injected between the "fingers" of the two materials to be bonded. The strength of the grip of these clasped fingers is determined by the number of molecular bonds that are converted from the pliable to the rigid cross-linked state as the resin hardens. Light is used to facilitate these conversions — and lasers, the purest form of light, are the most efficient tools for this purpose. The process can be done without them, but studies have shown that lasers convert more of the resin bonds, convert them faster, and make the resulting bond harder and stronger than any other option currently available. The resin is literally locked into both the tooth and the crown, resulting in a fusion material that hardens to a strength that may in some cases be greater than that of the natural interface between enamel and dentin.

"The new hard tissue Erbium laser can increase fusion strength by 50 percent," says Dr. Hansen. "It makes the bond stronger and more impervious to problems later, reducing the risk of marginal leakage. The drill leads to leakage because it produces micro-fracturing within the tooth structure and enamel crystalline rods. The laser helps overcome the objection I hear all the time from dentists, that they don't want to use ceramics because they aren't strong, won't last, and they are too hard to use. The new restorative materials bonded with laser fusion and the new adhesion techniques consistently surpass the strength of natural teeth. Ceramics can be used without lasers, using high-energy curing lights, provided the frequency of the light corresponds to that necessary for the conversion process. If not results may be inconsistant. Curing lights must be checked with meters every week since the bulb can degrade and lose its strength. Failures blamed on the material may be due to failures in equipment and technique. The laser has allowed consistently strong results with ceramics."

When these new bonding techniques are used, says Dr. Hansen, Degussa porcelain alone has proved to be strong enough for making crowns. It isn't as hard as gold or porcelain, but just like the tooth's enamel, it doesn't need to be.

Dr. Marshall explains, "The body is a carbon-cycle, fragile, biochemical, frail machine, fraught with pitfalls. We're not working on cadavers, where we're trying to preserve the structure for posterity. We're trying to put something in that will work without killing us. The net strength of an inlay or onlay of Degussa porcelain, when laser-fused to the tooth, is stronger than the original tooth. It doesn't need to be as strong as metal."

For bridges, stronger biocompatible materials are in the process of development.

The December, 1997, issue of Popular Mechanics Magazine featured a cover article titled, 'Bridges of Glass.' On the cover it stated, "Exotic materials are rewriting the rules of bridge building." The new materials consist of layers of glass fibers vacuum filled with new resins. The reason industry is moving to these new space age materials is simple. Even though they are more costly to build initially, "traditional steel and concrete bridges that cross roads, rivers, and gullies are corroding faster than their owners can repair or replace them" thereby greatly increasing the long term costs of the bridges. According to the article "42% of the nation's nearly 600,000 bridges need repair and are obsolete." "Steel rods embedded in concrete for reinforcement and concrete both corrode over time from moisture and salts that seep through cracks." "Replacing steel with glass fibers might extend the life of a typical bridge from 50 to as long as 200 years." It is no wonder that this new technology is being applied to dentistry since the mouth has much more chemical activity leading to corrosion and degradation of old metal restorations. If we are to achieve a long disease free life, we should want our teeth to survive with us.

The Rewards of True Biocompatibility

"With the new biocompatible materials and bonding techniques," says Dr. Hansen, "we can do tiny restorations that are of immediate, noticeable benefit to the patient. We don't have to grind the teeth all the way down anymore for caps or crowns that contain toxic metals or metal oxides and porcelains. I've had a number of patients express the feeling of suddenly getting a weight off their chests, a sense of relief, when their old dental work was removed and reconstructed with biocompatible materials."

Chronic Fatigue and Digestive Problems Alleviated

Dr. Marshall cites the case of a young woman in her early twenties who suffered from chronic fatigue, migraine headaches and digestive problems so severe she was unable to work. Many types of food made her ill, and she had lost her boyfriend over her illness. She had only four mercury amalgam fillings, but they were evidently the source of her problems, because when she had them replaced with Degussa porcelain, she recovered completely.

"I've never seen a case that dramatic in one so young," comments Dr. Marshall. "She felt better immediately. Then there was a crash — the detox. It took six months before she was perfect. But now she is super-healthy, and she can eat anything she wants. She looks great too. She used to have black circles under her eyes. Now she has a glow, almost like a halo — and a set of teeth I'd pay $100,000 for."

The most important thing to know about the "detox" phase mentioned by Dr. Marshall is what it is. When interference fields are suddenly eliminated, the body takes this long-awaited opportunity to reactivate its suppressed elimination system and dump toxins. You should avoid suppressing these "symptoms" with drugs. In fact, some authorities recommend encouraging them. We'll look at the detox phase and ways to speed and cope with it in Chapters 14 and 15.

Replacing Missing Teeth: Biocompatible Bridges

A trickier problem than making biocompatible fillings and crowns is replacing whole teeth biocompatibly. The traditional solution for replacing one or two or three missing teeth is the bridge. Bridges are either fixed or removable appliances that "bridge the gap" between missing teeth. The challenge is finding a material that is strong enough for this feat, flexible enough to allow for cranial movement, yet compatible with the body. When bridges are made of materials that are stiff and inflexible, they prevent the bones from moving, locking up the cranium.

"Each tooth corresponds to a cranial plate or section of the brain," explains Dr. Marshall. "When you chew, it actually respirates the brain. If the tooth is locked up with a bridge, or is extracted, the brain in that area slowly atrophies from lack of oxygen."

For this reason, even when bridges are made of apparently biocompatible materials, wearers can experience major adverse reactions. Dr. Hansen cites the case of a patient who complained of a bridge that had continued to bother her, although it had been constructed of Degussa porcelain reinforced with Golden Gate Gold (the system currently preferred by many "biological" dentists). When Dr. Hansen cut out the junctions in the middle of the bridge, the woman said she felt a great release, as if a weight had been lifted from her. Her distress was evidently caused by blockage of the energetic flow through her cranial bones, which had been bound together without flexure.

Dr. Hansen prefers to leave out the gold. He makes smaller bridges from unreinforced Degussa porcelain. As discussed earlier, larger bridges can be reinforced with glass fibers and veneered with Degussa ceramic. The new generation of biomaterials are flexible, nearly the strength of steel, and will not corrode. Newer materials that are both strong and biocompatible are in process of development. It is important that with newer material that the individual patient be tested for appropriate compatibility.

"We're looking at reinforcement with fiberglass," he says, "with injected ceramic polymer particles around the fiberglass itself — just like the 'bridges of glass'; As strong as steel without the deterioration and maintenance problems. Many possibilities are being researched. In the meantime, there is unreinforced Degussa; but it might not withstand a heavy bite. If that's a concern, the person needs to be informed that the bridge might periodically have to be replaced." Being a rigid structure even a bridge made with 100% Degussa will lock together the bony plates. The flexible framework of reinforced fiberglass veneered with Degussa ceramic is one possible solution. Figures 20 and 21 demonstrate one of the new fiberglass and ceramic bridges used in the mouth.

The Implant Alternative

A newer option for replacing missing teeth is the implant. Touted as the next best thing to your own teeth, implants are artificial teeth that have been anchored into the jawbone with metal screw-like fixtures. Technically, the "implant" is the part that replaces the root. It is usually made of titanium. The bone is first drilled as if it were wood being prepared for a screw; then the implant is screwed or tapped into place. The artificial tooth is attached to it three to six months later, after the bone integration to the implant.

Implants sound good in theory, but the procedure is quite invasive; and titanium is a metal. Dr. Peter Bennett, writing in the August/September 1997 Townsend Letter for Doctors, says that in his clinical experience, implants are the worst of the dental metals. He cites the case of a patient who developed full-blown MS within six to eight months of getting them.[2]

Dr. Hansen is also concerned about their potential toxicity. "Implants are very controversial," he says. "There are two concerns. One is that the material itself may be chemically harmful. That issue has been addressed by coating the implants with a plasma coating of hydroxyapatite, the major component of bone and tooth structure, so the body recognizes the material as being almost its own and bone grows into it very readily. But no matter how well coated it is, titanium is still a metal, which may adversely affect the electromagnetic fields of the body and the brain. If it does, we have to look for some other, non-blocking material. Sapphire has been suggested as a possible crystal to be implanted in the body, but it's not strong enough at present. We need a way to adequately attach it to other structures for support, or to load it with the bite and occlusion so as not to cause stresses within the crystal. The natural root is made of bone and is strong enough to hold the tooth, but it's put together in a very unique chemical pattern. If we could figure out that pattern, we could reproduce nature. We have to figure out not just what the material is but how it's interlinked and fused to make it strong in the body."

In the meantime, Dr. Hansen feels the safest alternative for replacing single missing teeth is still the Degussa porcelain bridge.

Blepharospasms Alleviated

He cites the case of a registered nurse who suffered from acute blepharospasms: her eyes involuntarily closed and stayed closed. She had this problem for years and was unable to drive a car. Her medical doctors wanted to perform surgery to attempt to preserve her eyesight. Her dental work included a wide range of mixed metals and metal bridges with corrosive by-products underneath. A year after Dr. Hansen redid not only her fillings but her metal bridges with wholly biocompatible materials, her condition had improved so much that she was able to drive again. She managed to avoid major surgery. Implants might have achieved the desired functional and aesthetic results, but they would not have transformed her health in this way.

Biocompatible Dentures?

When more than just a couple of teeth are missing, dentures are required. Traditional denture materials, however, contain components that may be quite toxic to the body. Many partials and some dentures have chrome cobalt metal frameworks to help add strength and support.

They may also have stainless steel, nickel or wire clasps that hold them onto adjoining teeth. Dentures may be made of methyl methacrylate, a hydrocarbon-based plastic; or of porcelain that contains metal oxides, giving rise to the same biocompatibility problems as reinforced porcelain crowns. Coloring, additives, and metal oxides are used to impart the aesthetic look of teeth and gums; but they may not be healthy permanent additions to the mouth. Dr. Marshall cites cases in which patients' electromagnetic fields tested strong when their dentures or partials were not in the mouth, but collapsed when the appliances were re-inserted.

A newer denture material that tests well on the Computron is a nylon-based material called Flexite or Valplast. Like with partials, however, biocompatibility isn't the only consideration. To be satisfactory, says Dr. Hansen, dentures also need to restore the collapsed vertical dimension of the bite. The relationship of the jaws and the face is a major concern for the elderly. As the bones shrink, a collapse results in the vertical dimension of the teeth, producing the typical "Andy Gump" look of the elderly patient. The concern is that a closed vertical dimension resulting from missing teeth gives inappropriate proprioceptive feedback to the neurotransmitting mechanisms, particularly the thalamus. It may also alter or block neurotransmitters to the brain. These concerns are currently being researched by Dr. Larry Lytle, a dentist in South Dakota. If verified, they will reinforce the importance of preserving the natural teeth at all costs.

Other Biocompatible Dental Materials

Besides the restorative materials themselves, there are bonding agents, resin-glass cements, temporary filling materials and other products used in the mouth that need to be compatible with the body. After testing a wide range of these materials, Dr. Marshall has found only a few that passed a four-hour tolerance test on the Computron.

Chapter 11

Salvaging the Root Canal

. . . I'd avoid root canals like the plague, because that's what they may turn out to be.
— Dr. David Williams[1]

There remains the question of a biocompatible root canal filling material. We've seen that conventional root canal materials may shrink when they dry, leaving spaces where toxic anaerobic bacteria can breed. Gutta percha, the most popular of these materials, is a water-proofing latex derived from the sap of trees. It was used in industry years ago because nothing sticks to it. In its pure state, gutta percha is a milky white latex which does not show up on x-rays. Mercury salts are added to give it the pink color that dentists can visually recognize inside the tooth. Barium and lead are then added to make the material radio-opaque on x-ray, so the dentist can see his work; but barium and lead leakage from the root canal may poison the body. The cements used in conventional root canal therapy may also be quite toxic. Some patients are so chemically sensitive that they can't tolerate the conventional materials and are forced to have their teeth pulled. In addition since nothing sticks to gutta percha, achieving a completely sterile, bacteriologic seal of the millions of dentin tubules may be impossible. Because of this, many times the bone surrounding the root becomes dead and necrotic especially where the nerve tissue has died and remained in the canal for some time. This dead bone (cavitation) may not heal and regenerate even with the best of the root canal procedures. On an x-ray it may appear normal, because it is still bone structure, but it has died, lost its blood supply, and remains a gangrene-like, septic source which can infect the otherwise healthy body.

Convinced of their toxicity, Dr. Price maintained that all root filled teeth should be extracted; but that approach, too, is problematic. Fortunately, a root canal filling material and sterilization procedure are now available that have solved these problems. After all why would we want to perform a treatment of last resort (extraction and surgery) first, before we attempt all viable alternatives. This is the very principle of alternative medicine.

A Material That Grows Like Natural Teeth

The filling material is one that has only recently been approved for use in the United States, but that has been used for nearly two decades in Europe. Called Biocalex 6.9, it is being marketed by Future Dentistry, Inc. in the U.S. and by Biodent in Canada. Unlike other filling materials, Biocalex actually expands to fill and seal the root canal and being a heavy calcium oxide, it is naturally bactericidal. Bacteria thrive in an acid environment, and Biocalex is the opposite, a base. Also, scientific research demonstrates that calcium oxide, not calcium hydroxide, can calcify the dentin tubules effectively occluding them preventing future bacterial invasion.

Biocalex is composed of calcium oxide, zinc oxide, and a special ethyl glycol/water liquid. Calcium oxide is unique in that it has an affinity for fluid: it absorbs liquids in the root canal and dentin tubules and expands, allowing the material to penetrate otherwise inaccessible canals. When calcium oxide combines with water, it forms calcium hydroxide, the most biocompatible material used in endodontic therapy. But when calcium hydroxide is used initially as a filling material, no expansion occurs. Only when calcium oxide is used as the initial material does its affinity for water cause it to penetrate devital dentin tubules, sealing areas that would otherwise be left as hiding places for bacteria to breed. The calcium hydroxide to which it is converted is then converted to calcium carbonate, creating a wall of calcification that further seals off these filled areas. Unlike with conventional root canal filling materials, no toxic chemicals or cements need to be used with Biocalex to sterilize and seal the canals.

In a 1990 Italian study, calcium oxide was found to produce perfect asepsis (absence of germs) in the root canals.[2] Questions were raised in another Italian study, in which Biocalex produced only 67 percent asepsis; but Dr. Hansen maintains that the problem wasn't with the material. It was with the procedure for preparing the tooth. When the root canal is sterilized with a laser, a nearly perfect asepsis is achieved, as shown in a recent German study.[3] Many additional studies have verified the sterility achieved by the laser and its ability to penetrate through the entire tooth, its millions of dentinal tubules, and even into the surrounding bone. Combining these two innovations assures a germ-free root canal.

"The Biocalex raises the pH to the point where it's bactericidal, which is good," he says; "but its main purpose is to induce the body to calcify and seal the canals. That's what the studies have confirmed — tubule occlusion. Several studies have shown that heavy calcium oxide continues to induce calcification of the millions of tubules that compose the tooth root, sealing off these tubules so that bacteria can no longer penetrate the tooth. When we combine virtually complete tubule occlusion from the Biocalex with nearly perfect asepsis from the laser, long term sterilization is no longer a problem."

Disinfecting with Light

The root canal, explains Dr. Hansen, is a two-step procedure. The first involves cleaning out all the necrotic, decaying, bacteria-filled, nearly gangrenous tissue inside the canal and sterilizing it. Then, because bacteria migrate and grow, the canal must be sealed with something. So the second phase of the treatment is to seal the sterile canals and tubules with something that will be not only biocompatible but will permanently seal and occlude all the microscopic tubules while maintaining the long term sterility. The problem in the past was that everything available to seal it with produced effects that were worse than taking out the tooth or having nothing done at all. Biocalex solved the problem of compatibility, but there remained concerns about sterility. These concerns have now been met with the laser.

"The canal is pure dentin," he observes, "with millions of tubules going out the sides in every direction, communicating with the body. The tubules are unbelievably small — about five microns across. There is no traditional way to clean or treat them adequately. Files have been used, but they can only access the larger main canals, not the smaller accessory canals and tubules. But now lasers and rotary-type cleaning instruments are available that can perform the procedure more effectively. Spiral-type nickel titanium instruments wind into the root canal with a rotary-type motion, scraping the sides of the tooth as they go in and pulling debris back out. The top layers of tubules, which are the most bacteria-laden, are removed first. A chelating agent, EDTA, is used to dissolve the debris, and open the tubules. After this solution is rinsed from the canals, the canals are dried. This is followed by the laser, which eliminates bacteria and their toxins and sterilizes the inside of the tooth, penetrating through the tubules and into the surrounding bone. A disinfecting rinse may also be used.

The procedure is very precise; the laser doesn't blow gases, toxins, or other materials out the end of the root or drive them into the tubules as some uninformed, non-laser dentists have speculated. With the appropriate power densities selected and when used properly, the laser light can penetrate through the canal, the tubules, and into the surrounding bone for additional sterilization. Then we use a spiral filler, which completely penetrates, forcing the mixed Biocalex material down, totally filling all the canals. Some dentists worry that they won't be able to see what's going on without barium to make the Biocalex radio-opaque. But the heavy calcium is a different density and actually provides a phase contrast, so it does show up quite well on x-ray, especially the computer enhanced digital x-rays that also reduce radiation by up to 90%. When the tooth is cleaned, sterilized and sealed right, there shouldn't be any problems with the Biocalex or the root canal. Biocalex has also been shown in several scientific studies to cause calcification of the microscopic tubules and effectively block future bacterial invasion."

Scoring on the Computron

Dr. Marshall agrees, after testing these laser-sterilized Biocalex root canals on the Computron. "The ones we've tested are perfect," he reports. "The other root canals always test bad. They're making people sick. With the use of the laser, light can go wherever there's a hole, right down to the smallest particle size, and can enter and do a thorough job of disinfection throughout the entire dentinal tubules. The Biocalex then goes into the dental tubules and fills them and seals them so that the tooth, instead of being a festering anaerobic breeding ground of poison. It solidifies, so there is no place for bacteria to be harbored. It also induces the dentinal tubules to calcify, solidify and harden so that they cannot be penetrated by future bacteria. Sealing with Biocalex has been very successful in cases where the conventional gutta percha has completely failed. When conventional methods are used to drill out the tooth, the inner side wall has to be drilled, costing calcium and tooth. But with this technique, you don't lose much of the side wall which is so critical for keeping the tooth's strength."

Surgeon's Hands Restored

Dr. Marshall cites the case of a 35-year-old opthalmological surgeon who had had to abandon her work due to chronic fatigue and a condition in her fingers that had left them barely movable. The advice of her medical colleagues was to have the nerves cut to her arms. She protested, "But I'll never work again!" Her colleagues responded, "At least you'll be out of pain."

She consulted with Dr. Marshall for nutritional therapy. He took a patient history and learned that she had had extensive dental work that included <u>eleven</u> root canals. He told her her teeth would all have to be redone with biocompatible materials: Biocalex in the canals, and metal-free Degussa porcelain in the fillings and crowns.

The surgeon found a dentist who was willing to do the work, but the dentist thought hydrogen peroxide would be sufficient to disinfect the canals. Dr. Marshall wasn't convinced. "The surface tension of a water droplet exceeds the width of a dental tubule," he reasoned. "What would make a droplet want to go into the tubule? Nothing. But wherever there's a hole, light will go."

Laser disinfection was the solution. Her dentist succeeded in replacing all of the patient's root canal fillings with Biocalex and in constructing Degussa porcelain crowns on her teeth, although in some cases there was virtually no tooth left.

Remarkably, the treatment worked. The patient's chronic fatigue went away, and she regained the use of her surgeon's hands.

Lame Leg Healed

In another case, redoing just one root canal with Biocalex after sterilizing the inner tooth canal with a laser caused striking improvements in health. The patient was a mechanic who sought help for a swollen leg so painful that he wasn't able to work. After being tested on the Computron it was determined that a root canal in one of his front teeth was affecting his kidney meridian. Nutritional supplementation was recommended, along with complete dental revision. The man was quite dubious about the dental part; he protested that he couldn't afford to get all his dental work overhauled. But he was impressed when the nutritional therapy made him feel much better. What it didn't do was to cure the swelling in his leg, so he finally agreed to get the root canal redone. When reconstructing this single tooth caused his leg to completely heal and his energy level to rise dramatically, he was so impressed that he decided to have all his teeth fixed. He found he could afford the work after all. It was just a matter of deciding what was really important in his life.

Back Pain Cured

While in some cases, fixing just one tooth has had dramatic results, in other cases symptoms haven't resolved until the last particle of toxic filling material was removed.

That was how it was in Raylene's case. She had suffered for years with severe back pain and neuromuscular problems. Treatment by holistic practitioners in a major medical center in New York had relieved her symptoms enough that she could function, but she was still symptomatic. All of her amalgam fillings and root-filled teeth were redone with biocompatible materials, yet her symptoms persisted. X-ray revealed one tiny bit of amalgam left at the end of a root canal filling, which could be removed only by going in surgically from the side. When Dr. Hansen did this operation, Raylene's symptoms instantly disappeared — a dramatic recovery.

Chronic Fatigue Syndrome Relieved

A woman from Arizona suffered from chronic fatigue syndrome so severe she could function for only a few hours a day. "Her mouth was a mess," says Dr. Hansen. "She had root canals with abscesses that were leaking, and lots of mixed metals." When he completely redid her dental work with Biocalex and other bicompatible materials, her symptoms abated and her energy rose to normal levels.

If Biocalex Is So Good, Why Aren't All Endodontists Using It?

Besides the objection that Biocalex won't show up on x-ray, endodontists have been slow to accept this new material because it departs radically from the way they have been taught to fill a root canal. Instead of compacting the material tightly in the canal and filling it to the top, the dentist using Biocalex spirals the material into the canal from the tip of the root up to the top, filling the entire canal and all it's hidden crevices. Conventionally-trained endodontists find this concept hard to accept, but the fact that it works has been demonstrated on film. Figure 22 is a photo of a tooth repaired by Dr. Hansen after it was broken off in an accident. The Biocalex can be seen seeping into the juncture between the viable and the broken parts of the tooth, actually rejoining and sealing these parts together — a hitherto unheard of accomplishment.

Avoiding Root Canals With Lasers

Lasers can be an effective tool not only for disinfection during the root canal procedure, but for avoiding the procedure entirely. Arabinda Das, M.D., wrote in the May 1994 Townsend Letter for Doctors that when a root canal was recommended for his 18-year-old son, he tried passive laser treatment on it instead. Dr. Das had a dentist open an access hole in the crown of the affected tooth. Then a helium and neon laser was applied to the opened tooth for ten minutes, and the hole was sealed. The biostimulation effect of a cold laser to induce biologic repair, speed healing, and for pain relief has been well documented in Japan. Dr. Das wrote that the preserved tooth has given his son no problem since that time, a period of twelve years.[4] However, this laser is not cleared in the United States for this purpose. Dr. Hansen, utilizing the newly approved Erbium; YAG laser, has completed over 30 cases of teeth that had large, infected, bleeding nerves. When treated with the Erbium laser, their pain and bleeding were not only gone, but the teeth have continued to remain healthy and pain free, thereby avoiding certain root canals or extractions. (See Figures 23-26.)

Avoiding Root Canals By Avoiding Amalgam

Dr. Hansen has another suggestion for avoiding root canals: avoid silver/mercury amalgam fillings.

"Most problems that we see today," he says, "are because of rampant decay that has gone unchecked, or because of large silver fillings that aren't adhesive and break the teeth or leak and decay. But rampant decay is getting less and less common. The vast majority of root canals and crowns are now done around large silver-filled teeth. If we could replace all amalgam with something biocompatible like Degussa porcelain, we could virtually eliminate root canals"

Lasers To The Rescue

Even when amalgam has done its insidious work, however, infected teeth can now be saved, thanks to laser disinfection.

"We've been doing laser techniques with the new Erbium laser on teeth that automatically in traditional dentistry would have needed root canals and crowns," says Dr. Hansen. "When you open the pulps, they're bleeding all over and heavily decayed and infected with bacteria. In traditional dentistry, 100% of these teeth would die. If you do a root canal right away, you prevent necrosis (or death) and the development of necrotic neurotoxic products at the ends of the roots. But most dentists don't do that. They put medications on the teeth in the hope of preserving the tooth. Usually, it dies anyway, if not immediately then over several years. Meanwhile, necrotic, toxic products accumulate in the root. With the laser, we can vaporize the decayed area — since decay is heavily filled with water and bacteria, which the laser attacks and literally vaporizes — with no trauma to the nerve and no drilling. The drill alone would kill an infected nerve by traumatizing it with heat, vibration, and pushing bacteria inside. Vaporizing the decay with a laser doesn't produce the heat and vibration of a drill, and it sterilizes the area instead of pushing the debris into the canal. We can literally vaporize the infected nerve tissue in this way without traumatizing it, and produce a bacteria-free zone, even with multiple bleeding sites. Then we seal over these infected nerve tissues that are now decay- and bacteria-free. In the thirty cases we've done, they've all healed up; and the patients have had no pain immediately afterwards. In the traditional case, pain goes on for days after treatment. Instead of grinding the tooth down for a crown or having to do a root canal, we now have a perfectly preserved tooth that formerly would have been destroyed and crowned or root-canaled."

Figures 23 through 26 show these dramatic results in two of Dr. Hansen's cases.

"We're pushing the new laser to new limits," he remarks. "Dentists say, 'You can't do that.' But I've got the slides and nerve tests to prove it. It's very exciting. All the young dentists I've shown this laser treatment to want to learn it, because it's so dramatic."

Chapter 12

Dentistry in the Laser Age: No More Drilling, Root Canals or Crowns!

Use of lasers in dentistry is medicine for the 21ˢᵗ century.

— Dr. Bruce Burlington, M.D.,
Director FDA Devices and
Radiologic Health May 1997[1]

Lasers are finding many other uses in dentistry. Their versatility is due to the fact that lasers of different frequencies target different tissues. Some target water; some target harder materials. All matter absorbs energy, which vibrates at a particular harmonic frequency. Like the opera singer who can shatter crystal if he hits the right note with the right harmonic frequency, the laser will affect only those tissues that resonate at its target frequency.

"The argon laser passes right through water as if it didn't exist and can target dark material and hemoglobin." Dr. Hansen explains. "In ophthalmology, it's used to target, shape and weld the dark retina in the back of the eye. The laser can pass all the way through the exterior of the eye, target the retina, and do surgery on it to re-attach it and weld it together, without affecting any other eye tissue. Whereas the CO_2 or the Erbium laser energy is absorbed primarily by the water in the surface of the eye and does not penetrate inside. Two different lasers with exactly the opposite effect.

If the laser frequency is matched, it will be absorbed and have an effect; if it isn't, it won't. You can literally vaporize a single cell, if 100% of the energy were to be absorbed by that single cell, and have the cell right next to it not feel or sense anything going on."

Dr. Hansen has demonstrated this effect on television by turning the power down on an erbium laser and burning just one side of a sheet of paper, leaving the other side untouched.

No More Drilling, Root Canals Or Crowns

A laser that targets decay can now vaporize the decay in the same way, without affecting any of the viable tooth underneath. For small cavities, the procedure actually eliminates the need for drilling, saving substantial amounts of tooth and preventing the tooth from being further traumatized by the drill's heat and vibration. The laser can also sterilize the interior of the tooth, making it less likely to decay or have further damage.

Another new technology that resembles sanding more than drilling is air particle beam abrasion. The equipment uses minute, almost invisible abrasive particles propelled by air to blast away certain areas of the tooth surface and the decay without the vibrations of drilling or the need for anesthesia in most cases.

That means cavities can now be filled when they are still very small, without jeopardizing the strength or structure of the tooth. "The long-term effect," says Dr. Hansen, "will be to virtually eliminate the need for crowns and root canals." Traditional dentistry allowed small cavities to progress because the alternative was to destroy the internal structure of the tooth while trying to fill them. Drills used to run at slow speeds and would not break through enamel very easily, so the dentist had to wait until the tooth was thoroughly decayed before they could clean out the decay with the old peddle or belt driven drill and place a filling. With the high speed air turbine handpiece, treatment could be performed earlier since their usual treatment is to drill away a large amount of the good tooth beyond the cavity just to hold the mercury filling. They do not inform the patient and intervene until the cavity and disease progress further, requiring larger, more invasive dental care. Now, cavities can be caught and repaired before structural damage has occurred.

"If we can start with children early on," he observes, "instead of having a tiny, little cavity that you just watch and let it become a big cavity, then have to rip the whole tooth apart and place a big silver filling, you can just pinpoint the cavity with a little air abrasive or the laser with no anesthetic and no discomfort. After the cavity has been removed, a little dot of the fusible, tooth replacement material can be injected into the prepared cavity, and fused to the tooth with a laser. This will truly restore the tooth, not just fill it — maybe to the point where the tooth may never need anything again. That's one way we can solve adult problems — by taking care of them when kids are small. If children have good nutrition, once they get out of their decay-prone era, they can avoid decay and gum disease later. If we can keep the structural integrity of the dentin solid, and pinpoint cavities while they're tiny and rebuild the outer surface or small openings, the tooth should never need a root canal or crown, barring accidental fracture or neglect. The neglect won't happen if we can change people's attitudes about going to the dentist. If we could eliminate crowns and root canals, and make people want to come in because the treatment is fast and painless, we could change the future of dentistry."

No More Pain in the Dental Chair

Toward the goal of treatment that is fast and painless, lasers also represent a major advance. When tiny cavities are pinpointed and vaporized with a laser or air abrasion, no anesthetic is usually necessary. The use of lasers to sterilize and seal blood vessels and nerve endings eliminates pain at the nerve.

Another pain relief innovation is electronic anesthesia. Transcutaneous electrical nerve stimulation (TENS), an acupuncture-like electronic treatment, effectively blocks the pain of dental work in susceptible patients by stimulating other sensory nerves.

Another method developed by British researchers called Targeted Electronic Anesthesia, anesthetizes without the use of needles. A thin receptor strip placed at the gum near the tooth neutralizes only the nerve fibers that transmit pain. The remaining fibers (those necessary for swallowing and other sensory perception) continue to function, eliminating the annoying swollen rubber-lip sensation. This device also causes the release of endorphins, which provide natural pain relief for about two hours after treatment.[2] The system is still in the early stages of development but has potential.

The latest system for delivery of the chemical anesthesia in a pain free manner, uses a computer to sense the resistance of the body tissue and deliver just enough anesthetic to produce numbness without any discomfort to the patient. This innovation is also important because recent evidence suggests that the chemical anesthetics break down into aniline compounds which may be carcinogenic. This device greatly reduces the amount of the anesthetic necessary to block pain.

Another feature of the Space Age dental experience is the use of 3-D virtual-reality glasses that engulf patients in sight and sound, distracting them from even the lengthiest procedures. They can watch full length movies and not even notice the dental treatment. Many patients are actually laughing while having dental treatment. A recent Newsweek article that featured Dr. Hansen quoted one patient as saying, "That's the most fun I've had in a dental chair."

Laser Bleaching

The laser is also being used for bleaching the teeth, a cosmetic procedure it has made faster, more efficient, and more controllable. Bleaching is an oxidation/reduction process traditionally done with hydrogen peroxide. A similar process occurs when wood burns. Full oxidation results in the total breakdown of organic matter into carbon dioxide and water. What we are trying to achieve is only partial oxidation to convert the organic matter into intermediary compounds that are lighter in color than the original elements. Only four percent of the enamel actually is organic; the rest is inorganic crystalline matter. However, because the crystalline part is translucent, the organic matter has a large influence on the color and shading of the tooth. If the oxidation/reduction process goes too far, full oxidation, this organic tooth matrix starts breaking down — and when bleaching is done at home, it's hard to tell if you've gone too far. Home bleaching can be a lengthy, tedious and risky undertaking, says Dr. Hansen, just because the bleaching agent is so weak and slow. In the office, the laser can add energy that assists the peroxide in releasing its free radicals, speeding the process so it can be completed in a single visit. The dentist can keep checking the rate of oxidation during this in-office procedure and keep it under control.

Instant Orthodontia

Another cosmetic use of the laser is in what Dr. Hansen calls "instant orthodontia." It involves laser-fusing biocompatible porcelain overlays to the tops of the teeth.

In the past, he observes, orthodontia was the only way to correct an insufficient vertical dimension or malalignment of the teeth; and it continues to be the best way for children, whose bones, muscles, and teeth are still developing and can be guided into their proper positions. Orthodontia is also the preferred option when the teeth are out of alignment. However, many adults do not want to wait the years it takes to complete orthodontics so for these individuals, the instant cosmetic option is selected. Also, when the teeth are in fairly good alignment and only the vertical dimension needs to be corrected to restore the harmony and balance of the jaw, occlusal overlays of biocompatible porcelain offer definite advantages. In older people, particularly where there are complications like periodontal disease or bone loss, correcting the bite orthodontically may be difficult and even dangerous. Laser-fused overlays are a quicker and safer option.

Dr. Hansen cites the case of a woman in her mid-sixties, whose jaw was massively overclosed. Her former dentist had recommended orthodontia to correct the problem, but the woman was already in the moderate to advanced stages of periodontal disease. She had root canals that had failed (become infected). Apical surgery, involving trimming off half the root and plugging it with amalgam at the base, had been tried to stop the ongoing infection, causing the roots to be shorter and more unstable. Any degree of orthodontic movement could have damaged the bone structure, so the teeth might not have survived the procedure. But the woman's jaw was so severely overclosed that something had to be done. Dr. Hansen's solution was to first correct and stabilize her periodontal disease. Then have a lab make overlays of ceramic that could be laser-fused to the tops of the teeth, giving them new biting surfaces.

"This type of overlay requires minimal tooth preparation," he says. "You don't have to grind the tooth off. You just modify the surface a little to accommodate a fusible porcelain. Then you have the lab make a whole new top to the tooth, and you fuse it permanently into place. Temporary overlays can be used first to determine the correct bite position. That's the beauty of this technique. Getting the relationship of the teeth right with orthodontics is largely guesswork; and once it's done, it's permanent. But if we begin with temporary overlays, we can make sure the bite is right before fusing the permanent overlays into place. We can muscle test to determine the correct position of the jaw, then build the teeth up to the approximately correct height and vertical dimension with temporary overlays. For that we can use either a laser-bonded splint or a removable splint. Then we can observe the patient for a week or a month or several months, to see if the ideal position has been found. If not, we can do little modifications until we get the height right. Once the ideal vertical height has been established, the teeth can have permanent new surfaces fused with the laser. So we can change the teeth position and height in the mouth, just and with orthodontia, but it's a very minimal, calculated, and just enough to change the height or vertical dimension of the visible part of the tooth without actually moving the tooth roots."

The procedure also has cosmetic benefits, creating the effect of an "instant face lift." Figures 27-28 consists of "before" and "after" photos of a woman whose facial muscles originally appeared collapsed, wrinkled and compressed due to a collapsed bite. In addition her front teeth were extremely crowded due to the facial collapse. In the "after" picture, a more ideal height has been restored to the face, transforming the woman's appearance merely by raising the bite. This allowed her front teeth surfaces to be made in an ideal alignment and appearance. This entire process took just about 2 weeks to complete!

A Promising Future

Dr. Hansen now uses six different lasers in his office and is excited about their possibilities; but he concedes that lasers may take awhile to catch on in dentistry, because they require training that isn't offered in dental school and they are very expensive for the average practitioner.

"You need to understand tissue interactions and laser physics," he says. "You have to know your parameters, your target tissue type, it's absorption spectrum, power densities and settings before you can make a good choice in what to do with the energy." We'll look at that question in Chapter 13.

Biocalex and Degussa porcelain also take special equipment and training. As a result, the "standard practice" is likely to take awhile to catch up to the cutting edge.

In the meantime, the patient is faced with the question, "What should I do about my mercury amalgam fillings?"

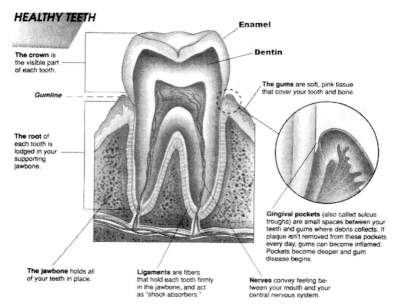

HEALTHY TEETH

Enamel

The crown is the visible part of each tooth.

Dentin

Gumline

The gums are soft, pink tissue that cover your tooth and bone.

The root of each tooth is lodged in your supporting jawbone.

Gingival pockets (also called sulcus troughs) are small spaces between your teeth and gums where debris collects. If plaque isn't removed from these pockets every day, gums can become inflamed. Pockets become deeper and gum disease begins.

The jawbone holds all of your teeth in place.

Ligaments are fibers that hold each tooth firmly in the jawbone, and act as "shock absorbers."

Nerves convey feeling between your mouth and your central nervous system.

Figure 1 (see page 17)
Cross section of a normal tooth showing enamel, dentin, nerves, gums and bone.

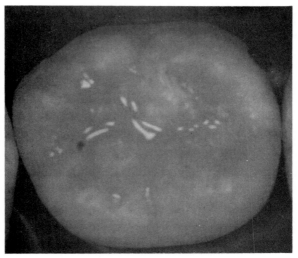

Figure 1A (see page 17)
Chewing surface of a healthy tooth.

Dental Systemic SYNERGISM

Zones	V	IV		III	II	I	I	II	III		IV	V
Paranasal Sinuses		Maxillary Sinus		Ethmoid Cells		Sphenoidal Sinus			Ethmoid Cells		Maxillary Sinus	
						Frontal Sinus						
Endocrine Glands	Anterior pituitary lobe	Para-thyroid	Thy-roid	Thy-mus	Post. pituitary	Inter med.	Pineal Gland	Post. pituitary	Inter med.	Thy-mus	Thy-roid	Para thy-roid	Anterior pituitary lobe
Sense Organs	Cavern-ous Sin	Tongue		Nose	Eye	Nose		Eye	Nose		Tongue	Cavern-ous Sin
Tonsils	Lingual	Laryngeal		Tubal	Pal	Pharyngeal		Pal	Tubal		Laryngeal	Lingual
yang	Heart	Pancreas		Lung	Liv	Kidney		Liv	Lung		Spleen	Heart
Organs	Duodenum Terminal Ileum	Stomach Esophagus		Large Intestine	Gallbladder Biliary ducts	Urinary bladder Genito-urinary area Rectum Anal Canal		Biliary ducts	Large Intestine		Stomach Esophagus	Duodenum Jejunum Ileum
yin												
Jaw Sections	HE SI CS	SI PA		LI LU	LIV GB	BL KI KI BL		LIV GB	LU LI		SP ST	HE SI CS

right 1 2 3 4 5 6 7 8 9 10 11 12 13 14 15 16 left

right 32 31 30 29 28 27 26 25 24 23 22 21 20 19 18 17 left

Jaw Sections	HE SI CS	LI LU		ST PA	LIV GB	BL KI KI BL		LIV GB	SP ST		LU LI	HE SI CS
yin												
Organs	Terminal Ileum	Large Intestine		Stomach Esophagus	Gallbladder Biliary ducts	Rectum Anal Canal Urinary bladder Genito-urinary area		Biliary ducts	Stomach Esophagus		Large Intestine	Jejunum Ileum
yang	Heart	Lung		Pancreas	Liv	Kidney		Liv	Spleen		Lung	Heart
Tonsils	Lingual	Tubal		Laryngeal	Pal	Pharyngeal		Pal	Laryngeal		Tubal	Lingual
Sense Organs	Ear Tongue	Nose		Tongue	Eye	Nose		Eye	Tongue		Nose	Ear Tongue
Endocrine Glands					Gonad	Adrenal Gland		Gonad				
Paranasal Sinuses		Ethmoid Cells		Maxillary Sinus		Frontal Sinus			Maxillary Sinus		Ethmoid Cells	
						Sphenoidal Sinus						

Figure 2 (see page 27)

Tooth and organ relational chart

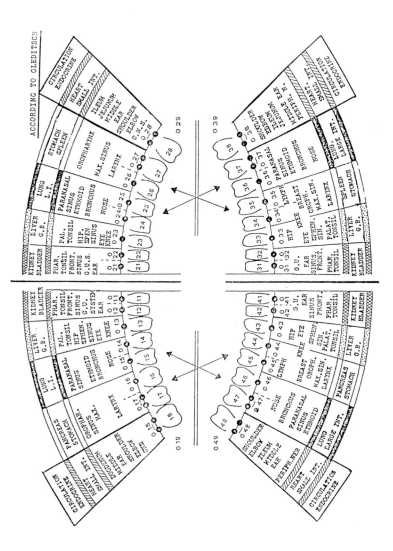

Figure 3 (see page 27)
Electromagnetic connection between teeth and organ systems

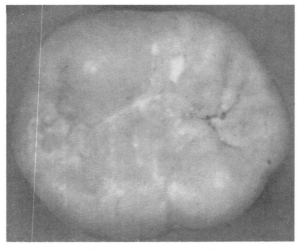

Figure 4 (see page 64)

Normal chewing surface of a back tooth. Note the reinforcing ridges and enamel structural struts that absorb the force of chewing and distribute the stresses throughout the entire tooth surface.

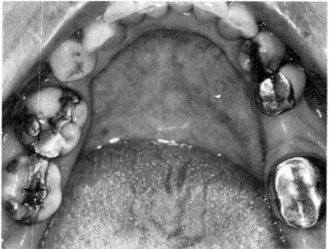

Figure 5 (see page 65)

An entire lower jaw restored the traditional way. Note the large, leaking, mercury alloys that are fracturing the teeth, the gold crowns on other teeth where previous fillings failed, and a missing space where a prior tooth fractured and was extracted.

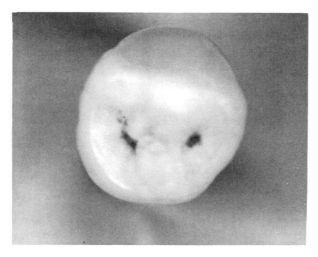

Figure 6 (see page 65)
Normal tooth with a small cavity.

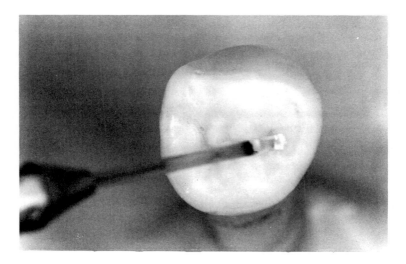

Figure 7 (see page 65)
Same cavity being vaporized with the laser.

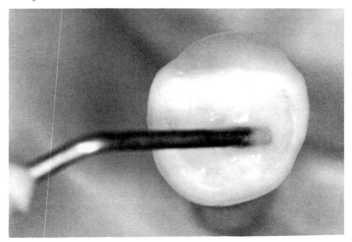

Figure 8 (see page 65)

Same tooth from previous page being restored with an injectable tooth replacement. It is then fused into the tooth with another laser.

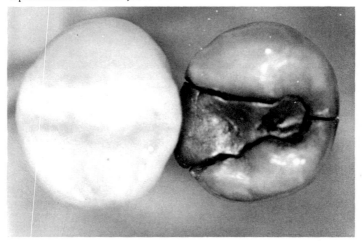

Figure 9 (page 65)

Two teeth - one filled with the laser and injectable tooth replacement, the other filled the traditional way with a drill and a mercury/silver filling. Note the expansion and fracturing of the tooth due to the metal filling.

Which would you rather have?

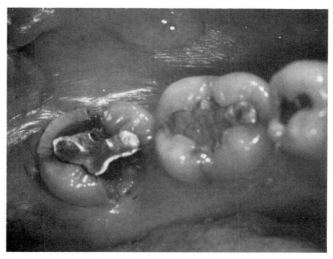

Figure 10 (see page 65)
Example of two silver/mercury fillings of equal size. The tooth on the right shows fracture lines throughout the tooth enamel. The tooth on the left shows what happens when these type of fractures progress and two major sections of the tooth have broken away.

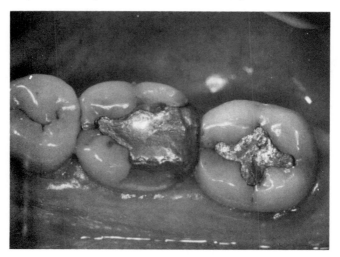

Figure 11 (see page 65)
Example of another large mercury filling that has broken off a section of the tooth.

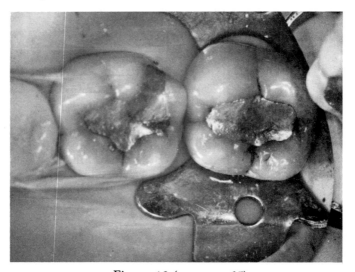

Figure 12 (see page 65)

Photo of mercury fillings before they are removed from the teeth. From the surface they look normal...

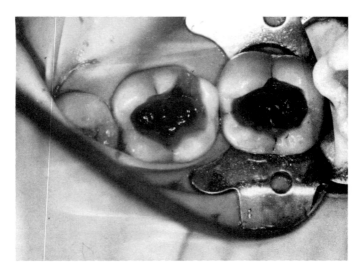

Figure 13 (see page 65)

Photo after fillings have been removed. Note the extensive decay and destruction inside that was hidden from the x-rays and the dentists view.

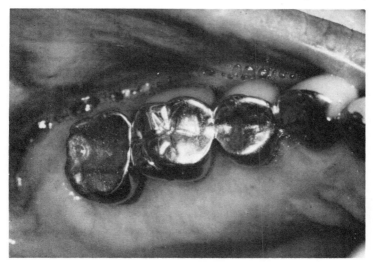

Figure 14 (see page 66)

As good as gold?

Normal looking gold restorations. No problems detectable from x-rays or visual examination.

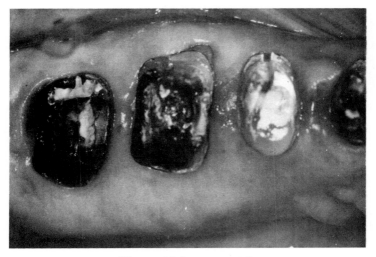

Figure 15 (see page 66)

After gold crowns have been removed there is massive oxidative corrosion caused by bacteria and the leaking cement. These metalic oxides, decay, and bacterial toxins have saturated through the dentin and into the living nerve tissue.

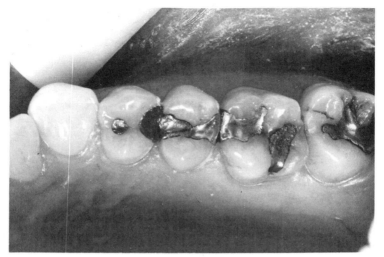

Figure 16 (see page 66)
Photo of a section of the upper jaw with large, traditional mercury fillings.

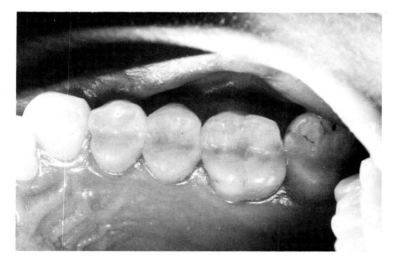

Figure 17 (see page 66)
Photo of the same teeth, reinforced and restored with beautiful biocompatable materials that strengthen the tooth back to natural condition.

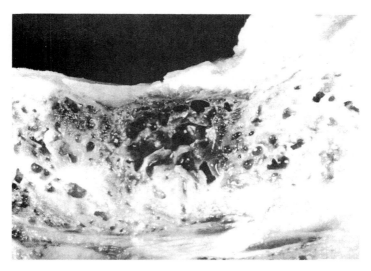

Figure 18 (see page 73)
Photo of a jawbone cavitation necrotic from an autopsy patient showing the necrotic dead bone.

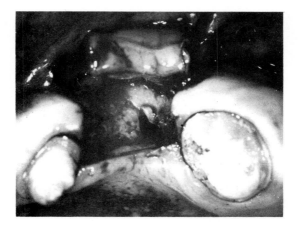

Figure 19 (see page 74)
Photo of a hole left behind into the sinus cavity after aggressive cavitational surgery was performed.

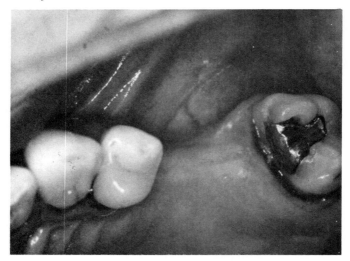

Figure 20 (see page 94)

Before photo of a section of the mouth with two missing teeth ad a large mercury filling in the back tooth.

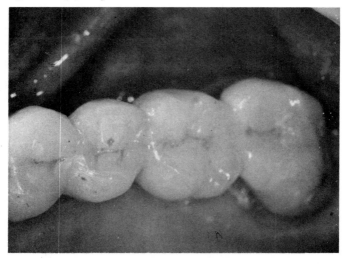

Figure 21 (see page 94)

After photo with the fiberglass and ceramic bridge fused in place between the existing teeth. The large mercury filling was removed and inlay extensions used to fuse the new teeth. This technique does not need to grind down and crown perfectly good teeth to make a bridge.

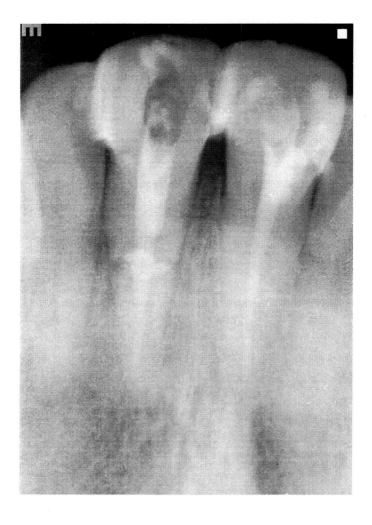

Figure 22 (see page 103)
Photo of a tooth that was fractured in half. The biocalex is shown seeping   into

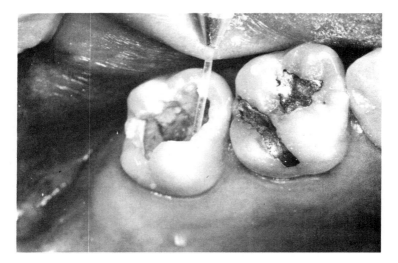

Figure 23 (see pages 104 and 105)
Erbuim laser vaporizing and sterilizing a very large decayed tooth.

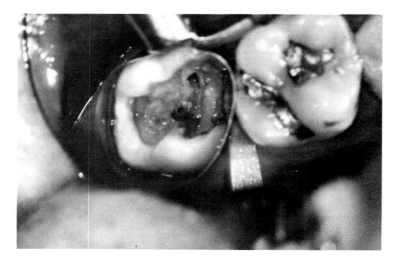

Figure 24 (see pages 104 and 105)
The same tooth showing the bleeding nerve after the decay and bacteria was removed. In traditional dentistry a root canal is always required because of the trauma created by the drill and the bacterial infection that the drill pushes inside the tooth.

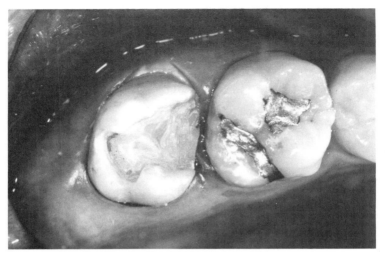

Figure 25 (see pages 104 and 105)
The same tooth sealed and rebuilt inside with an injectable tooth replacement, fused with the laser. This tooth will survive without a root canal and crown because the laser has cleared out and sterilized the tooth without trauma to the pulp. This will allow the natural blood supply in the tooth to repair the structure.

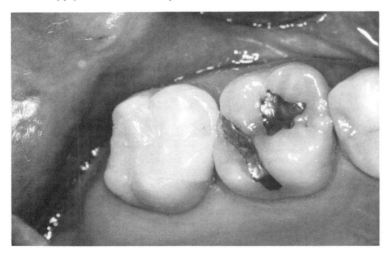

Figure 26 (see pages 104 and 105)
The same tooth with the final tooth-like inlay placed and fused with the laser.

Figure 27 (see page 111)
Before photo of a woman prior to dental correction.

Figure 28 (see page 111)
After photo showing the improvement in facial appearance with dental veneering the front and back teeth in order to restore function and improve esthetics.

Chapter 13

Removing Mercury Amalgam: The Importance of Protocol

> [F]indings suggest that the use of mercury as a restorative
> material is a health risk for dentists.
> — The Lancet (1982)[1]

Once you have decided to have your mercury amalgam
fillings replaced, the next question you face is, who is going
to do the work? Your family dentist, no matter how fatherly
and benevolent, may not be the right choice. Removing and
replacing mercury amalgam is a delicate business that requires
special education and training. Careful protocols are required
to prevent mercury from being dumped from your teeth into
your body, a process that some patients have reported made
them quite ill, permanently, since mercury once locked in
body tissue is difficult to remove.

Mercury amalgam removal can be a hazardous
undertaking not only for patients but for dentists. Horror
stories abound in the dental community concerning the
occupational hazards of mercury poisoning. Before composite
materials became available, mercury amalgam was used by
dentists without a second thought. But in 1989, the
Environmental Protection Agency declared amalgam a
hazardous substance under the Superfund law. Awareness
of mercury's dangers has now become so acute that if a
thermometer is broken in a classroom in California,
government regulations require that the room be evacuated
and a hazardous waste group be called in to clean up the

spill according to EPA standards. This heightened public awareness underscores not only mercury's hazards in the body, but the scrupulous caution necessary in its removal from the mouth.

There is another rub: even if the mercury in your mouth has made you ill, there is no guarantee that removing it will make you better. The procedure has worked on some patients but not on others. This may have been because the wrong replacement materials were used, as we have seen. But it may also have been because degeneration had gone too far to be reversed. There is insufficient data at the moment to distinguish between those cases.

Better to Let Sleeping Dogs Lie?

With all these provisos, you might wonder whether it wouldn't be better to leave well enough alone. The threshold question seems to be whether you are "well enough."

David Eggleston, D.D.S., suggests that if you have no obvious symptoms, you should have a "T" cell test run to determine whether mercury amalgam may be causing an immune deficiency in your case. The test is called an Immune Deficiency Evaluation (IDE) and is run by Smith-Kline, which has laboratories across the country. If there is a suppression of "T" cells, a "T"4/"T"8 test can be run as a follow-up. If these tests indicate an immune deficiency, you should seriously consider mercury amalgam removal[2] and a mercury detox program. You should also consider it if you have obvious health problems — particularly if you can trace your decline in health to a time when you had dental work.

Hal Huggins, D.D.S., who pioneered mercury amalgam removal for health reasons, ran a number of other tests to determine whether the patient's fillings needed to be removed. A "mercury toxicity porphyrin test" was used to determine whether a lack of oxygen transport had metabolically compromised the patient's system. A Complete Blood Count could suggest the amount of immune challenge the patient was suffering. Hormone levels might also be tested, since mercury can cause hormone disturbances. Other relevant tests included blood chemistry, hair analysis, retinal photography (which can detect mercury deposits in the eye), body temperature, and urinary excretion of mercury.[3] Simpler alternatives, if you know a practitioner with appropriate skills and equipment, are electro-dermal screening or kinesiology. (See Chapter 16.)

Dr. Huggins' Protocol For Mercury Amalgam Removal

Legal battles aside, Dr. Huggins' groundbreaking work has been relied on by so many other "biological" dentists that a discussion of the subject would be incomplete without mentioning his protocol. He claimed progressive improvement in his success in reversing chronic disease as he refined his procedures over twenty years of practice. He says his success with MS rose substantially after he began removing fillings in the proper order. It rose again after he came to appreciate the importance of proper diet and nutritional supplementation, and of clearing out chronic dental infections. Ailments besides MS that Dr. Huggins and his staff reported seeing respond to this protocol included not only chronic headaches, chronic fatigue and sinus problems, but such serious diseases as breast cancer, heart disease, leukemia, lupus, Parkinson's disease, Alzheimer's disease and Lou Gehrig's disease.[4]

Minimal standards recommended by Dr. Huggins in mercury amalgam removal include:

1. Use of a "rubber dam" (a piece of rubber that fits across the mouth and prevents the patient from swallowing amalgam).

2. Testing to determine what replacement filling materials are suitable for the patient's own body.

3. Laboratory testing to determine appropriate dietary changes and nutritional supplementation.

4. Appointment scheduling that avoids the observed drops in immune system strength on days 7, 14, 21 and 28 following major dental work.

5. An air filtration system that removes airborne mercury released by drilling. Dr. Huggins did his work in a thick cement cage and dome (called a "bubble operatory"), from which fans and a small filtering machine on the floor sucked

mercury out of the air. The system was designed for the protection not only of patients but of the dentist and his assistants.

6. In seriously ill patients, intravenous vitamin C and perhaps chelation infusions were used during the removal process, to facilitate mercury processing and excretion. The vitamin C was given in a four-hour drip beginning before the dental work was done. After the dental work, acupressure was used to balance the pulses and reduce swelling and pain.

7. Dr. Huggins also recommended removal of fillings in the proper order based on electrical readings, although other biological dentists have questioned the need for this step.[5] To test electrical potentials, Dr. Huggins used a simple machine that demonstrated the amount of electrical field that was coming through the teeth as a result of the metals in the mouth. The most electromagnetically active material was removed first. He divided the mouth into four quadrants and began with the quadrant with the greatest electrical potential.[6]

He points out that this is only about 30 percent of his actual protocol, which also included acupuncture, body work techniques for rebalancing and restoring body function, the removal of all root-filled teeth, and the routing out of cavitations.

Dr. Hansen's Protocol

Dr. Hansen uses a modified version of this protocol. "We supply pure compressed air that is given to the patient through a nasal canula," he says, "to help ensure that the patient does not breathe any unnecessary vapors during the procedures. We also have three vacuum systems that were specifically designed to remove particles and vapors from the air around the patient, again to ensure proper air quality. First a rubber dam clean system barrier is applied over the teeth. One large vacuum is placed directly in front of the patient's face area. This unique vacuum system changes the air in a 10' x 10' room every five minutes with two mercury vapor filters, a sub-micron HEPA filter and two additional filter units. This not only draws in all vapor from the treatment site but helps insure that the room air is as pure an environment as possible. Dr. Hansen feels that this vacuum system is critical since the mercury vapor from drilling may be inhaled by both the patient and the doctor. The rubber dam is designed to protect the patient from swallowing particles not from breathing vapor. Even with Dr. Huggins clean room the two foot space around the patient's head may be filled with mercury vapor. With this compressed nasal delivered air and powerful vacuum systems in front of the rubber dam, the area around the patient's nose and mouth is kept clear of hazardous mercury vapor. We also use six different lasers, digital occlusal bite analysis, electronic anesthesia, and computer designed restorations to enhance patient comfort and care. We use a Computerized EAV, Vega Test electro dermal screening, and applied kinesiology for material selection, a surgical microscope for precise treatment, and virtually noiseless, vibrational reduced electronic handpieces and lasers for patient comfort. These unique handpieces, designed in Germany, move at a slower speed without the noise, loss of torque, and vibration of the standard high speed air turbine drill. This further reduces the production and aerosol of mercury vapor. We have also developed microsurgical techniques with lasers to treat cavitational areas, sterilize and remove endotoxins, then fill the excavated voids with calcium sulfate or other bone inductive material to save teeth that need or have had root canals."

The Kinder, Gentler Approach to Infected Root Canals and Cavitations

Concerning root-filled teeth and cavitations, Dr. Hansen agrees that these hidden areas can be dangerous breeding grounds for bacteria. But he maintains that laser disinfection with cavitational microsurgery can now take care of the problem without invasive tooth-pulling or bone-drilling. For root canals, the old filling material is simply removed; the root canal is then cleaned and sterilized with a laser and refilled with Biocalex, which calcifies the root so that infection can no longer invade it. For cavitations, the threat of infection is also taken care of by disinfecting the area with a laser around the treated tooth root and performing microsurgery to remove and rebuild the necrotic bone.

To prompt the body to regenerate the area naturally, what is needed, Dr. Hansen asserts, is merely a supply of blood to regrow new bone. He suggests that the reason cavitations and root canals are dangerous is because of this lack of blood supply and the gangrene like necrosis that results from tissue death. Even a sterile Biocalex root canal can abscess and be toxic if it's surrounded by an area walled off by necrotic dead bone, where the bone can't regrow. Like a gangrenous limb, the festering blood-starved area has traditionally been treated by surgical amputation. But the more natural, less invasive approach is simply to develop a matrix, allow blood to return to the area, and regrow bone. This can be done by making a tiny hole in any layer of calcification that has built up around the infected area to induce bleeding and the formation of a blood clot matrix. He has documented cases in which this modest treatment alone has caused the surrounding bone to regrow. For more destructive lesions involving larger cavitational areas, microsurgical techniques and bone additive procedures may be necessary. He suggests that the beneficial effects seen from more drastic root canal and cavitational surgeries may actually have been the result merely of the bleeding caused by these procedures in the gangrene-like walled-off areas.

"Rather than going in surgically grinding away the necrosis and removing much good sound bone structure," says Dr. Hansen, "we now have bone fillers called calcium sulfates, a bit like plaster of Paris, that you can use to just fill in the hole; and they're osteoinductive materials, meaning they induce bone to grow. We now have the ability to go in, clean out the cavitational area, sterilize the area with the laser, fill in the void with a bone-growing material, seal it up, and solve the problem. Cleaning is done with the laser and hand instruments, but you're cleaning out necrotic (dead) bone and space, not vital bone; and you're not leaving a void open to a bacteria-laden environment as in traditional cavitational surgeries. With infected teeth, the problem, in standard dentistry, has traditionally been thought to be in the root. The treatment has been to go in surgically, cut the root, and fill the hole in the root with amalgam. I saw a case recently in which this was done, where not only the gums but the bone underneath had turned black from the amalgam. Now we can close the hole up and keep the area sterile, providing a more protected and confined environment to regrow bone in, while at the same time keeping the root, and keeping the jaw from dissolving away later in life to where the patient can't even wear synthetic dentures.

Traditional cavitational surgery isn't the way to go; it injects the body with toxic products while you're trying to clean them out. The drill pushes this junk back into the body where its picked up by the open blood supply and absorbed. Most traditionally trained cavitational surgeons have not accepted this new paradigm. They criticize saying things like, "the laser can't sterilize," "the laser will drive the toxins into the tubules," etc. None of these is true and usually indicates the lack of knowledge concerning the laser, it's absorption characteristics, and tissue interactions. Instead of criticism they should be excitedly researching with the hope that there may be a better way. Unfortunately most of these 'surgeons' only know how to pull teeth and grind away bone, and not how to perform microsurgery to repair and rebuild disease. It is like having a crushed or damaged hand. You can have the hand amputated and replaced by a prosthesis, or you can have the intricate, time consuming job of microsurgery to repair the damaged hand and make it functional. The same surgeon who performs the first procedure will most likely be unable to perform the more skilled second procedure.

The traditional standard for determining success of treatment for root canals has been: how do they look on an x-ray? That's why gutta percha is so popular — it shows up on an x-ray because it is composed of many heavy metals additives so you can see that the root has been filled. But the microtubules that don't show up are left to breed bacteria. The better standard should be: how do we induce health?

We do it by creating an environment that's sterile inside and that will calcify the canal, so the tubules are blocked and bacteria are precluded. Then we treat the environment on the outside to induce the regrowth of healthy tissue. We're currently conducting controlled studies to establish the long term effects of this treatment. We're trying to show two things: that you can seal, sterilize, and block the canals with the laser and Biocalex, and that you can eliminate necrosis and induce bone regrowth without aggressive, bone destroying, traditional, cavitational surgery. When I describe this process to groups of physicians who have been recommending cavitational surgery to their patients because they don't know there is any other alternative, they say, 'Thank God, I knew there had to be a better way!'"

The Role of the Health Practitioner

Dr. Hansen feels it is critical for the health-oriented dentist to work closely with physicians and other qualified health practitioners. Dr. Huggins got into legal trouble for ministering to the patient in ways normally reserved for the medical profession, opening him to charges of practicing medicine without a license. Dentists can avoid this problem by relying on referrals from and working in conjunction with practitioners with appropriate licenses.

In most cases, it will be the health practitioner rather than the dentist who initiates the work. A qualified practitioner can also test the patient to determine whether dental revision is necessary, and can administer supportive therapies. Nutritional counseling can be done to prepare the body for the stress of dental work using botanical medicine and supplements. Acupuncture can rebalance the energy meridians — the day before, the day of, and the day after dental revision. Chiropractic, homeopathy, and massage are other supportive possibilities.

Organizations and resources to help in locating qualified dentists and supporting practitioners are listed under "Resources." When selecting a dentist, it's good to ask what protocol he follows in removing mercury amalgam, and what material he will use to replace it as well as how it was tested for individual compatibility.

How Can You Be Sure?

This raises another question: how can you tell what your dentist is putting in your mouth? To the untrained eye, all tooth-colored restorative materials look alike. And you can't just pick up the package and read the label. Dentists and lab technicians who don't subscribe to the biocompatibility theory have been known to humor the practitioner with assurances that one thing will be used, then use another.

Dr. Marshall cites the case of a missionary who had been all over the world, who suffered from parasites and migraine headaches. The man's mouth was peppered with mercury amalgam fillings. Dr. Marshall worked on him nutritionally, but the man was advised that for optimum health he would need to get his amalgams changed to Degussa porcelain. The patient agreed, and went to the dentist Dr. Marshall was working with at the time to do the overhaul. When the patient's migraines continued, Dr. Marshall became suspicious. When he tested the man tooth by tooth on the Computron, one tooth "lit up the machine."

"It wouldn't scratch like Degussa," says Dr. Marshall. "It was rock-hard like regular porcelain. Degussa is a softer, gentler material."

Dr. Marshall then questioned the dentist, who admitted that his regular lab had been closed the day that particular restoration was sent out. The dentist had therefore given it to another lab, where he had been assured Degussa porcelain would be used. He asked the dentist to redo the tooth. When it was redone, the man's migraines ceased and his health problems resolved.

There is no ready way to guarantee that this scenario won't happen to you, other than locating a dentist you can trust and hoping he is working with a lab he can trust. But it's good to be alert to the problem.

Chapter 14

After Your Dental Overhaul:
Clearing Heavy Metals
from the Body

Later in life, metals stored in the bones will be released into the bloodstream during demineralization of the bones. . . . This can cause extreme agitation and mental insufficiency or dementia in the aging adult.

— Nancy Hallaway, R.N.,
Zigurts Strauts, M.D.,
Turning Lead into Gold[1]

Getting the mercury out of your teeth is only half the battle. To eliminate symptoms, you also have to eliminate the mercury that has accumulated over the years in your brain and other body tissues. Studies have now established that when you put something into the teeth, the substance gets absorbed into the body.

In an early European study, radioactive iodine was placed in the tooth pulp chamber of animals. The iodine was found in the subjects' thyroids several hours later. When the tooth was covered with silver amalgam and silicates, the radioactive iodine was still found in the animals' thyroids twenty hours later.[2]

Recent studies with sheep have confirmed this effect. When twelve amalgam fillings (a normal number for humans) were implanted in the mouths of sheep, the animals lost half their kidney function within thirty days. The mercury had evidently migrated through the body, passing into the kidneys and then into the brain.[3]

The same researchers found that when radioactively labeled mercury amalgam was placed in monkey teeth, the mercury could later be found in high concentrations in certain organs, particularly the kidneys, gastrointestinal tract and jaw.

It follows that the symptoms of mercury toxicity can be eliminated only with the elimination of mercury from body tissues. But how can this be done?

Sweat Therapy and the Niacin Flush

The simplest home option is to sweat heavy metals out through the skin. Interestingly, the original description of multiple sclerosis was that it was a disease caused by the suppression of sweat.[4] Dr. Murray Vimy, one of the Canadian researchers who conducted the sheep studies, observes that one of the primary modes for excreting mercury is through the skin by sweating. He suggests hot baths, saunas, steam baths, and perspiration through exercise.[5]

A still-experimental detox treatment not discussed by Dr. Vimy is the "niacin flush." It combines exercise and sauna therapy with the B vitamin niacin. The face turns red and the skin turns hot as the niacin flushes out toxins. In a California study, participants undergoing this treatment experienced significant drops in blood pressure, improvements in vision, increases in IQ points, and lessening of the symptoms of a number of physical ailments, including asthma, allergy, migraine, and hypoglycemia. Participants also reported re-experiencing the smells and physical effects of drugs taken in the past.[6]

The program was followed daily for a period of three weeks. It involved 20 to 30 minutes of vigorous exercise (jogging, stationary bicycling, rowing), followed by 30 minutes in the sauna, a 5 minute cooling off period, then 30 more minutes in the sauna. Sauna times could be gradually increased to 2 hours. Niacin dosage began at 400 milligrams (mg) spread throughout the day. The dose was then increased gradually to as high as 6,000 mg, depending on tolerance.[7]

If you're thinking of trying this program yourself, note that the niacin "flush" can be quite intense. Test your tolerance gradually! At high doses, niacin should be taken only with medical supervision. Even 400 mg is a large dose; starting at 100 mg would seem more prudent. It's also important to balance niacin intake with a B-complex containing the other B vitamins.

Vitamin, Mineral, and Diet Therapy

Besides exercise and sauna, Dr. Vimy's detox program includes vitamin and mineral therapy and a strict diet. Recommended supplementation includes:

1. General B-complex stress formulation (containing 15-25 mg of each of the B vitamins): one per day with breakfast.

2. Vitamin C (1000 mg, time-released): one with breakfast, one with dinner.

3. Zinc (amino acid chelate, 15-30 mg): one after dinner.

4. Selenium (150-200 micrograms): one after lunch.

5. Vitamin E (400 IU): one after lunch.

6. Vitamin A (5,000 IU): one per day.

7. Acidophilus: one capsule before breakfast, one before bed.

Dr. Vimy recommends that this supplementation program be continued for at least two months after mercury amalgam removal, and that it not be discontinued abruptly. He cautions that professional supervision should be sought when adding megadoses of vitamins. He also makes rather stringent dietary recommendations. They include:

1. Eliminating caffeine, high-sugar products, red and organ meats, refined fats, and alcohol. (Nutritionist Mary Buckley adds white flour to this list.)

2. Eliminating milk products, eggs and wheat products, foods that are highly allergenic for many people.

3. Eating at least two fresh fruits and one fresh salad with cold- or expeller-pressed safflower or olive oil daily.

4. Increasing intakes of fresh poultry and fish (except swordfish, tuna, shark, and other varieties known to be high in mercury).

5. Drinking eight glasses of water daily (including two with fresh lemon).

Other recommendations include getting more exercise; eliminating cigarettes; avoiding exposure to additional toxic metals (lead, aluminum, cadmium, copper, and mercury in sources besides dental amalgam); and eliminating chronic infections (fungal, bacterial, viral, amoebic, or parasitic). Before mercury removal, Dr. Vimy says to eliminate unnecessary chewing, which increases mercury vapor release into the mouth.[8]

A Comprehensive Detox Program

Vivienne Bradshaw, a British nurse suggests an even more comprehensive detox program. She says her interest in eliminating the effects of mercury poisoning, arose from her personal experience. She had suffered from a strange series of symptoms, including panic attacks, chronic fatigue and tachycardia, for which she had been hospitalized; but no cause could be found for her problems. Then she chanced to meet a doctor who diagnosed her as mercury poisoned. Amalgam removal was the turning point in her health, but the road back was a long one involving many therapies. Even with these therapies, she observes, eradicating all stored amalgam takes from twelve to eighteen months. Therapies she recommends include:

1. Vitamin and mineral therapy
2. Homeopathic and herbal detox remedies
3. Lymphatic massage from a qualified practitioner
4. Dietary modification
5. Digestive enzymes
6. Bacterial recolonization with "friendly" intestinal gut flora (acidophilus, bifido) in generous doses (those recommended on the bottle normally aren't sufficient)
7. Thyroid support (if recommended by a qualified practitioner)
8. Emotional stress release therapies
9. Structural rebalancing with manipulative therapies (chiropractic, osteopathy)
10. Attention to acid/base balance and food combining

11. Hydrogen peroxide therapy (oral or intravenous)
12. Kinesiological correction
13. Reflexology to break up crystalline accumulations
14. Fresh air, sunshine, and exercise (in moderation — recuperation being your first priority).

Concerning diet, Ms. Bradshaw says that in her experience, no one tolerates cow's milk well in its modern commercial form. Butter, cheese and yogurt are okay, but liquid, powdered or condensed milk is not. Other things she suggests omitting from the diet include margarine, hydrogenated oil, mushrooms, shellfish, and pork. She also recommends herbs for cleansing the bowels, liver and kidneys; herbal support for the organs; anti-parasitic herbs; coenzyme Q10 and ginkgo biloba to improve circulation and clear gum disease; and aloe vera.[9]

Water Therapy

Like Dr. Vimy, Ms. Bradshaw also stresses the importance of drinking at least eight glasses of pure water a day — not coffee, tea, soft drinks, or juices, but plain (filtered or bottled) water. Otherwise, she says, your detox program won't work. The lymphatic system can flush out tissue toxins stirred up by detox therapies only with sufficient water.

F. Batmanghelidj, M.D., in his groundbreaking book Your Body's Many Cries for Water, theorizes that the major chronic epidemics of modern life are diseases of water dehydration. Our mistake, he says, is in thinking we have satisfied our need for water by satisfying our thirst with other beverages. We need half our body's weight in ounces of water per day. (That means a 128 pound woman would need 64 ounces, or eight glasses of water.) Diseases Dr. Batmanghelidj says he has helped reverse with this simple therapy include high blood pressure, low back pain, asthma, allergies and ulcers, among others. The regimen is also a good way to lose weight. Wait ˝ hour before meals and 2˝ hours after meals for your heavy water doses, to avoid diluting your digestive juices. Dr. Batmanghelidj advises adding half a teaspoon of salt to your diet daily for every ten glasses of water added. Increase your water intake gradually to make sure your kidneys are functioning properly: output should increase proportionately with input.[10]

Chelation

Other authorities recommend eliminating heavy metals from the tissues through chelation. Intravenous chelation requires professional assistance and isn't considered necessary in the ordinary amalgam-removal case where patients are not symptomatic. However, some practitioners are so enthusiastic about it that it warrants a discussion here, not only for those people who do need it, but for what it says about the effects of heavy metals and their removal on human health.

What Is Chelation?

Chelation is actually a natural process in the body. It is the method by which metals necessary for body functions are transported through the body and in and out of cells. Iron in hemoglobin is a chelated metal; the chlorophyll in plants is a chelate of magnesium. Chelators are substances with extra electrons, or negative charges, that combine with the positive charges of a metal and hold it fast in a claw-like grip. ("Chele" means "claw" in Greek.) Temperature, acidity and other environmental changes affect this grip, causing the release and exchange of metals, allowing them to be picked up, transported, and released as needed.

IV Chelation with EDTA

EDTA (disodium ethylene diamine tetra-acetic acid) is a chelating substance that has long been used conventionally as a treatment for lead poisoning. Its effectiveness as a treatment for blocked arteries was discovered accidentally in the fifties, when an M.D. named N. E. Clarke used EDTA to treat tenants in a World War II tenement house in Detroit who had come down with lead poisoning from the paint used on the building.[11] The patients were all elderly, and many had cardiovascular problems. To Dr. Clarke's surprise, when the lead was chelated out of their arteries, their cardiovascular troubles went away.

Ray Evers, M.D., an early pioneer of intravenous chelation therapy, analyzed the heavy metal levels in his patients through hair analysis and 24-hour urine tests. He found that the vast majority of them had some abnormality in heavy metal content, with lead and mercury usually being the highest. Elevated levels of lead were present in nearly all his arthritis patients. Remarkably, chelation successfully relieved their symptoms.

Dr. Evers also found that diseases of the cardiovascular system — the number one cause of death in industrialized countries — were significantly alleviated with the therapy. These diseases are all caused by the same basic abnormality, a narrowing or closing off of the blood vessels. He postulated that the closing was caused by heavy metals that had built up in the vessels. Conditions that were helped by chelation included arteriosclerosis (hardening of the arteries of the heart), angina (chest pain), strokes and senility (hardening of the arteries of the brain), pain in the limbs (hardening of the arteries of the limbs), multiple sclerosis, cataracts, heart valve calcification, bursitis, hypertension, scleroderma, emphysema, Parkinson's disease, and muscular dystrophy. Dr. Evers reported that 90 percent of his patients with these conditions experienced improvement, and 75 percent experienced virtually complete recovery.[12] These observations throw additional light on the link between mercury and high blood pressure reported by Robert Siblerud, discussed in Chapter 4.

Dr. H. Richard Casdorph and Dr. Morton Walker in their book, 'Toxic Metal Syndrome' write, "I am never surprised to learn of medical practitioners who can accomplish successful patient outcomes in conditions in which the official pronouncements of consensus panels of leading professors indicate that cure is impossible." "In the case of dementia of the Alzheimer's type, I can tell you why Dr. Casdorph is able to provide case histories of successful treatments, when all the while the professors are telling you nothing can be done." The answer for his successes and the successes of the several thousand physician members of the American College for Advancement in Medicine, is chelation therapy. Drs. Walker and Casdorph document overwhelming evidence of the reversal of much degenerative and neurological disorders such as Alzheimers by the removal of accumulated metals such as aluminum, mercury, and lead.

One heavy metal removed by chelation is calcium — a potential problem, since calcium is necessary for strong bones and teeth. Dr. Evers maintained, however, that chelation removes only the unwanted inorganic calcium, not the organic, protein-bound calcium found in the skeleton. As the inorganic calcium is removed from the blood by chelation, calcium is pulled from other areas to keep the blood level constant. But this calcium is that which is most readily available and expendable, the calcium that has been abnormally deposited and is loosely bound — that in the inner walls of the blood vessels and around the tendons, joints, ligaments, skin, kidneys and pancreas. These extraskeletal calcium deposits are major offenders in arteriosclerosis, acting as cement-like binders that hold fatty substances and other unwanted materials in the arteries. When the extraskeletal calcium is chelated out, the remaining unwanted material becomes softer and can be absorbed or removed by the cleansing action of the blood.

Dr. Evers observed that a small increase in the diameter of a blood vessel increases the flow through it by a much greater proportion. An increase of one millimeter in diameter permits a fourfold increase in blood flow. Since symptoms of arteriosclerotic heart disease are not even detectable in the tissues until the diameter of the blood vessels that supply them is reduced by about half, a very small increase in blood flow can mean the difference between experiencing illness and experiencing health.

Note that intravenous chelation isn't recommended until all of the metals are out of the mouth. Otherwise, more metal will simply be pulled from the teeth into body tissues. For finding a practitioner in your area trained in intravenous chelation, see "Resources."

Oral Chelation

Dr. Evers suggested that the increasing levels of heavy metals to which people in industrialized societies are exposed may one day require routine chelation just to de-metal our bodies enough to stay alive. Children today absorb large amounts of lead simply by playing in dirt and dust, which has been exposed to the fallout from smog or winds carrying exhaust fumes from highways, freeways and industrial complexes. Aluminum is ubiquitous — in cans, cooking pots, underarm deodorants, and antacids. And more than 200 million Americans have mercury implanted in their mouths.

While patients with serious diseases need chelation treatment intravenously, Dr. Evers suggested that the arteries of children might be kept metal-free simply by regular oral ingestion of chelating substances like calcium oratate and magnesium oratate (Magora).

Unfortunately, after he wrote those suggestions, the FDA removed the oratates from the over-the-counter market. However, other oral chelators are still available.

Prescription Oral Chelators

In Heavy Metal Detox, Sam Ziff, Michael F. Ziff, D.D.S., and Mats Hanson, Ph.D., list several drugs that are oral chelators, of which DMPS (Dimaval) and DMSA (Chemet) seem to be the safest and most promising. The authors state that Dimaval is used in Europe for decreasing adverse effects during amalgam removal, as well as for treating neurological patients (ALS, MS); and that DMSA is being used very effectively for the same purpose during amalgam removal in the United States. They conclude, "The availability of DMSA in the U.S. dictates that serious consideration be given to its use during amalgam removal for all patients with neurological problems."

Both drugs are said to be very safe, even for young children. An oral DMSA dosage of 10 to 30 milligrams is recommended per kilogram of body weight. The authors caution that these chelators will also remove zinc, which should be supplemented during treatment. Glutathione, on the other hand, should not be taken during treatment. There is some evidence that oral supplementation with the amino acid glycine can increase the effectiveness of DMSA, Cuprimine, and EDTA in chelating out mercury, as indicated by increased mercury yields in the urine; and this is probably also true for DMPS. But glycine should not be taken without chelating agents, as it may only move the mercury around without facilitating its excretion.[13]

A 1997 study comparing the effectiveness of seven chelating agents in mobilizing mercury from renal tissue ranked their effectiveness as follows, from most to least: DMPS, DMSA, penicillamine, 1,4-dithiothreitol, glutathione, lipoic acid, and EDTA.[14]

At an International and American Association of Clinical Nutritionists (IAACN) Symposium in the summer of 1997, Dr. Dietrich Klinghart reported the results of testing with oral chelators. He found that <u>every subject</u> who previously had mercury fillings excreted large amounts of mercury when challenged with chelating agents like cuprimine and DMPS.

Autism and Hyperactivity Reversed

In <u>Turning Lead into Gold: How Heavy Metal Poisoning Can Affect Your Child and How to Prevent It</u> (Vancouver: New Star Books, 1995), Nancy Hallaway, R.N., and Zigurts Strauts, M.D., relate the remarkable saga of author Hallaway's two hyperactive, autistic children. Their conventional doctors had pronounced the condition hereditary and irreversible; but Dr. Zigurts ingeniously surmised that the problem was heavy metal poisoning resulting from a house remodeling and nearby freeway fumes. The children's symptoms were reversed simply by giving them an oral chelator called Cuprimine (D-penicillamine). A number of children in their neighborhood who were found to have the same condition were also helped by this prescription drug.

Herbal Chelators

DMSA, DMPS and Cuprimine are drugs that require a prescription, but there are natural oral chelators that can be obtained in the health food store or supermarket. The chlorophyll in plants is a natural chelator. Cilantro, a leafy green herb, is particularly effective. Japanese researchers writing in <u>Acupuncture Electrotherapy Research</u> in 1996 reported a case in which mercury deposits were detected in the organs of a patient where none were detected before, after three amalgam fillings had been removed from the patient's mouth. The mercury deposits were eliminated from these organs by the ingestion of a 100 mg tablet of cilantro (Chinese parsley) four times a day.[15]

The problem, cautions Dr. Marshall, is in finding a pure source. In the United States, most commercial cilantro has absorbed environmental toxins. An alternative option is the freshwater algae chlorella. The recommended dose is a 1/2 teaspoon a day, up to 1-1/2 teaspoons according to tolerance.

Other very useful natural products are the essential oils, particularly carvacrol oil (essential oil of oregano). The "blood of the plant," essential oils are aromatic and volatile liquids extracted from plants through distillation. They help open deficient pathways in the electromagnetic network running through the body by oxygenating the tissues.

For all of these products, purity of source is particularly important. (See "Resources.")

Homeopathic Remedies

Homeopathy is another non-toxic, non-prescription alternative used by many practitioners for pulling dental metals out of the tissues. It functions on a vibrational rather than a physical level, and its effectiveness is controversial; but Ziff, et al., maintain that "in the hands of a skilled practitioner — it works."[16]

The basic principle of homeopathy is that the symptoms of a disease are the body's attempt to heal itself. Where "allopaths" (conventional doctors) suppress symptoms, homeopaths encourage them, on the theory that they represent the body's attempt to flush out toxins. Homeopaths aid the healing process by administering minute amounts of substances which, in larger amounts, would produce the same symptoms as the disease. But side effects are avoided, because the remedies are so diluted that no molecule of the original substance is likely to be left in solution.

Homeopathy is currently quite popular in Europe, and it was popular in the United States in the nineteenth century.

But it was overtaken at the turn of the twentieth century by allopathic medicine, which was more lucrative and afforded its practitioners greater political leverage. The allopathic approach also seemed to make more sense scientifically. The current renaissance of homeopathy in the United States is due in part to the fact that a series of studies has finally brought scientific credence to its rather unlikely premises. A meta-analysis (a systematic review of a body of research) of 107 clinical studies of homeopathy was published in the British Medical Journal in 1991. In 81 of these studies, the remedies were shown to be effective.[17]

The chelating properties of homeopathic remedies were demonstrated in a laboratory study in which rats were given crude doses of arsenic, bismuth, cadmium, mercury chloride, or lead. Animals pretreated with homeopathic doses of these substances before and after exposure to the crude substances excreted more of the toxic crude substances through urine, feces, and sweat than did animals pretreated with a placebo.[18]

Tom Warren attributes his recovery from Alzheimer's disease to a mercury amalgam removal protocol that included homeopathy. He describes its graphic effects like this:

> Homeopathic remedies to remove mercury and lead seemed to work very well for me. They drove the metal that had accumulated within my body directly to my skin. Small black particles appeared on my skin under my heart in a shot-gun pattern with a circumference about the size of a coffee-can lid.[19]

Chapter 15

Taking It Slowly

Hours or days after the removal of amalgams, there is commonly an acute occurrence or aggravation of symptoms, as there may be again during the chelated removal of mercury from the body.

—Stephen Edelson, M.D.,
director of the Environmental and
Preventive Health Center in Atlanta[1]

Even if you have become convinced of the benefits of replacing your old dental work with biocompatible materials, you may want to take it slowly. Cost may be a factor; you may feel your health can't withstand the stress of a dental overhaul; or you may be waiting for developments in technology, or for a properly trained practitioner to move into your area. In this chapter, we'll look at the pros and cons of some proposed alternatives for neutralizing the effects of toxic dental metals in the meantime. We'll also look at the wisdom of proceeding with caution even if you can afford to go full speed ahead, to ease the "detox" phase of dental revision.

Stopgap Measures: Neutralizing the Battery Effect

Various treatments have been tried for reversing the battery effect without actually removing the offending metals. One practitioner did it by literally grounding the patient, taking away the built-up electrical currents with a metal plate grounded to the floor at night. Many people were reported to be helped; but the procedure was inconvenient, and it did not work during the day.

A popular alternative that may work on the same principle is the copper bracelet. Pure copper linked bracelets, preferably touching all the way around the wrist, act as a conductive material. The metal conductor may allow vagrant currents to be dispersed down the arm and out the fingers. Better yet is pure gold, but proponents say it should be eighteen karat; fourteen karat gold works only if it is the right alloy. However, even if the bracelets may help discharge static charges within body tissue, current discharges between metals in the mouth would still be present.

Many arthritis patients swear by copper bracelets, but do they really work? Dr. Ray Walker, of the University of Newcastle in Australia, decided to put them to the test. Half of the 300 arthritis sufferers in his study had previously worn copper bracelets. They were asked not to wear them for a month. The other subjects had never worn the bracelets. They were given two indistinguishable ones, one made of copper and the other a placebo made of aluminum. They were instructed to wear each for a month. Group I, the previous copper-bracelet users, reported that their symptoms were significantly worse when not wearing the bracelets; while Group II reported feeling best during the month when they wore the bracelets that proved to be the copper ones.[2]

Arguably, these effects were due to absorption of trace amounts of copper from the bracelets; but an alternative explanation is that the bracelets were discharging electrical distress produced in the mouth by dissimilar metals. In Chinese medicine, the meridians that service the jaw and the teeth run down the arm. The bracelet may deal with the electrical short-out caused by the vagrant currents built up in the mouth.

Short-circuiting the Circuit

Dr. Marshall suggests another alternative for short-circuiting the battery effect, which worked for a patient who complained that he was able to sleep only an hour at a time. The man said he was constantly "wired." An examination of his mouth revealed a large collection of mixed metals. Dr. Marshall suggested that he buy a rubber splint, the unfitted kind available for a dollar or two used for athletic sports. The first night the patient wore the splint, he reported that he slept a full five hours — still not enough for most people, but to him it was a miracle. The splint had evidently separated the metals in his mouth sufficiently to defuse the battery effect that had kept him "wired."

Other options for counteracting electrical short-out include treatments like acupuncture, which revive and rebalance the body's energy fields; and energy-generating devices like the Accuscope, which produce beneficial wave lengths in the body. Chiropractor Dr. Linda Forbes explains that the electrical systems of sick patients are weak. Micro-frequency machines help eliminate the deficiency by generating an electrical current that is quite similar to the body's own. The problem with these alternatives is that symptoms return when the patient stops doing them.

Neutralizing Dental Metals with Homeopathy

Should homeopathic remedies be given for neutralizing dental metals before all the mercury is out of the teeth? Authorities disagree on this question. Tom Warren says they shouldn't. Fuller Royal, M.D., H.M.D., of the Nevada Clinic in Las Vegas, however, reports using homeopathy quite successfully for that purpose. In an interview quoted by Betsy Russell Manning, he gives this example:

> I had a psychiatrist that came to see me who had Meniere's syndrome and he was extremely ill. He was vomiting, his eyes were jerking, and someone had to bring him to the clinic. I checked with the instrument [an electro-dermal screening device] and I found that his problem was that he was reacting to gold in his mouth. I said, 'Open your mouth,' he did, and I looked in there, and he had a solid gold bridge on the right side, where I was getting the bad reading. I said, 'You have an electric generator in your mouth. You

are having terrible problems with the gold.' So, we found the correct homeopathic dose of oroment, which is a gold remedy, and I gave him an injection and in less than a minute, all of his dizziness disappeared, his symptoms disappeared.[3]

Dr. Lynne Walker, a pharmacist/homeopath/acupuncturist in Sun Valley, Idaho, also feels homeopathy can be an effective neutralizer of dental metals while metal is still in the teeth — although she agrees that the ideal solution is to have the metal removed. She cites the case of a man with dangerously high cholesterol levels, who had been given medication for that symptom. The drugs had dropped his cholesterol to normal, but his blood pressure and thyroid levels had then shot up. His thyroid hormone level was so high that his doctor had proposed surgically removing his thyroid. A patient history revealed that the man had had a great deal of trouble with his teeth. His mouth was a shiny mixture of mercury and nickel. He'd had caps that had been filed down to make a bridge, but the bridge didn't fit right. Dr. Walker proposed having his dental work reconstructed with biocompatible materials, but the man had already invested $20,000 in his teeth and couldn't bring himself to have them redone. She therefore recommended homeopathic remedies and natural oral chelators instead. The latter included chlorella, barley, a green drink called "Ultimate Green," and zinc. Remarkably, the man's thyroid and blood pressure levels returned to normal, allowing him to avoid a devastating surgery. More than three years later, he reported that he was still in good health. Dr. Walker concedes that his symptoms may eventually return and eventually the man will have to deal with his dental limitations to ultimate health.

The homeopathic medicines she uses are part of a new line of combination homeopathic products designed specifically for neutralizing heavy metal poisoning, dental work, and environmental toxins. "Oratox" by Deseret is recommended for two or three weeks after dental work. Other Deseret combination homeopathics include "Enviroclenz" and "Metox." A remedy by Apex called "Mercury Antitox" helps clear mercury from body tissues after its removal from the teeth. Other combination products include "Dental Detox" and "Amalgam" by PHP.

In addition, Dr. Walker recommends homeopathic medicines to reduce the trauma of dental work. She suggests taking homeopathic arnica before going to the dentist, to help control shock, pain and bruising. Homeopathic calendula is given for tissue healing after tooth extractions. Homeopathic phosphorus is given to eliminate the anesthetic from the system. Hypericum helps with nerve pain after injury to the head. Bellis helps with bruises and injuries. Alumina is given for metal detoxification and is particularly indicated in cases of senile dementia.[4] Supplemental zinc is also good, to help counteract mercury and nickel absorption. Dr. Walker also recommends a detox program specifically designed for cleaning the liver.

The Long-range Goal

Although homeopathy and other stopgap measures can help stave off symptoms, as long as the precipitating cause remains in the body, Dr. Forbes warns that you will simply be bailing water out of a leaky boat. The ultimate goal should be to have toxic materials removed from the teeth and replaced with biocompatible materials. Where the hurdle is money, the work can be done gradually, tackling only one or two teeth at a time. It can be financed the way cars and colleges are. It's a matter of priorities — and of being convinced you are investing in a long and healthy old age.

If you can afford to upgrade only one or two teeth, results can still be quite dramatic, since clearing a single tooth can open an energy pathway through an imbalanced quadrant. Electro-dermal screening can help zero in on the most productive area to tackle first. Dr. Marshall and Dr. Forbes cite a number of cases in which fixing only one or two teeth transformed the patient's health:

Chronic Fatigue Reversed

A 50-year-old male hairdresser complained he was so exhausted he could hardly get through his work day. A careful patient history revealed that his health had started to fail after the installation of two gold crowns alloyed with palladium. He insisted he couldn't afford a complete dental overhaul, but he agreed to get the two gold crowns replaced with Degussa porcelain. When this modest modification made him "a new man," he was so impressed that he sold some family assets to finance a complete dental upgrade — not only for himself but for his wife.

Scoliosis And Chronic Nasal Congestion Alleviated

A private investigator in his early forties suffered from scoliosis (curvature of the spine) and frequent colds, flu and nasal congestion so bothersome he had trouble sleeping. He had been to many therapists without relief. Remarkably, when a root canal in one of his front teeth was cleaned out, his upper spine, which had been bowed to the side, began straightening out.

The man's sore throats and colds, however, continued. As fall approached, he remarked that he hated this time of year; he always caught one cold after another throughout the winter. Dr. Forbes asked if he would be willing to have just one silver filling replaced, and he agreed. She looked in his mouth and picked out his largest amalgam.

Several weeks after the amalgam was replaced with Degussa porcelain, the man returned again complaining of symptoms. He said he was tired and had a sore throat. Dr. Forbes maintained that this was a good sign; it was the healing crisis. The man decided she was right, when he didn't get a single cold or flu as the season progressed. He couldn't believe it; his nasal passages were clear and he was sleeping well.

"He had other silver fillings," Dr. Forbes observes, "but eliminating just this one was apparently enough to upregulate his immune system and break the flu cycle."

Angina Eliminated

A third case involved a 74-year-old multi-millionaire with heart symptoms. He had chest pains, arm pains, and an irregular heart beat. He was on nitroglycerin for angina and

Verapamil for high blood pressure. He spent two days in the hospital undergoing tests, but the medication he was given for his irregular heart beat had only made his symptoms worse. Dr. Marshall had been telling him for months that he had an infected tooth that was sitting on his heart meridian, but the man didn't want to spend the money to have it fixed. He stalled until there was no alternative but to have the tooth extracted. When he did, all his symptoms disappeared. He got off his heart medications and onto a nutritional maintenance program. He said he had never felt stronger.

"That's typical," Dr. Marshall remarked. "It's not like our patients rush out to get their dental work done. They're all highly resistant to the idea. And after they do it, they all say, 'Why didn't I do it sooner!'"

The Virtues Of Restraint

Even if you can afford to have all your dental work upgraded at one sitting, proceeding slowly is generally recommended, since having too many teeth done in a short time can traumatize the jaw and stress the immune system. Seriously ill people are advised to wait four to eight weeks between sessions and limit them to one or two fillings each.[5]

Practitioners report that a detoxification phase follows the replacement of toxic dental work with biocompatible dental materials, even when revision is done gradually. The more toxic you are to begin with, the more you are likely to be symptomatic during the clearing of old interference fields. You should anticipate alternating between feeling exceptionally good and re-experiencing old complaints (fatigue, digestive ills, nasal congestion, body aches, etc.). The important thing is to recognize what this experience is — a clearing of toxins from an energy field that is being revitalized — and to ride it out without suppressing it with drugs. Acupuncture to balance the energy meridians, nutritional support, and herbs may be recommended by your health practitioner to ease and speed the process. Better yet, detox and build up your body nutritionally <u>before</u> your dental overhaul.

Dr. Marshall also advises getting your bone status checked. If you are in a state of bone loss, calcium levels should be built back up before proceeding. Poor bone status can indicate a weakness in the kidneys, which control bone metabolism and calcium absorption. Without proper kidney function, mineral supplements won't be absorbed. If kidney function is poor, a kidney detox program is recommended.

Dr. Marshall also stresses the importance of increasing water intake to improve kidney function. "Elderly women with urinary incontinence tend to reduce their water intake," he observes. "They leak, so they stop drinking water. But your kidneys are forced to filter 2,000 liters of blood a day. If that blood is dirty and there's no water to flush it, you fry the nephrons. The kidneys control the bones. That's why those women lose bone so fast."

Chapter 16

Precision Diagnostics

> Measurement of changes in the electrical parameters of
> acupoints . . . will ultimately prove to be the diagnostic
> avenues of the future.
> — Richard Gerber, M.D.[1]

In an article in the February 1997 Reader's Digest titled
"How Honest Are Dentists?", William Ecenbarger skeptically
observed that in a 28-state investigation, he received estimates
for fixing his teeth that ranged from $500 to $29,850. Are
dentists intentionally ripping us off? Or is dentistry simply an
inexact science — so inexact that dentists relying on
conventional training and equipment have no way of knowing
the true condition of the teeth or what truly needs to be done
to them? Therefore they are ignorant of hidden problems and
erroneously tell their patients everything is fine.

Dr. Hansen subscribes to the latter theory. "Dentistry
until now has been largely guesswork," he says. "Fillings can
look fine on the outside, while slow corrosion, bacterial
leakage, and decay are going on underneath. The first sign
of trouble is when the tooth cracks or breaks or dies and
needs a root canal, or has visible decay around a filling. We
need better ways of diagnosing cavities. We need accurate,
quantifiable means of diagnosing early problems, to
document the need for replacing defective restorations that
are no longer serviceable or are heading toward major, more
invasive dentistry. Until now, there has been no real way of
having measurable results with a high degree of accuracy."

All that, however, is changing. New diagnostic
techniques promise to turn dentistry into the most exact of

sciences. Dentists finally have accurate means of diagnosing early problems and documentable reasons for replacing mercury amalgam and other defective restorations.

The Downsides of Conventional X-rays

X-rays, the diagnostic tools most often used by dentists, have to date been valuable diagnostic procedures. But they don't detect everything that is going on inside the tooth. Conventional x-ray machines are also leading sources of man-made radiation. At one time, dentists were advised to take x-rays every six months; but the FDA now recommends limiting them to only once every two years for children in good dental health, and once every two to three years for adults.[2]

New research indicates that even that exposure may be hazardous. Dr. John Gofman, a professor at the University of California at Berkeley, concluded in his 1995 book Preventing Breast Cancer that about three-quarters of the current cases of breast cancer in the United States are caused by previous exposure to non-ionising radiation, primarily from medical x-rays. The x-rays that girls were given in the fifties, he maintains, are killing the women of the nineties.[3]

Dental x-rays are most often done on children, who are far more sensitive to radiation injury than adults. Children's bodies are growing rapidly, providing more opportunity for the disruption of growing cells; and since children have longer life expectancies, they have longer to produce visible cancers, which take many years to develop. Studies have shown not only that children have higher cancer induction rates than adults, but that women have higher rates than men. In a 1986 study, girls under ten exposed to one REM of radiation were found to be 39 percent more likely to develop breast cancer after the age of thirty than girls not so exposed. One REM of radiation is the amount provided by a single major spinal or gastrointestinal x-ray series.[4]

David Kennedy, D.D.S., says that overuse of dental x-rays can be blamed largely on legal and insurance requirements. Dentists who try to limit x-ray exposure in their patients risk malpractice suits if they miss something that might have been detected by x-ray, and insurance companies will refuse to pay for fillings unless they are accompanied by current x-rays.[5] The result has been excessive and unnecessary exposure of patients to radiation.

State-of-the-art Solutions

While x-rays from the conventional equipment found in most dental offices may be harmful to the body, there are state-of-the-art machines now available that focus the beam so precisely that there is no scatter and very low exposure to radiation. Computerized dental radiography substitutes a microchip for the traditional bite-wing used to take dental images. The microchip can reduce the need for x-ray exposure by up to 90 percent. It can also help the dentist detect cavities and other problems difficult to see on standard x-ray film. Computer-enhanced x-rays have become a major radiological innovation.

"You can now take an image like you would with an x-ray," says Dr. Hansen, "using 90 percent less radiation, and enhance that image with a computer so that it's much clearer and more precise than you could ever get with a manual x-ray. There's even a program now to quantitate the gridding on the x-ray, so that when the patient comes back, the computer can tell the dentist if there has been any change in density or structure in the tooth. That means we now have the ability to see if there is any demineralization or loss of tooth structure, something we couldn't tell before even with an x-ray."

Intra-oral cameras can now magnify the tooth surface 30 times on a television screen, in front of the patient, for easy inspection by both the doctor and the patient. Dr. Hansen explains that "I can now see things happening in the mouth at an early, very easily treated stage rather than wait till we have to use aggressive more destructive treatment. I think any dentist who does not use an intra-oral magnification camera is just working with blinders on. They seem to want to be an ostrich, bury their head in the sand, and pretend everything is fine so that they do not have to inform the patient of any potential problems and deal with the confrontation. They ignore the problem and pretend it doesn't exist. Until the patient bites on something, breaks the tooth, and now the problem has to be faced. The trouble with this scenario is that the patient could have avoided the fracture, the associated pain, inconvenience, and costs if the dentist would have informed the patient earlier and treated the problem rather than ignoring it."

Computer-imaging techniques can detect incipient caries at a stage when the teeth could potentially be remineralized rather than having to be removed or restored. That and other innovations are turning dental diagnostics into a quantifiable, precision exercise.

Other Innovations for Diagnosing Decay

"Cavity detector dyes are now available," says Dr. Hansen, "that will stain the protein material and detect if there's even a tiny cavity in the tooth. We've learned from looking at slides of electron microscope examination of cavities that have been stained, that the decay doesn't just run down the middle of the tooth, like we've been taught. The decay runs off to the sides, through micro cracks in the tooth, and can destroy much of the inside of the tooth before we ever see it in the surface.

Our society has used fluoride for over 30 years which has increased the resistance of the surface enamel to decay. However, the inner part of the tooth, the dentin, has been unaffected by fluoride. So our traditional model of diagnosing and treating decay has changed. We used to be able to see decay on the surface of the tooth with an explorer or an x-ray. Now, however, we no longer see this surface decay yet the tooth may be rotting away inside. The dentist does not "see" anything from the surface and tells the patient everything is OK. By the time the dentist discovers the problem much of the tooth has been destroyed and requires an invasive large filling, a crown or a root canal. When we're doing micro-dentistry, we can use an air abrasive to clean out the small micro crevices of the tooth, pinpoint its exact location with a caries detector dye and an intra-oral camera, and do much smaller restorations. We can target and remove the decay in a tooth like this with a laser or air particle beam abrasive, with no anaesthetic or pain, and inject in and fuse, with the laser, a biocompatable tooth replacement."

He is also in the process of developing a digital caries indicator that measures electrical resistance and potential. It will detect leakage into the tooth by following metallic dyes into the crevices and determining changes in electrical potential.

Researchers at the University of Dundee Dental School in Scotland have also been testing a procedure for detecting decay with an electric current. The current is shot through the tooth to detect tiny pores signaling decayed spots too small to be detected by x-ray. The technique hasn't yet been tested on humans, but the ADA says it's promising.[6]

Materials Testing

Besides diagnosing decay, new techniques have been developed for testing the biocompatibility of dental materials. Materials testing kits are available for practitioners who do this type of testing on their patients. Three major vehicles are currently being used:

(1) blood serum compatibility testing — the Clifford and Huggins diagnostic systems, which test blood serum response and immuno-response;

(2) electro-dermal screening — particularly the Vega, Computron, and Listen systems; and

(3) muscle response testing, or applied kinesiology.

The first two vehicles were discussed in Chapter 3. Muscle testing is a system that has been criticized as being highly subjective, but it has the advantage that it involves no "drugs or devices" requiring FDA approval. It uses nothing more than the patient's own arm or leg. And experienced practitioners report getting consistently accurate results.

Muscle Testing

The principles of applied kinesiology, or muscle testing, were discovered largely by accident. Dr. George Goodheart, a Detroit chiropractor, found that some of the standard chiropractic muscle tests provided clues to the workings of the whole body. His new system combined chiropractic principles with Eastern ideas about energy flow. Weaknesses were identified by muscle-testing techniques, then treated to correct imbalances in the body's energy systems. Where energy was found to be restricted or excessive, Dr. Goodheart discovered that either the muscle might be weak or the patient might be reacting to certain foods or other irritants. Kinesiologists have been particularly successful in locating and treating allergies. Dr. Goodheart also discovered that muscle weakness or strength could be used to indicate the compatibility of a remedy.

John Diamond, M.D., observed in a book on the subject:

> Over the years, Dr. Goodheart had achieved many amazing results — results that had far-reaching implications. . . If a particular nutritional supplement was given to a patient and the muscle tested strong, it was the right supplement for that patient; if the muscle remained weak, it was not. Other methods of treatment could be similarly evaluated. With Applied Kinesiology, doctors had a really useful tool, a system of feedback from the body itself. If they gave a patient the proper treatment, the body would respond immediately as if to say, "Yes, that is what was needed."

Salivary Analysis

Saliva is one of the most important components in the oral environment for not only protecting the dental tissue from disease but for rebuilding and remineralizing damaged teeth. Saliva also is the important first step in digesting foods and adding enzymes and minerals to help break down foods and allow nutrients to be utilized. Normal saliva has a slightly basic ph. However, in diseased states the saliva turns more acidic and instead of protecting teeth and tissues, helps decay and destroy them. Measuring the ph, enzyme, and mineral content of the saliva can be a very important diagnostic test for assessing disease and disease potential. More on saliva composition and its importance to health is discussed in Chapter 17.

Future Diagnostics

For testing the biocompatibility of materials, Dr. Hansen feels that, electro-dermal screening may hold the key; but it has to be made universally acceptable. He is currently designing and implementing double-blind studies for that purpose.

More advanced techniques are projected for twenty-first century dentistry. "The key for the future," he maintains, "will be diagnosing on a molecular, chemical, or neurological level to find out the individual's needs based on a whole range of factors, environmental and genetic, and tailoring a program to meet those needs. Scanners can check various parameters — ultrasound, digital x-rays, chemical scans of composition of saliva, and electronic scans of the teeth and bone. In Europe, an electronic scanner is already available that checks tooth density to determine if a cavity is present.

Once you've identified a problem, another micro-manipulator can be placed in the mouth to correct it. The saliva can be modified to become more basic and more enriched with the minerals and enzymes for not only stopping disease, but which can actually remineralize and rebuild damaged tissue. If it's disease in the form of a cavity, a targeted laser can pinpoint the cavity area. If it's a very small cavity, the laser will be able to vaporize the decay and literally weld the tooth back together without any replacement material. The disease within the tooth will be removed, not the tooth structure itself. If it's a larger decayed area or breakage or other problem, the scanner could calculate what type of replacement is needed. For a tiny area, you could use injectable tooth substitutes — cloned enamel to replace enamel, cloned dentin to replace dentin. For a larger area — including a whole tooth that needs to be replaced — you could have the computer design and make up a tooth-like replacement from tooth-like biomaterials that could then be fused into the mouth with a laser. Much of the treatment could be done without a dentist ever putting his hand in the patient's mouth, using anesthetics, drills, or grinding any good tooth away."

The Millennial Soul

In Section III, we'll explore research pointing toward another millennial ideal — preserving the teeth by natural means, without drills, metals, plastics, or even dentists.

SECTION III
BEYOND DENTISTRY:
PERFECT TEETH/PERFECT HEALTH

Chapter 17

The Nutritional Approach

It is store food which has given us store teeth.

— Anthropologist Dr. Ernest A. Hooton[1]

A recent TV news program showed a clip suggesting that the current epidemic of dental problems is due to a general inability to afford dental insurance. People who can't afford their dentists are waiting to visit them until their dental problems have become so bad that only the more complicated, expensive and hazardous procedures will repair the damage.

Contrast this story with a one circulating several years ago in Africa. A beneficent young dental graduate set out in his jeep with his dental equipment, intending to repair the teeth of poor Africans in the bush who could not afford dental treatment. He found himself without work. The African bushmen had the finest teeth he had ever seen. The only dental care they received was to chew on certain tree branches to clean the teeth.

Other research has shown that many "primitive" people around the world have teeth that are free of cavities, gum disease, and orthodontic defects, although they do not have the benefit of dentists, orthodontists, fluoride, or even toothbrushes.[2]

What is their secret? Research reveals that the key to prevention has actually been known for decades. In the forties, Harold Hawkins, D.D.S., showed that if the mineral levels of the saliva were raised to sufficient levels, cavities could be totally eliminated. This was true for children who never used fluoride or even brushed their teeth.[3] In the same decade, Weston Price, D.D.S., documented cases of spontaneous regeneration of teeth that originally were so decayed that the inner pulp was exposed. After the children's nutrition was improved, the teeth reincased themselves in secondary dentin (the tooth tissue under the hard outer enamel), drawing on the minerals in the saliva and the pulp to rebuild themselves.[4]

Dr. Price was the innovative dentist who spent 25 years implanting root-filled teeth into rabbits. He also conducted extensive orthodontic research. He found that tooth and jaw defects once thought to be hereditary can be related to nutrition. He documented cases in both animals and humans in which mothers who ate deficient diets produced offspring with insufficiently formed jaw structures and other "congenital" defects. These same mothers, when switched to mineral-rich diets, went on in the same generation to produce offspring having normal jaws. In a monumental 1948 work called <u>Nutrition and Physical Degeneration</u>, Dr. Price published studies showing that defective bone growth patterns can be corrected in a relatively short time by nutritional means.[5]

His work was corroborated by Francis M. Pottenger, M.D., in a ten-year study with cats. We'll look at the work of Dr. Price, Dr. Pottenger, and Dr. Hawkins here in turn.

Nutritional Reversal of Jaw Defects

Dr. Price's orthodontic investigations began with the clinical observation that some children seemed to have dental problems not experienced by their parents. The children's teeth were not only more decayed but did not fit properly into the dental arch and were crowded and crooked. Suspecting a nutritional cause, Dr. Price traveled around the world studying primitive cultures. He found that when people from "underdeveloped" areas moved to the city, their offspring tended to have narrow jaws and crowded teeth. People with wide, ample jaws produced children with small jaws and crowded teeth after adopting a Western diet of sugar, white flour, and other refined, processed, chemicalized foods — a phenomenon sometimes referred to as "short-term genetics."

Dr. Price also made the remarkable discovery that the damage caused by an improper diet could be reversed nearly as quickly as it appeared. Mothers who had produced offspring with deficient jaw structures and other "genetic" defects when they were eating deficient diets produced other children without these defects when the mothers were switched to adequate diets before and during gestation. In animal studies, even the defective offspring went on to produce offspring without structural defects, when the defective generation was fed an adequate diet before and during gestation. Dr. Price also documented cases of too-small pelvic bones among women whose mothers had eaten inadequate diets. The result was difficulty in delivering children.[6]

These effects could not be explained by normal genetics. Bone structure is undoubtedly programmed into DNA, but defects not found in the parents must come not from "nature" but from "nurture": deficient nutrition.

Nutritional Reversal of Dental Caries

Dr. Price made another revolutionary discovery: a proper diet could result in the spontaneous repair of teeth that had already started to decay. During the Great Depression, when tooth decay had reached epidemic proportions, he treated 27 children with rampant caries. In many cases their teeth were so decayed that the inner pulp was exposed. Improvements in their diets actually helped stop the decay and caused these teeth to be reincased in secondary dentin. The teeth evidently drew on the minerals in the saliva and the pulp to rebuild themselves.

What were the magic ingredients in Dr. Price's cavity-repairing diet? He considered its most important component to be a food which today has acquired a bad name, but which featured prominently in primitive nutrition. It was butter — but not just any butter would do. He found that the most potent butter was produced by dairy animals fed on rapidly growing grass that was green or had been rapidly dried. It contained a critical factor that he originally thought was vitamin D, but that he later identified simply as "activator X." Whatever this mysterious factor was, it had these features: it was synthesized by the mammary glands; it could be demonstrated not only in butterfat but in the eggs of fishes and the organs and fats of animals; and it was essential for the maximum utilization of body-building minerals and tissue components.

Dr. Price concocted a butter product with even greater potency, by melting a high-vitamin butter and allowing it to crystallize for 24 hours at a temperature of about 70 degrees, then centrifuging it and mixing the upper oil with equal parts of a natural high-vitamin cod-liver oil. The children in his study were fed one supplemental meal a day that included a teaspoonful of the special butter-oil concoction. It also included four ounces of tomato or orange juice, a pint of rich vegetable and meat stew (made largely from bone marrow and fine cuts of tender meat, finely chopped vegetables and very yellow carrots), cooked fruit, freshly ground whole wheat rolls spread with high-vitamin butter, and two glasses of fresh whole milk. A single helping of each course provided a total of 1.48 grams of calcium (twice the recommended calcium allowance) and 1.28 grams of phosphorus. No change was made in the children's home diets or care of the teeth besides this single daily meal.

> "The clinical effect," wrote Dr. Price, "was apparent complete control of dental caries for the entire group, as shown in the x-ray films. In many of these cases, the open cavities were left without fillings; and, in all such cases, the exposed dentin took on a hard glassy finish." The x-ray films showed a progressive filling in of the pulp chambers . . . from a deposition of secondary dentin, making a roof over the pulp and thereby providing a protection which enabled the pulp to remain vital and useful for an extended period. This is frequently experienced as a result of reinforcing the diet with high-vitamin and high-

activator butter, together with reducing the carbohydrate intake to a normal level as supplied by natural foods and by increasing the foods that provide body-building and tooth-forming minerals. The condition that obtains in the tooth is one in which the minerals cease to be taken in minute amounts from the tooth structure and, owing to the change in the saliva, the minerals in ionic form pass from the saliva bathing the tooth cavity into the demineralized dentin, in many cases a hard and even glassy surface resulting."[7]

Later research augmented these findings. Dr. Ralph Steinman of Loma Linda University Dental School demonstrated that when the diet is adequate, the fluid always moves from the pulp outwards to the surface of the tooth, keeping bacteria out of the teeth. But when the diet is unbalanced or contains too much refined sugar or other carbohydrates, the fluid movement through the teeth reverses. Small microorganisms — viruses, fungi, etc. — are then pulled into the tooth through the dental tubules all the way to the pulp. Dr. Steinman found that when saliva mineral and enzyme levels are high, cavities do not form.[8]

Dr. Pottenger's Cats

Dr. Price's findings concerning nutrition and structural defects were confirmed by Frances M. Pottenger, M.D., in a classic ten-year study involving 900 cats. The experiment grew out of the observation that laboratory cats who were fed cooked-meat leftovers from an institutional kitchen were poor operative risks, while those fed raw-meat scraps were not. The cats fed cooked meat in Dr. Pottenger's study developed dental malformations like those seen in children of mothers eating the modern diet, including narrow dental arches, crowded teeth, underbites and overbites, and protruding and crooked teeth.

One group of cats was fed a diet of two-thirds raw meat, one-third raw milk, and cod-liver oil. The second group was fed the same diet except that the meat was cooked. The cats eating the raw meat reproduced normally and had good resistance to infections and parasites. Their organic development was complete and they functioned normally. The cats eating cooked meat, on the other hand, developed a number of defects and diseases familiar in human medicine, including not only dental malformations but cardiac lesions (damaged heart tissue), cirrhosis of the liver, and degeneration of the brain and spinal cord. Skin lesions and allergies were common and became progressively worse from one generation to the next. Intestinal parasites abounded. Spontaneous abortion was common, running as high as seventy percent in the second generation. Deliveries were difficult, and many cats died in labor. Mortality rates of the kittens were high, frequently due to the failure of the mother to produce milk. Pneumonia and empyema (pus in the lung cavity) were among the principal causes of death among the adult cats. By the third generation, the entire strain had died out.

In a follow-up experiment, the meat was raw but the milk was cooked or otherwise treated. Again, the cats fed raw milk grew and reproduced normally, while those fed pasteurized or metabolized vitamin D milk developed bone disturbances. The mothers showed lessened reproductive efficiency, and the kittens showed developmental deficiencies. Cats fed evaporated milk showed even more damage. The most marked deficiencies occurred in the cats fed sweetened condensed milk.[9]

The Research of Dr. Hawkins

Dr. Price's findings concerning nutrition and dental caries were confirmed by Harold Hawkins, D.D.S., in a 1947 book called Diet and Nutrition. Dr. Hawkins identified four defects that can lead to tooth decay:

1. Insufficient ptyalin

One was a shortage of the enzyme ptyalin. The popular conception is that tooth decay results when sugar forms a breeding ground for bacteria on the teeth; but Dr. Hawkins maintained that the culprit is starch that hasn't been broken down into simple sugar. When the body's tooth-preserving systems are working properly, starch is broken down by ptyalin into sugar, which is then dissolved in the saliva and washed away. When this system fails, the starch remains trapped around the teeth, feeding harmful bacteria that release enamel-destroying acids, which then cause tooth decay. Eating sugar and other refined carbohydrates is still hazardous, but for a different reason. Forming sufficient ptyalin requires sufficient B vitamins, which are found naturally in unrefined carbohydrates. These vitamins are lost when carbohydrates are refined, as most carbohydrates are in the modern diet.

2. Insufficient alkaline buffers in the saliva

Once the enamel-eating acids have formed on the teeth, the body's second line of defense is to neutralize them with alkaline buffers in the saliva. Its alkaline components include calcium, magnesium, potassium and sodium. If these minerals (particularly calcium) are in short supply, the saliva's buffering capacity is lost and caries result.[10]

3. Insufficient formation of saliva

The saliva's buffering capacity is lost not only when its minerals are in short supply but when the saliva itself is insufficient. Dry mouths can be caused by diets that are low in fruits, vegetables and liquids, and high in cereals; by insufficient vitamin A; or by low thyroid levels. Dr. Hawkins reported that improving the body chemistry usually normalizes the amount of saliva.[11]

4. Decreased alkalinity and increased acidity in the saliva

An acid condition of the saliva can also cause tooth decay. The effect of acids on the skeleton is suggested by a popular children's experiment: if a hard-boiled egg is soaked in vinegar for three days, the shell will become soft and spongy like rubber. The reason is that the acid has leached the calcium out of the shell. An increase in acidity does the same thing to the teeth: it causes calcium to become more soluble. The dissolved calcium then washes away and is lost through the urine.

What causes the saliva's alkalinity to drop and acidity to increase? Usually, the effect comes from ingesting too much of certain substances that produce an acid reaction in the body, including sugar, flour, bread, legumes, grains, and meat. When these foods are included in the diet, they should be balanced with alkalinizing foods, particularly vegetables and seaweed products.[12]

Dr. Hawkins observed that a drop in alkalinity can also be brought about by infection, kidney obstruction, a faulty splitting of fats that leaves an acetone residue, and a deficiency of the hydrochloric acid required for digestion. Without sufficient hydrochloric acid, organic acids — particularly those found in acid fruits — aren't oxidized properly. The saliva then turns acid, decreasing its buffering capacity.

Preventing Cavities Through Proper Mineral Balance

Like Dr. Price and Dr. Steinman, Dr. Hawkins found that with adequate levels of minerals in the saliva, tooth decay simply does not occur. He also observed that while calcium is the most important mineral for protecting the teeth, salivary calcium is the mineral level that changes most slowly. Merely ingesting calcium will not raise salivary calcium to proper levels unless other factors are changed as well. Dr. Hawkins listed thirteen factors that determine the calcium level:

1. The amount and type of calcium in the diet,
2. The buffer pH of the saliva,
3. The amount of phosphorus assimilated,
4. The amount of potassium assimilated,
5. The amount of magnesium assimilated,
6. The basal metabolic rate,
7. The influence of vitamin D,
8. The rate of growth in the case of a child,
9. The hydrochloric acid level,
10. The amount of bile secreted,
11. The level of iron in the body,
12. Overactivity or underactivity of the parathyroids, and
13. The rate of intestinal activity.

All of these factors must be at appropriate levels to maintain the calcium level. Trouble results when they are not in balance with each other.

One element that has gotten out of balance in the modern American diet is phosphorus. Phosphorus is a necessary nutrient, but our diets now include far more of it than our great grandparents' did. Phosphorus is the chief mobilizer of calcium, drawing calcium from the bones and causing it to be excreted in the urine. Our principal sources of phosphate (the assimilable form of phosphorus) are carbonated soft drinks and protein, particularly meat protein. Protein acidifies the blood, dissolving calcium from the bones. In a University of Wisconsin study, people on a diet containing 102 grams of protein a day (a typical American intake) excreted almost twice the amount of calcium as people on a diet containing only 44 grams of protein (the Recommended Daily Allowance).[13] In another study, children's serum calcium levels rose and serum phosphorus levels dropped significantly after they discontinued soft drinks for thirty days.[14]

Vegetarian expert Annemarie Colbin reports that calcium balance also seems to be affected by the nightshades, including tomatoes, potatoes, eggplant, peppers and tobacco. Consuming nightshades on a dairy-free diet can result in a loss of calcium that is evidenced by brittle nails, painful gums, and dental caries. Alcohol consumption can also cause calcium loss. Social drinkers are 2-1/2 times as likely to develop osteoporosis as non-drinkers, and alcoholics are known to lose significant amounts of bone.[15]

Coffee is another culprit, particularly if the coffee isn't balanced with dairy foods. In a 1994 study, non-milk drinkers who drank more than two cups of caffeinated coffee per day had a lower bone density than those who drank less than two cups. However, women who drank _four_ cups of coffee accompanied by a glass of milk each day had average bone density.[16] The researchers concluded that coffee's effect on bone density is due mainly to calcium excretion. Caffeine is a diuretic, which stimulates the kidneys to excrete fluid. Most coffee is also acidic, drawing calcium as an alkaline buffer.

Chapter 18

Does Every Body Need Milk?

The next time you savor that Kentucky Fried or 'fresh' Washington State Poultry think about the fact that this animal hasn't seen sunlight, can't move, is given chemicals to fatten it, calm it, and kill its gut microbiology. . . . A chicken 100 years ago was a chicken; a chicken in 1995 is a miserable creature that has never enjoyed a natural day in its life.
— Jonathan Collin, M.D.[1]

To Dr. Hawkins and Dr. Price, milk and butter were among the most valuable foods for preserving the teeth. But both doctors were writing in the forties, when you could still get raw milk and butter from cows that grazed in green pastures. Milk, eggs, and many other staples are not the same products today. Modern commercial dairy products do not come from pastured animals, and raw milk is hard to obtain. Dairy cows are now raised in confinement, where they are surrounded by their own excrement, routinely injected with antibiotics and hormones, and fed dry foods that are deficient in nutritional value.

The Hazards of Pasteurization and Homogenization

Dr. Hawkins wrote, "Raw milk from healthy cows that have been suitably tested is of the highest biological value." But pasteurized milk, he observed, "greatly increases the difficulty of calcium assimilation as well as injuring vitamins and probably hormones. . . Homogenized milk is usually pasteurized from 165 to 186 degrees F by the flash method. This type of milk is not suitable for a growing child or invalid as only about half the theoretical calcium is assimilated by the average child according to our tests."[2]

Live enzymes are necessary to aid the body in assimilating the minerals in milk. When milk or any other calcium source has been heated above 125 degrees F, these enzymes are lost. In 1946, Dr. Edward Howell, in <u>The Status of Food Enzymes in Digestion and Metabolism</u>, cited numerous studies demonstrating the superiority of raw over pasteurized milk.[3] They included:

* A study conducted at London Hospital finding that raw milk conferred immunity to dental caries. No incidence of caries was found in forty children fed over a 3-1/2 year period on a diet that was rich in refined carbohydrates but in which the milk was raw.

* A study in which six premature infants at the University Pediatric Clinic in Leipzig fared very well on raw human milk fed over a sixteen-day period. When they were fed sterilized human milk for the next sixteen days, their growth rates decreased and they developed diarrhea, catarrhal conditions of the respiratory tract and impaired utilization of protein and other nutrients.

* A study finding a higher content of calcium and phosphorus in the bones of rats fed raw milk than in rats fed pasteurized milk.

* A study finding that body weights of rats fed pasteurized milk were about ten percent lower than those fed raw milk.

Other evidence of the damage done by the heat treatment of milk comes from certain epidemiological studies implicating it in heart disease. In the United Kingdom and in Oslo, Norway, at different times and in different regions, a sudden steep rise in coronary heart disease was seen within two years of the introduction of Holder pasteurized milk. Holder pasteurization involves heating for a period of thirty minutes at not less than 145 degrees Fahrenheit. In the United States, the consumption of milk products that were extensively heated, such as evaporated milk and ice cream, doubled from 1931 to 1945; and the consumption of cheese that was pasteurized, processed, or cooked came close to doubling in the same period. Heart disease deaths increased twelvefold during that time. Meanwhile, populations that consumed no milk products (including the Yemenites, the South Vietnamese, the Atiu Mitiaro, and the Hunja), all remained free of arteriosclerotic heart disease.

Other primitive peoples manage to remain free of heart disease although they consume great quantities of milk, including the African Masai, the rural Zulu, the Samburu, the nomads of Nigeria and Somaliland, the West Africans of Gabon, and the Congolese Pygmies. But their milk is preserved by fermentation (e.g. as yogurt) rather than by pasteurization.[4]

There is evidence that homogenization (the even disbursement of fat through the milk) further increases the risk of arteriosclerotic heart disease. Researchers at Fairfield University in Connecticut found that homogenization causes an enzyme to enter the bloodstream that damages the arteries. This enzyme, called xanthine oxidase, is present in all milk; but when milk is drunk raw, the enzyme is digested and passes through the system without harm. When milk is homogenized, the enzyme is protected from digestion by tiny droplets of fat that surround it. It gets carried into the bloodstream, where the fat droplets are broken down and the enzyme is freed, producing a chemical that damages the arteries. Plaque then builds up where the arteries have been injured, contributing to atherosclerosis.[5] This may explain why very young children in the United States already have signs of hardening of the arteries.[6]

The alternative is to drink raw milk, but many people question whether it is safe. Outbreaks of food poisoning have been attributed to it. Certified raw milk producers counter that more outbreaks of food poisoning can be traced to pasteurized milk. But for most people, the issue is moot in any case, since the sale of raw milk has been banned in more than half the states in the U.S., and the FDA has banned its interstate sale.[7]

Other Downsides of Milk

Milk has other drawbacks besides its denaturing by heat and homogenization. Populations that have not traditionally relied on animal milk after infancy are liable to be deficient in lactase, the enzyme necessary to digest lactose, or milk sugar. The result can be acute adverse reactions, including diarrhea and stomach cramps. Milk allergy is one of the most of common food allergies. Dairy products are also high in fat, which is hard on the heart; and in protein, which pulls calcium from the bones. Non-fat milk isn't the solution either, since butterfat seems to aid in the assimilation of calcium and in the digestion of protein. Dairy products also contain nine times as much calcium as magnesium, so ingesting them in large quantities can upset the body's calcium/magnesium balance. A too-high calcium/magnesium ratio can contribute to cardiovascular damage and functional abnormalities, and can lead to irritability, blood clots, vascular spasms, and angina pectoris.[8]

Drugs are also routinely given to cows. Antibiotic residues in milk and meat have contributed to the alarming growth of antibiotic-resistant strains of bacteria. Worse, cows are being bred to produce enormous amounts of milk by giving them growth hormones. The hormones survive cooking and can affect the consumer. This factor may help explain why offspring of Oriental immigrants to America are often two or three inches taller than their parents. George Schuchard, D.D.S., a dentist in Chino, California, observes that what growth hormones in milk and meat don't do is to increase the size of human teeth. The calcium in pasteurized, homogenized milk is largely non-assimilable, causing the quality of the bones to deteriorate as the bones themselves are getting longer. Children are getting insufficient minerals to grow a normal-sized mouth complex.[9]

Calcium from Vegetables

According to a recent large-scale study conducted by Dr. C. Campbell of Cornell University, levels of osteoporosis and cardiovascular disease in China are among the lowest in the world.[10] Yet the Chinese don't drink milk, and they consume only about half the calcium Americans do. The explanation for this anomaly may be that the Chinese also consume a third less protein than Americans, and that only seven percent of it comes from animal sources. The Chinese diet is composed principally of carbohydrates from plant foods. Protein, particularly animal protein, leaches calcium from the bones.

The most balanced, assimilable source of nutrients remains the plant kingdom itself. The cow gets calcium directly from the plants that get it from the soil. Non-dairy foods that are high in calcium include beans and nuts, greens (especially broccoli, collards, kale, mustard and turnip tops, parsley, watercress, and dandelion), sea vegetables, sesame seeds and tahini, canned salmon and sardines with bones, and soup made with bones and vinegar. High-calcium foods are listed in Table 1 in order of calories per 300 milligrams of calcium.[11]

One of the best sources of assimilable minerals is fresh-squeezed vegetable juice. New juicers now on the market make the process a quick and easy one.

Caution must be exercised since many plants, fruits and vegetables have been treated with chemicals containing fertilizers and toxic pesticides. Much of the farming methods and feed lot practices for raising animals actually may contaminate the very foods we come to expect as pure and nutritious. This has been dramatically illustrated recently in the book 'Mad Cowboy: Plain Truth From the Cattle Rancher Who Won't Eat Meat' by Howard F. Lyman. This chronicles his family's history through generations of natural organic farming methods in Montana and the devastating effects that occurred when he transformed into a modern chemical farming operation. Mr. Lyman also describes the continual process of adding one more chemical, pesticide, or fertilizer after another to correct the problems created by the last ones he had added. When he added raising cattle and a feed lot operation, the problems amplified. The disease in the animals seemed uncontrollable, and he was forced to continually add more chemicals, growth hormones, and antibiotics just so the cattle would survive and grow big and fat. His book, excerpted and published in the April 1998 issue of Self magazine, helps underscore the devastation that has occurred in the production of our food supply. In Chapter 19 this will be discussed further.

Table 1. High-calcium Low-calorie Foods

FOOD	CALCIUM (mgs)	CALORIES
1 cup cooked bok choy	300	25
1 cup cooked collards	300	60
1-1/4 cups other greens, cooked	300	60
2 cups cooked broccoli	300	80
1 cup skim milk	300	90
1/2 cup plain low-fat yogurt	300	95
1 cup buttermilk	300	100
2-1/2 tbsp. blackstrap molasses	300	110
1/4 cup grated Parmesan cheese	300	115
1 cup low-fat milk	300	120
1-1/2 ounces cheddar, Swiss or American cheese	300	150
1 cup whole milk	300	150
8 ounces tofu	300	150
1/2 cup part skim milk ricotta	300	170
3-1/2 ounce can sardines drained	300	200
3-1/2 ounce can sardines in sauce	300	230
1 cup fruit flavored yogurt	300	200-280
5 ounces canned salmon	300	235
1-1/2 cups ice milk	300	325
2 cups low-fat cottage cheese	300	410
7 corn tortillas	300	420
1-1/4 cups ice cream	300	450-1000

Chapter 19

The Need for Supplements: Fruits and Vegetables – Not What They Used to be

> Apparently we can no longer think of foods as having a fixed value; for such value varies according to the soil content.
>
> — Dr. Henry Bailey Stevens[1]

Natural, unprocessed plant foods may be the theoretical ideal, but these foods can no longer be relied on to fully satisfy our nutrient requirements either. At one time, everything the body needed was furnished by the foods of the earth. But today, the earth seems to be as depleted as our bodies are.

Canning and other methods of preserving shelf-life have further decreased the biological value of our food. The most controversial of the modern food-preserving innovations is irradiation, a procedure that involves bombarding food with ionizing radiation. The gamma rays used for irradiation come either from naturally occurring cobalt 60 or from a waste product of nuclear weapons manufacture called cesium 137. Although the FDA has concluded the procedure is safe, the issue continues to be hotly debated.[2]

There is also the problem of pesticides, which interfere with metabolism and prevent the proper assimilation of minerals. Since the 1940s, pesticide use in the United States has increased by a factor of ten. Ironically, crop losses from insects have managed to double during the same period. One problem is that 25 to 50 percent of the pesticides dropped from the air miss not only the insects but the very fields that are their targets. These pesticides enter the surrounding environment, including the ground, water and air. For consumers as well as field workers, the dire result can be acute poisoning or latent cancer. Nearly 50,000 cases of poisoning due to pesticides are reported every year.

Even if all our food were organic, raw, and unprocessed, we would still have trouble getting sufficient nutrients at today's dinner table. A U.S. Department of Agriculture report concluded that our soils and the crops grown on them are so mineral deficient that the only way to prevent and cure the resulting deficiency diseases is by taking mineral supplements — and that was in 1936.[3] The situation has declined significantly since.

Not only does the modern-day city dweller need to rely on nutritional supplements, but the products must be chosen with care. Nutrients need to be in an absorbable form. Since high pressures required to compress them into tablet form generate heat and reduce the biological value of the supplements, capsules are better than tablets. Vitamins and minerals work together synergistically, so the proper balance of nutrients is required. Essential fatty acids generally must be added, since most people's bodies are deficient in them. The high temperatures used in processing commercial fats interfere with fat metabolism, and so does the mercury leached from the teeth.

Calcium from Pills

Only a few studies have shown that calcium supplements have any effect on bone density. In those few, the calcium sources were particularly bioavailable (available for use by the body).[4]

Calcium carbonate is a cheap form of calcium contained in certain antacids, but it's an inorganic form that is only about five percent absorbed. A more bioavailable option is calcium citrate. Absorption from a combination chelate called calcium citrate-malate (CCM) is better yet.[5]

Another bioavailable source is animal bone. Primitive meat-eating people consume the calcium-containing bones along with the animal's flesh. The Eskimos eat small birds, bones and all. The hardy Vilcabamba in South America are essentially vegetarian, but they supplement their calcium intakes by cooking beef bones all day with vegetables to make a calcium-rich soup. Vinegar or acidic vegetables like tomatoes help get the calcium out of the soup bones.

Civilized man's teeth are no longer capable of grinding up raw bone, but processors have solved this problem by grinding up bone meal mechanically and pressing it into tablets. The ideal bone meal is a cold-processed product that has not been heated above 125 degrees F. A downside of bone meal is that it may be contaminated with lead, but this problem is avoided in a highly bioavailable bone calcium called microcrystalline hydroxyapatite compound (MCHC). MCHC is the organic protein calcium matrix found in the raw young bones of cattle and sheep raised on insecticide- and pesticide-free pastures. It differs from bone meal in that it is not heated in the reduction process or washed with chemical solvents. In two recent studies comparing MCHC with calcium gluconate and a placebo in the treatment of osteoporosis (age-related bone loss), only the MCHC groups experienced a significant increase in cortical bone.[6]

What About Colloidal Minerals?

"Colloidal minerals" are currently popular products touted as containing a broad range of minerals in a highly absorbable form. The marketing accompanying them is clever and informative, and it has done much to interest and instruct the public in alternative medicine; but researcher Dr. Alexander Schauss maintains that the products themselves leave something to be desired as mineral sources. He observes that colloidal minerals are basically clays dispersed in water. Something colloidal (suspended in water) is insoluble by definition, and insoluble minerals are generally less absorbable than soluble minerals. An analysis of five of these products showed they averaged only fifteen elements each, not the seventy or more claimed; and the mineral balance was poor. Four of the five contained aluminum (a toxic element linked to Alzheimer's disease) as their first or second element by weight. Other toxic trace elements included arsenic, barium, cadmium, mercury and lead. Assuming the absorption rate is actually 95 percent as claimed, Dr. Schauss asks why you would want to absorb 95 percent of these toxic elements.[7] Moreover, colloidal mineral products contain only small amounts of calcium and magnesium, the body's main mineral requirements. Trace minerals should be taken only in trace amounts. If they overpower the macro-minerals (calcium and magnesium), they can throw mineral balance into chaos.

Ionic Minerals

A better way to get your macro- and trace minerals is in ionized form, the form in which plants and mammals are designed to absorb inorganic minerals. To be absorbed, calcium must be reduced to the ionized state (charged particles of elemental calcium). If you take your calcium in this form, it can be immediately absorbed without intermediate processing. Converting calcium requires stomach acid — something in which many people, and particularly the elderly, tend to be deficient.

A more balanced mineral source than the rocks from which colloidal minerals are derived is the "coral water" drunk by certain Japanese islanders reported to have unusual longevity. Their drinking water has a high content of ionized minerals leached from the coral on which the island was built. The result is a highly alkalinized water that keeps the body alkaline and resistant to disease. Researchers have found that this "coral" water can actually neutralize waste products contained in it, including bacteria, heavy metals, fluoride and chloroform.

A balanced ionized mineral product made from this water is available from Pacific Research Laboratories. The recommended daily dose is 1/4 teaspoon of "Coral Legend" mixed with 1/4 cup of "Aloe Balance," an organic aloe vera juice fortified with negative ions that improves the bioavailability of ionized minerals taken with it. (See "Resources.")

Balancing Calcium with Magnesium

Dr. Hawkins observed that preserving the teeth requires not only calcium but certain factors necessary to its utilization, including magnesium and vitamin D. Vitamin D is necessary for the absorption of calcium and phosphorus, and magnesium helps move calcium out of the bloodstream and into the skeleton. When magnesium is out of balance with calcium, the calcium you eat may never make it to your bones.

Guy E. Abraham, M.D., a research gynecologist in Torrance, California, succeeded in increasing bone density in postmenopausal women by 11 percent in one year, by decreasing their calcium intakes to 500 mg per day, and increasing their magnesium intakes to 600-1000 mg per day. These results were significantly better than in studies involving calcium alone. The dose of magnesium was based on bowel tolerance: diarrhea was the limiting factor.

Magnesium is abundant in whole grains, beans, nuts, seeds, and vegetables. But fertilizers reduce its content in the soil, and sugar and alcohol increase its excretion through the urine. Although the RDA for magnesium is only 350 mg for women of all ages, Dr. Mildred Seelig, Executive President of the American College of Nutrition, suggests that older people eating a good diet can benefit from magnesium supplements of 700-800 mg per day.[8]

Vitamin D

For vitamin D, neither supplements nor food turns out to be the ideal source. Vitamin D is produced in the body only after sunlight striking the skin initiates a series of reactions there.[9] The sun is the most readily available source of vitamin D, which is essential for strong bones. Ultraviolet (UV) light from the sun aids calcium absorption into the skeleton. When calcium is ingested but isn't absorbed into the bones, extraskeletal calcium can wind up getting deposited in the tissues and along the walls of the arteries, contributing to arteriosclerosis (hardening of the arteries). Phototherapy pioneer John Ott showed that laboratory animals raised under artificial lighting developed excessive calcium deposits in their hearts, lost their hair, and developed large, fast-growing tumors.[10]

A study of elderly veterans showed that indoor UV lighting significantly increased their ability to absorb calcium from the diet. One group's living quarters contained full-spectrum lighting, which contains UV. The other group's quarters had ordinary indoor lighting, containing no UV. All of the men received approximately 200 IU per day of dietary vitamin D, but the group exposed to UV absorbed 40 percent more calcium from their diets than the group not exposed to it.[11]

Studies also show that blood levels of vitamin D are only weakly correlated with dietary intake. A much stronger correlation has been shown with exposure to sunlight. The evidence for this association is particularly compelling because it comes from England, where the sun rarely shines. British studies show that the sun is the principal source of vitamin D even when it isn't shining. A summer holiday at the beach, even for the British, affords better protection against vitamin D deficiency in the winter than vitamin D supplements. Residents of an old people's home who could spend some time in the garden were found to have normal vitamin D levels, while those confined indoors did not.[12]

The vitamin D produced commercially, called vitamin D2 (ergocalciferol), isn't the same as the vitamin D manufactured by the body (vitamin D3). Vitamin D3 isn't a true vitamin; it's a hormone (cholecalciferol) produced in response to ultraviolet radiation. Taking vitamin D2 orally, it seems, is not only largely ineffective and unnatural but can be dangerous in high doses.[13] Cod liver oil remains the best food source of the vitamin for people who can't get out in the sun.

If you're worried about skin cancer, it's good to know that only modest exposure to the sun is necessary to avoid vitamin D deficiency. Researchers at Tufts University have shown that in the summer, minimum vitamin D requirements are met by exposure of just the hands, face, and arms for ten to fifteen minutes a day, three times a week.[14] These recommendations were made specifically for the elderly, one of the two groups most likely to need vitamin D supplementation.

The other likely group is young children. Supplements may be necessary for children if they are under six years old and live in northern industrial areas that are often cloudy. Rickets, caused by vitamin D deficiency, was a common problem at the turn of the century in these areas, partly because air pollution from burning coal filtered out the already scarce ultraviolet rays. The problem was virtually eliminated in the 1930s by fortifying milk with vitamin D and giving children supplements of cod liver oil. In some studies, exposure to sunlight alone has proven to be an effective treatment for rickets.[15]

Sunlight: Threat or Therapy?

Some dermatologists, concerned about skin cancer, have gone so far as to recommend lathering up with sunscreen every morning, no matter what the weather, just to make sure the skin is protected from any sunshine that might chance to befall it. But other experts maintain we have gone too far. Dr. Samuel Berne asserts that studies linking sunlight and ultraviolet light to skin cancer were flawed. Massive doses of UV exposure were used on animals to create skin cancer and cataracts. The data were then extrapolated to apply to the more normal exposures of humans to sunlight.[16]

A 1982 British and Australian study found that the incidence of malignant melanomas (serious skin cancers) was significantly higher in office workers than in people whose lifestyles or occupations regularly exposed them to sunlight. Office workers who worked all day under fluorescent lighting had twice the risk of melanomas of other people. Surprisingly, the lowest risk of developing skin cancer was actually in people whose main outdoor activity was sunbathing. These results were confirmed in two controlled studies conducted at the New York School of Medicine.[17]

Zane Kime, M.D., in a groundbreaking book called Sunlight, demonstrates that the sun creates free radical damage only in the absence of protective antioxidants and the presence of harmful fats. The antioxidants he discussed were vitamins A, C and E and the mineral selenium, but there are many others. Harmful fats included hydrogenated oils, refined oils, and saturated fat; i.e., the fats in the standard American high-fat diet.[18]

Ultraviolet light from the sun helps not only in building strong bones but in killing infectious bacteria. Early in the twentieth century, sunbathing and UV therapy were considered the most effective treatments for many infectious diseases, including tuberculosis. Then in 1938, penicillin was discovered. Sun therapy was forgotten, as drugs became big business.[19] But antibiotics have now been so overused that they are losing their effectiveness and may soon be obsolete. Nature herself is forcing us to return to her own remedies, including prudent sun bathing.

Controversies About Salt and Fat

Besides those nutrients already mentioned, nutritional researcher Dr. Ray Peat adds the following factors as necessary for protecting the skeleton: hormones (thyroid, DHEA, progesterone, and pregnenolone), vitamins A and E, and various minerals including sodium.[20]

He points out that sodium (salt), though widely considered harmful, serves several necessary functions, including the "sparing" of magnesium. It aids in the cell's retention of albumin, "a first line of defense against toxins." It also acts under some conditions as an antioxidant, and it helps to regulate the water content of the blood. When the blood is unable to retain sufficient water because of insufficient sodium and albumin, the blood volume is reduced, the tissues become water-logged, and the blood's delivery of oxygen to the tissues is slowed.

Dr. Hawkins, too, stressed the importance for the teeth of getting sufficient salt. But like with milk, he was talking about salt in its raw, natural form. Modern processed salt has been heated to very high temperatures to make it pour easily. This heat treatment has turned it into a foreign substance the body has trouble assimilating. Heat-treated salt winds up getting deposited in the arteries, where it contributes to arteriosclerosis and high blood pressure.

Dr. Peat also diverges from mainstream thinking in recommending saturated oils like coconut oil. He postulates that the widespread use of coconut oil is one factor responsible for the low rates of osteoporosis in tropical countries. He agrees, however, that unsaturated oils should be avoided: they promote aging of the bones and other tissues, decrease respiration, and increase damage from stress.

Chapter 20

Teeth, Bones and Hormones

> Many people forget that teeth are bones too. Osteoporosis is strongly linked with the loss of teeth. Women tend to lose more teeth than men, especially after menopause, putting them at increased risk for an eroding jawbone.
>
> — Dr. JoAnne Allen, spokesperson for the Academy of General Dentistry[1]

Hormones are other factors vital for preserving the teeth and bones. Dr. Peat cites the case of a sixty-year-old woman who had osteoporosis in her jaw bone that was causing her teeth to loosen. A few months after she began applying a solution of natural progesterone to her gums each day, she reported that her teeth had again become firm.

The fact that elderly women are six times as likely to suffer from osteoporosis as elderly men is thought to be due to the loss of female hormones after menopause. Accompanying this bone loss is tooth loss.[2] These effects are generally attributed to loss of the ovarian hormone estrogen, but Dr. Peat and other researchers have questioned the theory. They note that bone loss typically starts about fifteen years <u>before</u> menopause, when estrogen levels are still high. And estrogen supplementation after menopause doesn't reverse bone loss. It merely slows the process down. New research suggests that progesterone, which is also produced by the ovaries, may actually be the missing catalyst. Progesterone acts as estrogen's antagonist and regulator in the body.[3] Progesterone raises blood albumin and makes blood circulation more efficient, reducing stress. Estrogen has the opposite effect.

Dr. Peat postulates that the reason bone loss is greater with age in women than in men is that the hormone prolactin, involved in milk production, increases in women with age. Prolactin is promoted by estrogen and inhibited by progesterone. He suggests that prolactin and estrogen actually pull calcium out of the bones.[4] The adage "for every child a tooth" reflects the common wisdom that a woman's body will sacrifice her own calcium for that of her unborn child.

Progesterone Can Rebuild Lost Bone

An eight-year study conducted by John R. Lee, M.D., reported in the <u>International Clinical Review</u> in 1990 and in <u>Medical Hypotheses</u> in 1991, showed that natural progesterone not only retards age-related bone loss but actually reverses it. Within a three-year period, bone density was brought back to safe levels in 100 percent of the patients treated, something not even estrogen would do.[5] The product used in this study, however, was not the synthetic progesterone found in popular hormone replacement therapy regimes. It was a natural progesterone derived from Mexican yams, applied in an absorbable skin cream form originally developed by Dr. Peat.

The women rubbed natural progesterone cream on the skin at bedtime for twelve days out of the month (or the last two weeks of estrogen use, if estrogen was being used). One-third to one-half of a one-ounce jar of progesterone cream was used per month, applied to the softer skin under the arms or of the neck and face, alternating sites each night. The women were also instructed to take the following measures known to counteract bone loss: they were to get sufficient exercise, vitamins, calcium and other minerals; eat a low-protein diet high in calcium-rich leafy green vegetables and low-fat cheeses; avoid cigarettes, excess phosphates (especially in soft drinks), excess protein, and certain drugs (excess thyroid hormone and corticosteroids); and limit alcohol intake. The following nutritional supplements were taken: vitamin D (350-400 IU), vitamin C (2,000 mg in divided doses), betacarotene (15 mg or 25,000 IU), and calcium (800-1000 mg by diet and/or supplements). In addition, a modest exercise routine was prescribed (twenty minutes per day, or thirty minutes three times a week).

As a result of this program, bone pains were relieved, muscle and bone strength and mobility increased, osteoporotic fractures dropped to zero, and regular fractures healed unusually well. No unwanted side effects were reported. Expected bone loss in the women over a three-year period was 4.5 percent. At best, estrogen would have slowed this loss down; but the natural progesterone regimen actually put bone back on. In the 63 tested patients, bone density over three years increased by an average of 15.4 percent. The women's bones typically got 10 percent thicker in the first 6 to 12 months and increased 3 to 5 percent per year thereafter. Several patients' bone densities jumped 20 to 25 percent during the first year. This increase occurred regardless of age. The patients who started out the worst actually improved the most. Bone density also increased regardless of whether estrogen supplements accompanied the progesterone. In many of the women, bone density eventually stabilized at the levels of healthy 35-year-olds; and in all of them, it stabilized at safe levels. The women also lost weight and had more energy, and many volunteered the observation that their lost libido (sex drive) had returned. Blood pressures dropped, and there were anti-cancer effects. Unlike in studies with synthetic progestins, cholesterol levels did not rise. So far, says Dr. Lee, natural progesterone has reversed bone loss in every woman on whom he has tried it (beginning in 1982), so long as the other essential factors were included: proper diet and exercise, supplemental micronutrients, etc.[6]

Natural progesterone has been overlooked by the media, probably because it's outside the major pharmaceutical loop and little known. Manufacturers of natural remedies lack the massive funding required for FDA approval; and until recently, they were prohibited by FDA regulations from making claims about their products. But drug companies are now taking an interest in natural progesterone, which may soon be in the pharmaceutical domain.

Hormone Precursors

Another natural hormone supplement that has recently taken the market by storm is DHEA. DHEA is actually a hormone precursor, which is converted in the body to other hormones. DHEA levels are high in youth and decline with age. Dr. Marshall reports that supplemental DHEA has tested out for many patients on whom he has checked it on the Computron.

Pregnenolone, a less well known precursor, also aids in restoring hormone levels.

The precursor at the top of the body's hormone pyramid, however, is cholesterol. All things in moderation . . . .

Hormones, Bone Loss, and Dental Materials

Not only do hormones affect the teeth and bones, but the teeth can affect hormone levels. The diagnostic testing of Hal Huggins, D.D.S., showed that hormone levels were depressed by mercury amalgam fillings.[7] Other research suggests that mercury may cause bone loss. It does this by interacting with the osteoblasts, the cells that build new bone.[8]

Recent studies have also linked bone loss to fluoride use. Fluoride has been linked to other degenerative conditions of old age as well, including wrinkled skin, arthritis, and cancer.[9] We'll look at the fluoride question more fully in the next chapter.

Chapter 21

Fluoride: Blessing or Bane?

[F]luoride causes more human cancer death, and causes it faster, than any other chemical.

—Dean Burk, Chief Chemist Emeritus,
U.S. National Cancer Institute[1]

Mention natural ways of avoiding tooth decay, and most people immediately think of fluoride. Most toothpaste manufacturers obviously think this additive is not only safe but prevents cavities, since it's hard to find a toothpaste anymore without fluoride in it. Most politicians must think so too, because 53 percent of Americans now have fluoridated water supplies. The ADA is such a staunch defender of this approach that an article in the ADA Journal branded as a "quack" any dentist who "says fluoridation is dangerous."[2] In fact, one of the only requirements needed to get 'ADA approval' of a toothpaste product, is the addition of fluoride. With it the manufacturer gets approval; without it they do not.

Like with mercury, however, the hazards of fluoride were a serious concern of conventional dentistry before the ADA mounted its campaign to promote fluoridation in the fifties. The October 1, 1944 issue of the Journal of the American Dental Association warned:

> We . . . know the use of drinking water containing as little as 1.2 to 3.0 parts per million of fluorine will cause such development disturbances in bones as

osteosclerosis, spondylosis and osteopetrosis, as well as goiter, and we cannot afford to run the risk of producing such serious systemic disturbances in applying what is at present a doubtful procedure intended to prevent development of dental disfigurements among children.[3]

Disquieting new research links fluoride to cancer, hip fractures, and kidney dialysis deaths.[4] Ironically, whether it actually does what it's touted for — preventing cavities in children — has also been disputed by recent research. Among other studies, one from the University of Arizona in 1992 involving 23,000 elementary school children in Tucson found that "the more fluoride a child drank, the more cavities appeared in the teeth!"[5] A study of 22,000 schoolchildren living in naturally fluoridated areas in Japan also found increasing cavity levels with increasing levels of fluoride. Similar results were reported in a study of 400,000 children in India, and in a study of 26,405 children in New Zealand.[6]

In 1997, the union of EPA scientists, engineers and attorneys who assess the scientific data for Safe Drinking Water Act standards and other EPA regulations went on record as opposing fluoridation of the public water supply. Endorsing the California State Drinking Water Initiative, the organization stated that "there is substantial evidence of adverse health effects and, contrary to public perception, virtually no evidence of significant benefits" from fluoridation. The scientists were concerned about causal links between fluoride and cancer, genetic damage, neurological impairment, and bone disease. They were particularly concerned about recent epidemiological studies linking fluoride exposure to lowered IQ in children.[7]

Fluoride Linked to Birth Defects and Bone Deformities

The 20th Conference of the International Society for Fluoride Research, co-sponsored by the World Health Organization and held in Beijing, China, in September of 1994, addressed the prevalence of fluorosis (fluoride poisoning) in China. Of 100 million people living in areas of "endemic" fluorosis, 43 million were reported to have toxicity symptoms of varying degrees of severity, including 2.4 million with skeletal fluorosis, a disease involving crippling bone deformities. Adverse effects were found not only in the teeth and bones but in the soft tissues. More disturbing, they were found at fluoride levels equivalent to those in artificially fluoridated areas of the United States. Symptoms included an increase in fracture rates and poor fracture healing, central nervous system disturbances, thyroid dysfunction, heart disease, lowered IQ, chromosomal abnormalities, decreased immunity, cataracts, increased rates of cancer, higher infant death rates due to congenital abnormalities, and higher death rates generally. Early signs of fluoride poisoning included gastrointestinal discomfort, back stiffness and joint pain.[8]

Why haven't these dire effects shown up in the United States? Experts suggest it's because Americans get adequate dietary calcium, magnesium and vitamin C. Deficiencies of these nutrients are known to increase the severity of fluorosis.[9]

Despite this nutritional protection, studies in the United States, England and New Zealand have linked a higher incidence of hip fractures to fluoridation. Five studies reported in the last decade all showed that fluoridation, far from increasing the strength of the bones, actually increased the incidence of hip fractures. In the most recent of these studies, the fracture rate among women aged 55-80 in an Iowa town with fluoridated water was about 30 percent higher than for comparable women in a town with unfluoridated water; while the fracture rate for men was 40 percent higher.[10] These findings may help explain why the U.S. hip fracture rate is now the highest in the world.[11]

The findings were particularly surprising, since fluoride has been prescribed to <u>treat</u> osteoporosis. Osteoporosis researcher John R. Lee, M.D., explains the puzzling discrepancies in its effects like this:

> The fact is that fluoride may slightly increase the X-ray appearance of bone mass but the resultant bone is of inferior quality and actually increases the rate of hip fracture. . . . Fluoride is a potent enzyme inhibitor

and, in bone, causes pathologic changes leading to increased risk of fracture.

Dr. Lee concludes, "Fluoride, in all forms including tooth pastes, should be avoided."[12]

Fluoride and Brain Impairment

Following up on the link between fluoride and birth defects found in China, Harvard Medical School researchers conducted a study on rats, reported in 1995. The behavior of rats given fluoridated water was recorded by video and analyzed with a computer program. Very young female rats who drank fluoridated water developed unusually high concentrations of fluoride in the hippocampus, the part of the brain generally linked with hyperactivity and cognitive defects. The researchers concluded that fluoride could cause motor dysfunction, lowered IQ and learning disabilities not only in rats but in humans. They observed that theirs was "the first laboratory study to demonstrate that CNS [central nervous system] functional output is vulnerable to fluoride, that the effects on behavior depend on the age at exposure and that fluoride accumulates in brain tissues."[13]

Justifying Fluoridation

Half the water supplies in the United States are now fluoridated, although only 0.06 percent of this fluoride winds up in the target population: children under 12. That means that for every $1,000 spent on fluoridation, less than fifty cents worth of fluoride goes where it is intended. Most of the rest of this toxic chemical is discharged into the environment, where it constitutes a significant source of pollution that is harmful to plants, fish, and land animals. Fluoride is more toxic than lead and only slightly less toxic than arsenic.[14]   How is this massive multi-billion dollar government program justified? A recent article in the Los Angeles Times, calling fluoridation "a shining public health success," pointed to the huge drop in dental caries since the program was instituted in the fifties. The article observed:

From 1971 through the mid-1980s, three national surveys of children's oral health showed a continued decline in cavities attributed to the use of fluoride, according to the dental institute, which is part of the National Institutes of Health.

The most recent survey, taken in 1986-87, found that American children had 36% fewer cavities than they did at the beginning of the 1980s, a decline similar to one shown during the 1970s.

Today, half of the children entering first grade have never had a cavity thanks to fluoridation, according to the American Dental Assn.[15]

Other researchers, however, maintain that this data needs to be reinterpreted. They observe that comprehensive studies show that cavities have dropped drastically not only in fluoridated but in unfluoridated areas, and that there is no correlation between dental caries and the ingestion or use of fluoride.[16] Stanley Heifetz, writing in the Journal of the American Dental Association in April of 1988, confirmed:

> ...the current reported decline in caries in the U.S. and other Western industrialized countries has been observed in both fluoridated and nonfluoridated communities, with percentage reductions in each community apparently about the same.

The 1986-87 oral health survey, involving 39,207 U.S. schoolchildren, found a continuing decline in caries prevalence in both fluoridated and unfluoridated areas, leading the researchers to conclude that "caries is no longer a public health problem."[17] The only significant difference found between study populations was for five-year-olds; and by age six, that advantage had disappeared.

A suggested explanation for the discrepancy was that tooth eruption is delayed in fluoridated five-year-olds. Yet a later report used only the data for five-year-olds in this survey to "prove" a significant advantage for fluoridation. Other studies have also looked only at five-year-olds without following up in older children, skewing the results. Other study flaws noted by analysts include comparing two areas of different socioeconomic status. When a poor unfluoridated area is compared to a rich fluoridated area, differences in tooth decay may be due not to fluoridation but to differences in diet, hygiene, and dental care.[18]

Statistical Analysis

It seems that research, like Scripture, can be quoted for one's own purposes. For every study finding that fluoride reduces dental caries, another can be found reporting the reverse. In an effort to resolve these discrepancies, Dr. Rudolph Ziegelbecker, Director of the Institute for Environmental Research in Graz, Austria, took all of the published studies available in 1981 that investigated the relationship between fluoridation and dental caries and fed them into a computer. He found that statistically, there was no relationship between these two variables.[19] When he followed up with a more comprehensive study in 1993, he found that at that time in most countries there was indeed a relationship, but it was a direct rather than an inverse one: dental caries increased with systemic fluoridation.[20]

The Historical Context

Chroniclers of the story of fluoridation in America contend it's another instance of science being colored by politics. They observe that the studies on which fluoridation was based in the fifties contained statistical errors and inadequacies and failed to meet acceptable experimental criteria. Dr. F. B. Exner, author of a 1955 report for the City of New York titled "Fluoridation of Public Water Supplies," described earlier reports as unscientific and inaccurate. He raised the spectre of fraud. Dr. Philip Sutton of the Dental School of the University of Melbourne, in a 1960 monograph titled "Fluoridation, Errors and Omissions in Experimental Trials," also concluded that the studies leading to adoption of fluoridation in the U.S. were "confounded by uncertainty." But Dr. Sutton's report was suppressed in the U.S., the printer's type of edition was destroyed without authority, and it was omitted from the Index to Dental Literature published by the ADA.[21]

Further investigation reveals that fluoride is a toxic waste product of aluminum manufacture, and that one of the giants of the chemical/industrial complex — the Aluminum Co. of America (ALCOA) — was instrumental in convincing the American Dental Association to campaign for mass fluoridation in the 1950s. Before studies had been completed to determine whether fluoride was a safe and effective means of reducing tooth decay, the ADA initiated a political crusade to promote its addition to the water supply.

Journalist Joel Griffiths observes:

> Industry and government have long had a powerful motive for claiming an increased dose of fluoride is safe for the population. Maintaining this position has not been easy because, of industry's largest pollutants, fluoride is by far the most toxic to vegetation, animals, and humans. . . [M]ost of the fluoride added to drinking water has been recycled waste . . . . The same concentrations added to human drinking water for cavity prevention can be fatal to freshwater fish.[22]

The Politics of Fluoridation

During the Second World War, fluoride evidently became a "protected pollutant" when the aluminum industry (which then consisted solely of ALCOA) took on a crucial economic and military role. Fluoride safety research was funded by the top fluoride emitters. A book written by an industry-funded researcher which became a basic international reference work. Included among its purposes to "aid industry in lawsuits arising from fluoride damage."[23]

In 1947, ALCOA lawyer Oscar Ewing was appointed head of the Federal Security Agency (later HEW), a position that placed him in charge of the Public Health Service. In 1952, Dr. A. L. Miller, a United States representative from

Nebraska and Chairman of the Special Committee on Chemicals in Foods, complained:

> I sometimes wonder if the Aluminum Co. of America, and its many subsidiary companies might not have a deep interest in getting rid of the waste products from the manufacture of aluminum, because these products contain a large amount of fluoride. In this connection it is interesting to know that Oscar Ewing, who now heads the Federal Security Administration. . . represents the Aluminum Co. of America.[24]

Ewings' public relations strategist for the water fluoridation campaign was Sigmund Freud's nephew Edward L. Bernays, the "father of public relations." Bernays applied his uncle's theories to advertising and government propaganda. In his book Propaganda, he explained "the structure of the mechanism which controls the public mind, and how it is manipulated by the special pleader who seeks to create public acceptance for a particular idea or commodity." Bernays wrote, "Those who manipulate this unseen mechanism of society constitute an invisible government which is the true ruling power of our country."[25]

The government's fluoridation campaign was considered one of Bernays' most stunning and enduring successes. Bernays created a demand for fluoridation so wild that a two-city Michigan experiment designed to scientifically test its safety and effectiveness was prematurely terminated, on the ground that it was unfair to deny the unfluoridated control population the chemical's benefits.[26]

The Overlooked Matter of Cancer

That was how the matter stood until 1975. Then Dr. Dean Burk, chief chemist emeritus of the U.S. National Cancer Institute, along with biochemical editor Dr. John Yiamouyiannis, began a series of studies comparing cancer death rates in fluoridated and unfluoridated populations. Deaths in the ten largest fluoridated cities were compared with those in the ten largest unfluoridated cities that had comparable death rates in 1940-50, a decade when neither group was fluoridated. The result: in a mere 13-17 years, fluoridated cities showed an approximate 10 percent increase in cancer deaths over those in unfluoridated cities. The researchers concluded from this and other evidence that fluoridation may account for more than 30,000 deaths a year in the United States, of which more than 10,000 are due to cancer. To make matters worse, the researchers demonstrated that adding fluoride to the water supply had no significant impact on dental caries.[27]

The response of the U.S. National Cancer Institute (NCI) was to peremptorily dismiss the cancer increases as due to other alleged differences in the compared populations. The fluoridation of water continued unabated. Citizens seeking pure water for their cities then protested in two lawsuits, one in Pennsylvania and the other in Illinois. Persuaded by the evidence of Drs. Burk and Yiamouyiannis, both courts rejected the contentions of the NCI and ruled that fluoridation is, indeed, a serious threat to the public health.[28] Said Pennsylvania Supreme Court Justice John P. Flaherty:

> The evidence is quite convincing that the addition of sodium fluoride to the public water supply . . . is extremely deleterious to the human body. A review of the evidence will reveal that there was no convincing evidence to the contrary. . . [T]he proponents of fluoridation do nothing more than try to impugn the objectivity of those who oppose fluoridation. I seriously believe that few responsible people have objectively reviewed the evidence.[29]

This sentiment echoed an earlier one of Dr. A. L. Miller, Chairman of the House Special Committee on Chemicals in Foods, who stated for the record in 1952:

> Mr. Speaker, despite my best efforts, and from the evidence before my committee, I cannot find any public evidence that gave me the impression that the

American Medical Association, the American Dental Association, or several other health agencies, now recommending the fluoridation of water, had done any original work of their own. These groups were simply endorsing each other's opinions.[30]

The findings of Drs. Burk and Yiamouyiannis triggered congressional hearings in 1977. Disturbingly, testimony revealed that the government had approved the mass fluoridation of water without ever having tested the chemical's cancer-causing potential. The National Toxicology Program (NTP) was promptly ordered to make this determination, but more than a decade passed before any data were released.

While the U.S. government was dragging its feet, European governments were taking steps to eliminate fluoride from their water supplies. "If it's entirely safe," asked the San Francisco Examiner in 1983, "why has fluoridation been banned or abandoned in such enlightened European countries as Norway, Sweden, Austria, Belgium, Holland, Denmark, France, Italy, and West Germany?" Noted one European researcher, H. C. Moolenburgh, M.D., of the Netherlands:

> Fluoridation causes a low grade poisoning which stays beneath the surface in most people, but in some, and especially in those whose health is deteriorating, produces clinical symptoms.[31]

Another 1990 Watershed: Refueling the Debate on Fluoride

In February of 1990, the NTP finally released its data. They showed that rats given fluoridated water have a significantly increased incidence of a form of bone cancer called osteosarcoma. The finding, observed a February 1990 Newsweek article, rekindled a debate long thought settled.[32]

In February of 1991, the U.S. Public Health Service (PHS) reported corroborating findings in humans. The PHS observed that nationwide evidence "of a rising rate of bone and joint cancer at all ages combined, due mainly to trends under the age of 20, was seen in the 'fluoridated' counties but not in the 'non-fluoridated' counties. . . . The larger increase in males under the age of 20 seen in the aggregate data for all bone and joint cancers is seen only in the 'fluoridated' counties. . . . For osteosarcomas [bone cancers] in males under 20, the rate increased 70 percent in the fluoridated areas and decreased four percent in the non-fluoridated areas."[33]

An official commission appointed to study the findings of the PHS concluded merely that "further studies are required." But many observers contended that science had been obscured by politics. According to EPA environmental scientist Robert Carton, "The level of fluoride the government allows the public is based on scientifically fraudulent information and altered reports."[34]

Joel Griffiths graphically illustrates the bone disease caused by fluoride with a description of cattle stricken with it:

> Cows crawled around the pasture on their bellies, inching along like giant snails. So crippled by bone disease they could not stand up, this was the only way they could graze. Some died kneeling, after giving birth to stunted calves. Others kept on crawling until, no longer able to chew because their teeth had crumbled down to the nerves, they began to starve . . . .[35]

The Mohawk Indians filed a $150 million lawsuit against the nearby Reynolds Metals Co. and ALCOA for fluoride damage to themselves and their property. Bankrupted by legal costs, they settled for $650,000 in damages to their cows; but the costlier damage was probably to themselves. The USDA Handbook states, "Man is much more sensitive than domestic animals to fluoride intoxication."[36] The symptoms were more evident in the cows only because they were grazing directly on polluted ground.

Fluoride and Tooth Decay

The final irony is that research now suggests that dental problems may actually be made <u>worse</u> by the fluoride intended to prevent it. When former fluoride advocate John Colquhoun of New Zealand gathered statistics to prove fluoride's benefits, he found, much to his chagrin, that the percentage of children free of tooth decay was higher in the unfluoridated than the fluoridated parts of most health districts in New Zealand.[37] His findings were corroborated by researchers in Tucson, which contains areas with groundwater having a naturally high fluoride content. When the Tucson researchers plotted the incidence of tooth decay against the fluoride content in neighborhood drinking water, they found that the more fluoride a child drank, the <u>more</u> cavities he was likely to have.[38]

Again, the findings weren't new. In 1954, researchers at the University of the State of New York found that in Newburgh, New York — one of the first cities to be fluoridated — 3 out of 5 children suffered from some oral problem, as compared to 2 out of 5 in a comparable neighboring non-fluoridated city. The dental arches of the fluoridated children also tended to be deformed. Dr. Samuel Charles Miller, Professor of Oral Medicine at New York University, reported that after fluoridation, a radical increase was observed in malocclusion — the improper meshing of the teeth of the two jaws when the mouth is closed.[39] Malocclusion can cause pain in the head, ears and face. It has generally been assumed to be genetic; but the theory fails to explain the dramatic increase in malocclusion seen in a single generation when primitive societies have adopted "civilized" lifestyles — or when cities have become fluoridated.[40]

"If this is all true," asks David Kennedy, D.D.S., "why are some pushing fluoridation more than ever?" His answer:

Apparently officials of the U.S. Public Health Service, the American Dental Association, and Procter & Gamble, as well as others, are more concerned with their reputations than they are about the health and welfare of the very people they claim to serve . . . Fluoride is . . . a major world pollutant . . . . The marketing campaign is powerful and political, and filled with scientific fraud and public deception.[41]

The Middle Ground

Dr. Hansen takes a middle road on the question of fluoridation. The decision, he maintains, should be left to the individual.

"The controversy is due to the fact that fluoride is a cancer-causing element that can harm the body. The dental community says it's within safe limits, and that it will combine with the tooth structure to harden the tooth; and it can actually have this effect. But it's only good for developing teeth and only within the enamel. The biggest problem with wholesale fluoridation is that the only people who benefit from it are three- to twelve-year-olds. After that your teeth are formed, and taking fluoride internally won't do you any good at all. Contact of fluoride with the tooth surface may not help significantly either. Fluoride has to be taken up into the enamel of the teeth to do any good. Brushing, drinking, or rinsing the teeth with fluoride has minimal effect. There are other explanations besides fluoridation for the decrease in cavities since the fifties. Television since then has bombarded us with the importance of brushing and otherwise taking care of our teeth. Brushing wasn't done routinely before that. We now have two sets of populations: those who eat decently and those who don't. Cavities will occur in the latter with or without fluoride. Ingesting fluoride should be a matter of parental choice: if they want fluoride for their children, they can add a drop or two to their water, or buy bottles of fluoridated water, or give drops or tablets. It should not be forced on an entire population, most of whom will see no positive effect. The alternative is for everyone else to buy bottled water. We shouldn't be drinking city water anyway, since all city water contains unhealthy contaminants."

Many times dentists will prescribe a brush on fluoride to help control sensitivity of teeth, usually to cold. This compound contains ions that can plug and block the hydraulic fluid movement in the dentinal tubules, thereby effectively stopping the temperature sensations. If any of these are used they should not be brushed on as the manufacturer recommends. This is good for the manufacturer since it wastes a lot of material, yet it will lead to an excess being present in the mouth that may be swallowed and ingested. They should only be used with precise placement, such as with a cotton applicator, only on the affected areas, and rinsed out after use.

Chapter 22

Preventing and Treating Periodontal Disease

> Many primitive peoples not only retain all of their teeth, many of them to an old age, but also have a healthy flesh supporting these teeth. This has occurred in spite of the fact that the primitives have not had dentists to remove the deposits and no means for doing so for themselves.
>
> — Weston Price, D.D.S.[1]

Most authorities agree that the teeth and gums need to be kept clean by brushing, flossing, and using mouthwashes . . . most authorities, but not all. Dr. J. E. Phillips, a dentist in Osseo, Wisconsin, warns that even these bastions of good dental sense may be hazardous. We'll look at his reasoning and his proposed alternatives in this chapter, after a preliminary discussion of the tooth and gum diseases oral hygiene has helped avoid.

Tooth Decay and Periodontal Disease

Thanks to the zeal of toothpaste advertisers, most people are aware of the relationship between tooth decay and "plaque," the white mouth debris found along the necks of the teeth and in the crevice between the teeth and gums. Tooth decay is considered to originate when food forms a sticky substance on the tooth which harbors bacteria. Carbohydrates and sugars then encourage the bacteria to multiply. The bacteria release acids and enzymes which, if not removed, can digest and dissolve the calcium and protein layers of the enamel. Normally, these acids are diluted and washed away by the saliva, preventing them from becoming strong enough to dissolve the enamel. But damage results in the presence of plaque, which protects the acids so they can't be washed away and do become strong enough to dissolve the teeth.

Not only the teeth but the gums around them can become diseased if not properly cleaned. Periodontal (gum) disease results when the "periodontium" (the gum tissue and bone supporting the teeth) becomes inflamed, attracts bacteria, and becomes infected. (Other names for periodontal disease or closely related conditions are pyorrhea, gingivitis, trench mouth, and periodontitis.) Eventually, the gum fibers and the underlying bone that hold the teeth in place may disintegrate. The teeth can then actually fall out.

Periodontics and Gum Surgery

Preventing that dire result is the business of periodontics. The bread and butter of periodontists is scraping tartar or calculus (hard stone-like deposits) from the teeth and their roots and curetting the gum tissue. Surgery is done in advanced cases to eliminate pockets of infection and irritants. "Gingivectomy" involves actually cutting away gum tissue. "Open-flap" surgery is done to eliminate deep infection. Where the bone has been eaten away, bone grafting or regenerative procedures are performed.

These procedures are lengthy, uncomfortable, and require a high degree of technical skill. Scraping the gums can take from four to eight hours. Common complications of periodontal surgery include sensitivity of the teeth to heat, cold and sweets caused by the additional exposure of the roots; and an unaesthetic appearance of the teeth, which tend to retain food around them after meals. But what is the alternative?

Dr. Phillips' simple home solution turns some conventional assumptions upside down.

Questioning Anti-bacterial Mouthwashes

One premise he challenges is that periodontal disease is best attacked by attacking the bacteria in the mouth. Most of these bacteria, he observes, are beneficial ones. The watchdogs of the oral cavity, they keep molds and fungi from growing there. When these organisms are destroyed, worse problems result. Like the indiscriminate use of antibiotics, which wipe out friendly as well as unfriendly bacteria, anti-bacterial mouthwashes destroy the friendly bacteria in the mouth that hold down the fort against unwanted invaders. Dr. Phillips blames an increase in gum disease partly on the indiscriminate use of these products.

Hazards of Flossing and Brushing

He also cautions against the indiscriminate use of dental floss, toothpicks, rubber tips, and even toothbrushes. While beneficial if used correctly, these tools, he says, can be hazardous if not used very carefully. The gum tissues can be damaged by snapping floss between the teeth so that the gums bleed, or by the forceful use of a rubber tip or toothpick to clean the base of the teeth; and toothbrushes and irrigating devices can drive bacteria deeper into the gum crevice. The result is to transform the early stage of gum disease (recognizable by bleeding) into the slow, chronic, secondary stage having no obvious symptoms. Simple toothbrushing will do an adequate job of cleaning the teeth, says Dr. Phillips, so long as the teeth and gums are healthy. But once the gums have swollen and the crevice has deepened — when the gums start to bleed when brushed or show other signs of breaking down — more thorough cleaning is required and additional periodontal therapy may become necessary.

Blotting

For this more thorough cleaning, he recommends a simple procedure called "blotting." It is done with an especially absorbent pocket-sized soft-bristled brush, used dry to blot up the plaque in the gingival crevice the way a painter blots up excess paint on his canvas. The brush is moved vertically from the gums toward the teeth. The goal is not only to remove plaque but to stimulate blood flow to the gums. Healthy teeth are maintained by healthy gums, which require a sufficient blood supply. Many people make the error of brushing horizontally with a hard-bristled brush that is abrasive to the teeth and gums, if the gums are reached at all.

"[If] the teeth, gingival crevices, gums, inside cheek surfaces, hard and soft palate (roof of the mouth), tongue, and throat . . . are cleaned adequately [by blotting] twice a day," Dr. Phillips asserts, "mouth diseases such as gingivitis (gum disease), periodontitis (pyorrhea), tooth decay, and halitosis (bad breath) disappear practically in every instance."[2]

As evidence, he has published over 100 photographs of teeth that in the "before" pictures manifest all of these diseases; but in the "after" pictures, they are remarkably pink and healthy. They include the teeth of a smile-conscious teenaged girl who brushed five or six times a day. Her gums had formed "Stillman's Clefts" where they had been worn away by excessive brushing. The "after" pictures demonstrated that the girl's Stillman's Clefts had been reversed and her gums restored simply by blotting. This result, says Dr. Phillips, is conventionally considered impossible.

He adds that toothbrushing is still good for polishing the teeth. But it should be done carefully — with a soft-bristled brush, so as not to injure the gums, and with a minimum of dentifrice. Brushing should be followed by blotting, which also minimizes the need for flossing. "Ordinary tooth-brushing plus dental floss cleans 10% of the mouth," he maintains, "while blotting of the teeth and crevices with total mouth hygiene cleans 98% of the mouth without floss."

However, his techniques will not remove calculus or other mineral deposits from around teeth. These deposits trap and protect more harmful strains of bacteria around the teeth and gums that are responsible for very destructive, aggressive bone disease. These techniques likewise cannot repair, augment, or regenerate damaged gums and bone.

Mouthwash Alternatives

Blotting is also Dr. Phillips' answer to antibacterial mouthwashes. Rather than killing bacteria with chemicals, he says, this simple mechanical procedure removes the plaque on which harmful bacteria feed. Bacteria multiply only when they have something on which to feed and a protected environment in which to grow. Cleaning up the oral environment eliminates harmful bacteria while allowing for the growth of beneficial ones. He cites research showing that the cleaner the mouth, the greater the number of beneficial bacteria that are found there.

The best natural mouthwash is found within the mouth itself: the saliva. Swishing the saliva around in the mouth allows the salivary enzymes to kill harmful bacteria while leaving beneficial organisms unharmed. Blotting also helps, says Dr. Phillips, by increasing the amount of saliva available for mouthwashing. If you want to gargle for a sore throat without causing good bacteria to perish along with the bad, you can use an old-fashioned hot water and salt or baking soda rinse. Hot water increases the flow to the infected area of blood, the best healer known. Salt and baking soda also have stimulating properties. But if you have high blood pressure or are otherwise disinclined to use them, hot water alone can be quite beneficial.

For bad breath, there are also natural home alternatives. One is to mix a tablespoon of allspice with a cup of hot water and use the mixture as a mouthwash and gargle. A tincture of the common garden plant Calendula also has antiseptic properties that make it an effective gargle for mouth ulcers and sore throats.

Reversing Periodontal Disease

Periodontal disease is usually blamed on calculus deposits, but Dr. Phillips maintains that these deposits are the result rather than the cause of the disease. As proof, he offers photo evidence of patients who were cured of periodontal disease by blotting, although calculus remained on their teeth. His policy, in fact, is to refrain from cleaning calculus from the teeth until his patients have restored their mouths to health by blotting — just to convince them it was their own efforts, not the dentist's, which brought about that beneficial result. In his practice, he says, gingivectomy (cutting away of infected gum tissue) has almost never been necessary when the blotting procedure was followed. Other forms of surgery might be necessary in extreme cases; but even then, his approach is to refrain from performing the procedure until the mouth has been cleaned and restored to health through blotting. After that, the more drastic procedures need be done only once. Mouth health so acquired can then be maintained for a lifetime, by blotting to preserve a clean oral cavity and good circulation to the gums.

Other Approaches to Periodontal Disease: The Gums and Mineral Balance

Weston Price, D.D.S., had another explanation for gum disease. He maintained that pyorrhea and gingivitis are the result of a borrowing of minerals from the teeth and bones in order to boost deficient mineral levels in the blood. The teeth then loosen and the surrounding tissue becomes susceptible to infection. Observing that many primitive peoples managed to retain healthy teeth and gums through old age without the benefit of dentists or toothbrushes to remove calculus and tartar from their teeth, he postulated that the key was in their diets. Deficient nutrition in "civilized" peoples causes low mineral levels in the blood and body fluids. The body compensates for these low levels by borrowing minerals from the bones and teeth. The result is not only fractured hips and bones but tooth loss. Pyorrhea and gingivitis, said Dr. Price, are actually nutritional problems that can be corrected by correcting the diet.[3]

Periodontal Disease and Amalgam

New research suggests another insidious cause of periodontal disease: the mercury amalgam used to repair dental caries. Periodontitis (which progresses to the destruction of connective tissue and bone) begins as gingivitis (gum disease); and gingivitis is one of the classic clinical signs of chronic mercury exposure. Ironically, the evidence suggests that gingivitis and periodontitis are simply additional autoimmune diseases that are induced, at least in part, by mercury.[4]

Beyond Toothbrushing: Oral Hygiene from the Inside out

While toothbrushing cleans the teeth from the outside, the ultimate in oral hygiene would be a procedure for clearing decay from the inside out. There is evidence that the body itself can bring about this result, if left for a period of time without the burden of digesting and assimilating food.

Like sun therapy, fasting was a once-popular natural therapy that was largely forgotten with the advent of more lucrative "quick fix" remedies aimed at the effects rather than the cause of disease. Fasting was recommended at the turn of the twentieth century for just about anything that ailed you, including tooth decay. R. B. Pearson, writing in the twenties, reported that after a fast of forty days, not only was the foul taste in his mouth replaced by a very sweet and pleasant taste, but "teeth with black cavities became white and clear, all decay seemed to be arrested by the fast, and there were no more toothaches." Although Pearson admitted to a fondness for candy bars and milkshakes, after this "complete" fast (abstention from food until the tongue was clear and hunger forcefully returned), he found that "an enema and a little fasting would entirely cure the toothache." He also found that after fasting, it was impossible to catch cold — at least, until he had fallen into so many dietary indiscretions that his system was again clogged with mucus. Not only germs but mosquitos seemed to have lost their hold. Mosquito bites produced no swelling, itch, or inflammation.[5]

Dr. Paavo Airola, another fasting expert, explained that after the first three days of a fast, your body lives on itself, burning and digesting its own tissues; but it eliminates the dispensable ones first. That means that diseased, aging or dead cells, morbid accumulations, tumors, abscesses, damaged tissues, and fat deposits are the first to go. During this time, the individual loses his craving for food. But when the non-essential tissues have been exhausted and the body is reduced to eating its own essential tissue, hunger suddenly returns with a vengeance. This is the physiologically correct time to end the fast.[6]

Pearson fasted on water only, but Dr. Airola, writing later in the century, recommended fasting on vegetable and fruit juices — and that not for more than 7 to 10 days, unless under medical supervision. It seems that our environment has become so polluted and our bodies so laden with drugs, pesticides and industrial wastes that water fasts can now be quite dangerous. Cleansing can proceed so rapidly that the released toxins overwhelm the body. Both authors also felt that daily enemas were essential to speed the elimination of toxins.

The V. E. Irons fast promoted by Dr. Bernard Jensen adds supplements (chlorophyll, beet, etc.), psyllium (plant fiber), and bentonite (a natural colloidal absorbing solution). The prescribed regimen is a seven-day fast once every seven weeks for seven weeks, a relatively painless endeavor that promises a return to youthful health and radiance. Before undertaking a fast, it's best to read Dr. Jensen's book <u>Tissue Cleansing Through Bowel Management</u> or another detailed reference for guidance.[7]

Dr. M. O. Garten wrote that each time he fasted, "I always felt like shouting to the entire world about this true panacea of recreating or maintaining the genuine pleasures of living."[8]

Chapter 23

Twenty-first Century Dental Health

> [O]ur job, as health-conscious individuals, is to make sure
> our bodies are able to function under the conditions best
> suited to allow them to cure themselves.
> — Dr. M. Ted Morter, Jr.[1]

At one time, the teeth were thought to be solid,
independent bony structures that could be rebuilt with metals
without affecting the health of the rest of the body. But,
today, the teeth are known to be parts of a living system,
and toxic substances placed in them are known to leak into
the rest of the body. These materials can damage the teeth,
block the body's electromagnetic fields, and create breeding
grounds for highly toxic anaerobic bacteria that travel
through the bloodstream and impair the overall health.

Dr. M. T. Morter Jr., a pioneer in the field of energy
medicine, observed that all illness involves a slowdown or
blockage of energy. Illness is characterized by decreased
electromagnetic flow through the diseased area. If the
electrical messages can get through, the body can heal itself.

Reinhard Voll, M.D., found that the majority of the
body's energy blockages arise in the teeth and jaw. The
necessary electromagnetic signals cannot get through unless
these interference fields are eliminated.

Even if all the blockages to nerve supply are removed,
however, the body will not function optimally unless the
requisite raw materials are supplied. These raw materials

include vitamins, minerals, amino acids, enzymes and hormones. For the body to heal itself, not only must its electromagnetic flow be unblocked but it must be supplied with appropriate building blocks. Adequate mineral levels in the saliva also serve to protect the teeth from decay. When saliva and blood levels of minerals and other nutrients are sufficient, our long-term health will naturally improve.

The Dental/Medical Coalition

Although Dr. Voll was an M.D., he considered the most important member of the healing arts to be the dentist, who works with the body's major interference fields. For a dentist to suggest dental work for health reasons is now considered unethical; but for nearly 2,000 years before dentistry became a recognized dental specialty, the two disciplines were joined. Recent contributions to our understanding of the intimate relationship between the teeth and the rest of the body suggest that they should be joined again. Dentists should be trained as M.D.'s and M.D.'s as dentists. Advances in technology, equipment, and theory promise to revolutionize both disciplines.

For doing routine monitoring of health parameters, dentists are actually in a better position than doctors are, since most people visit their dentists more regularly than their doctors. People go to M.D.'s only when they are sick. They go to dentists for routine annual checkups, whether or not they are aware of having dental problems.

"The dentist of the future may provide routine diagnostic screening along with his dental checkups," suggests Dr. Hansen. "Besides blood pressure readings and other standard tests, salivary readings are simple tests that could be inputted into a data base. The saliva is an excellent barometer of chemical levels. Sensors placed in the mouth can determine alkalinity, pH, and enzyme activity. Other scans — of the skin, eyes, etc. — could also be readily inputted into a computerized data bank of medical records."

He observes that a medical records institute is currently working toward worldwide global access to medical records on a security basis. The goal is for all medical and dental offices to have local Internet personal computers as part of their clinical work station environment. Each time a patient is treated, his computer-based record will be accessed and the new data entered. Doctors even in remote locations will then be able to find the patient's records and access them. Doctors will also have access to worldwide medical authorities. Radiographs and other diagnostic readings can be inputted and read remotely. Diagnosis and treatment recommendations can then be relayed back to the treating doctor via the Internet.

One additional benefit of this Internet based medical record is that we would now have the ability to compile data for real-time research. Imagine that when each patient presented with a given set of symptoms; had a given set of values from the measurements, tests, and other records gathered; and had a diagnosis and treatment prescribed for the symptoms. The results of the treatment could be tracked on the Internet and compiled with all other patients would wide for the effectiveness of the treatment. This data could be used to modify and direct treatment decisions to improve the patient's quality of care. Practitioners who utilize alternative treatment modalities i.e. nutritional, herbal, acupuncture, spiritual, and other methods of working with the body's natural healing potential, can document treatment regimens and successes. This method of real time research, formerly called "anecdotal," is nothing more than uncontrolled clinical studies and nothing less than live patient research conducted world wide with instant results that can be statistically correlated.

The Millennial Ideal

Simple, routine diagnostic readings of that type could also help lay the groundwork for the future ideal: a body so in balance that it can heal itself. If we knew early on how our body systems were out of balance, we could correct problems before they turned into irreversible degenerative disease.

"Space Age" dentistry is increasingly becoming more painless and less toxic, encouraging treatment when dental problems are still small and making revision of faulty dental work less daunting, more feasible, with longer lasting results. When dental and other interference fields have been removed and nutritional and other needs have been fulfilled, our bodies will be able to function optimally with little or no dental or medical attention needed. The long term cost savings in both medical care and dental care will be substantial.

Dentistry to date has consisted of stop-gap, patch-and-fill measures to keep the teeth from falling apart until we learned how to maintain them holistically, by supporting the body's own efforts to preserve their integrity. That day seems finally to have arrived. Children born to enlightened parents in the twenty-first century should be able to maintain healthy teeth while avoiding the dentist's drill entirely.

Chapter 24

Selecting a Health Practitioner

"Kill As Few Patients As Possible."
—Oscar London, M.D.

I believe that all of us as patients desire to have good health. I also believe that all of us as doctors, or other health practitioners, desire to provide the finest health care possible. So how do we select a health provider that will give us the care we desire? And how can we be sure that our selected provider is actually providing *all* the available treatment appropriate to our unique individual needs?

Answer: We don't!

Not unless we, as informed patients, do our homework and learn about the varied choices that we now have in health care. Only then can we begin to become a partner with our provider in making informed decisions to achieve and maintain optimum health. That is the first step to selecting a practitioner. Become informed! Learn about the varied treatment modalities available, not only with conventional, allopathic medicine, but with the more natural, alternative therapies. Learn also how the alternatives can be integrated and combined with conventional medicine. The Advantage Health Research Foundation can assist you in learning about all the appropriate treatment modalities. They cannot give diagnosis or treatment advice, but they can provide needed information to help the patient become more informed. They can be reached at 1-888-792-1102.

After you decide on which style of care seems most appropriate, the second step will be to select practitioners to provide treatment and become a partner in achieving your health goals. I refer to 'becoming a partner' because in order for any patient to achieve optimal health it is vital that they be willing to take shared responsibility for their health and their health care decisions. In order to achieve optimal health and wellness, we need to look at many areas of care and fully integrate them into our total health picture. Selecting practitioners can be a time consuming and uncertain task. One of the most important criteria is to make sure the practitioner is both knowledgeable in their field as well as informed on all appropriate areas of alternative health. Recommendations from other health professionals, patients, and organizations can also guide the patient in their decision. The Advanced Health Research Foundation, a non-profit organization, has a listing of advanced health care providers in a variety of fields along with their credentials, specialties, and advanced education.

Once a practitioner is selected, the third step is for the patient to interview the practitioner and be willing to develop a partnership in order to accomplish their health goals. The patient likewise must develop a high degree of trust, confidence, and rapport with their provider so that their mental energies can assist and not hinder their health efforts. Also the patient must be ready and willing to evaluate and correct their nutritional/biochemical, physical, emotional, and spiritual being if they want to achieve ultimate health.

Selecting a dental practitioner can indeed follow the same sequence as for any health care provider with the following additions. First ask to see the mouth of the dentist. A dentist who has silver/mercury fillings, gold or other influencers to optimal health may not believe in the value to the extent that the patient needs. It becomes difficult to trust the recommendations of a practitioner if they themselves do not believe in their own advice and treatment. Next, check out the advanced training, background, and experience of the dentist. Ask what additional readings, seminars, and training protocols they have attended. Also ask how long they have been practicing alternative, metal free dental care and what specialized equipment and techniques they employ. It is likewise important to find out with which organizations they participate. The Advanced Health Research Foundation can provide a listing of practitioners and their credentials along with answers to many of these questions.

Resources

Organizations and Literature

For referrals to mercury-free dentists and information on safer, less toxic dentistry:

Advanced Health Research Foundation
1031 Rosecrans Ave., Suite 105
Fullerton, CA 92833
1-888-792-1102

International Academy of Oral Medicine
and Toxicology (IAOMT)
P.O. Box 608531
Orlando, FL 32860-8531

American Academy of Biological Dentistry
P.O. Box 856
Carmel Valley, CA 93924

American College for Advancement in Dentistry
14742 Beach Blvd., Suite 133
La Mirada, CA 90638
714-738-6201

Foundation for Toxic-Free Dentistry
P.O. Box 608010
Orlando, FL 32860-8010

The Price Pottenger Foundation
LaMesa, CA
Telephone: 1-800-366-3748

For fluoridation questions:

The Safe Water Foundation
6439 Taggart Road
Delaware, Ohio 43015

Safe Water Coalition of Washington State
W. 5615 Lyons Ct.
Spokane, WA 99208-3874
Telephone: 509-328-6704

For referrals to practitioners knowledgeable in heavy metal detoxification protocols, including chelation:

American College for Advancement in Medicine (ACAM)
23121 Verdugo Drive, Suite 204
Laguna Hills, CA 92653
Telephone: 714-583-7666
              800-532-3688
Fax: 714-455-9679
[3000+ scientific references available on chelation]

American Academy of Environmental Medicine
10 E. Randolph St.
New Hope, PA 18938
Telephone: 215-862-4544
Fax: 215-862-4583

American Holistic Medical Association
4101 Lake Boone Trail, Suite 201
Raleigh, NC 27607
Telephone: 919-787-5181
Fax: 919-787-4916

American Preventive Medical Association
459 Walker Road
Great Falls, VA 22066
Telephone: 703-759-0662
Fax: 703-759-6711

For information on electro-dermal screening:

BioSource Inc. LISTEN System
1388 West Center Street
Orem, UT 84057
Telephone: 801-226-1117
Fax: 801-226-1147

BioEclectic Research Group VEGA-Test
Box 3505
Santa Rosa, CA 95402
Telephone: 707-537-0777
Fax: 707-538-7731
Attn: Scott Moyer

Synergy Health Systems Computron
Santa Monica, CA
Telephone: 310-394-6497

To test the toxicity of root-filled teeth or cavitations:

Affinity Labeling Technologies Inc.
Attn: Dr. Curt Pendergrass
138 East Reynolds Road
Lexington, KY 40517
Tele.: 606-257-2300, ext. 246

For nutritional counseling:

International and American Association of Clinical
Nutritionists (IAACN)
5200 Keller Springs Road, Suite 410
Dallas, TX 75248
Tele.: 972-250-2829
Fax: 972-250-0233

International Academy of Nutrition and Preventive
Medicine
P.O. Box 18433
Ashville, NC 28814
Telephone: 704-258-3243

Footnotes

Preface

1. See T. Levy, M.D., "Teeth — the root of most disease?", <u>Extraordinary Science</u> (Apr/May/Jun 1994); A. Tanchyk, "Patient- or physician-initiated amalgam removal for treatment of arthritis," <u>General Dentistry</u> (July/August 1994), pages 354-58.

Chapter 1

1. J. Kluger, "Medicine: Can we stay young?", <u>Time</u> (November 25, 1996).
2. D. Chopra, M.D., <u>Perfect Health: the Complete Mind/Body Guide</u> (New York: Harmony Books, 1990), pages 171-75.
3. Andrew Weil, M.D., et al., "Roots of Healing: The New Medicine" (audiotape).
4. See "Suppression and obstruction to cure," <u>Townsend Letter for Doctors</u> (June 1995), pages 112-13.

Chapter 2

1. M. Muir, "Current controversies in the diagnosis and treatment of heavy metal toxicity," <u>Alternative and Complementary Therapies</u> (June 1997), pages 170-78.
2. D. Chopra, M.D., <u>Perfect Health: the Complete Mind/Body Guide</u> (New York: Harmony Books, 1990), pages 8-9.
3. W. John Diamond, M.D., W. Lee Cowden M.D., with Burton Goldberg, <u>An Alternative Medicine Definitive Guide to Cancer</u> (Tiburon, California: Future Medicine Publishing, Inc., 1997), chapter 25.
4. See T. Warren, <u>Beating Alzheimer's</u> (Garden City Park, New York: Avery Publishing Group, Inc., 1991); T. Warren, "Reversing Alzheimer's disease" [Web Page:http://www.halcyon.com/alzh9/]; T. Warren, "Beating the diagnosis: The case for unlocking brain disease," <u>Townsend Letter for Doctors and Patients</u> (April 1997), pages 50-60.
5. T. Levy, M.D., "Teeth — the root of most disease?", <u>Extraordinary Science</u> (Apr/May/Jun 1994).
6. W. Price, D.D.S., <u>Dental Infections—Oral and Systemic</u> [vol. 1] and <u>Dental Infections and the Degenerative Diseases</u> [vol. 2] (Cleveland, Ohio: Penton Publishing Co., 1923).
7. M. Hassan, M.D., <u>Prevention and Cure of Cancer</u> (Smithtown, New York: Exposition Press, 1983), pages 46, 165-67.
8. Interview with George Schuchard, D.D.S., a dentist in Chino, California.
9. H. Gelb, D.M.D., <u>Killing Pain Without Prescription</u> (New York: Harper & Row, 1980), pages 43-44.
10. R. Williams, "Perfect smile replaces tin grin," FDA Consumer (March 1, 1995).

Chapter 3

1. R. Becker, M.D., <u>Cross Currents</u> (Los Angeles: Jeremy P. Tarcher, Inc., 1990), page 70.
2. See D. Ullman, "Conceptualizing energetic medicine: A beginning," <u>American Journal of Acupuncture</u> 9(3):261-64 (1981); L. Riscalla, "Principles of physics and their influence

in medicine," ibid. 9(2):157-60 (1981); E. Lund, Bioelectric Fields and Growth (Austin, Texas: University of Texas Press, 1947); H. Burr, The Fields of Life (New York: Ballantine Books, 1973).

3. V. Hunt, Infinite Mind: The Science of Human Vibrations (Malibu, California: Malibu Publishing Co., 1995); V. Hunt, "The Human Energy Field" (video), 1993. See J. Klotter, "Linking science and spirit," Townsend Letter for Doctors & Patients (January 1996), pages 124-26.

4. B. Owens, D.D.S., et al., "Localized galvanic shock after insertion of an amalgam restoration," Compend. Contin. Educ. Dent. 14(10):1302-07. See also S. Olsson, et al., "Release of elements due to electrochemical corrosion of dental amalgam," Journal of Dental Research 73(1):33-43 (1994); M. Marek, "The effect of the electrode potential on the release of mercury from dental amalgam," Journal of Dental Research 72(9):2325-19 (1993); R. Meyer, et al., "Intraoral galvanic corrosion: Literature review and case report," Journal of Prosthetic Dentistry 69:141-43 (1993).

5. R. Meyer, et al., op. cit.

6. E. Lain, "Electrogalvanic lesions of the oral cavity produced by metallic dentures," J.A.M.A. 100:717 (1933).

7. B. Owens, et al., op. cit.

8. M. Van Benschoten, "Acupoint energetics of mercury toxicity and amalgam removal with case studies," American Journal of Acupuncture 22(3):251-61 (1994).

9. T. Warren, "Beating the diagnosis: The case for unlocking brain disease," Townsend Letter for Doctors and Patients (April 1997), pages 50-60.

10. F. Royal, M.D., H.M.D., "Are dentists contributing to our declining health?", Townsend Letter for Doctors (May 1990), pages 310-15.

11. B. Russell Manning, How Safe Are Silver (Mercury) Fillings? (Calistoga, California: 1983), page 13.

12. F. Royal, op. cit.

13. B. Manning, op. cit., pages 35-36.

14. Ibid.

15. Charts furnished by Dr. Linda Forbes.

16. T. Warren, "Beating the diagnosis," op. cit.

17. R. Gerber, Vibrational Medicine (Santa Fe, New Mexico: Bear & Co., 1988), pages 206-10.

18. See W. Tiller, "What do electrodermal diagnostic acupuncture instruments really measure?", American Journal of Acupuncture 15(1):15-23 (1987).

19. S. Rosenblatt, "The electrodermal characteristics of acupuncture points," American Journal of Acupuncture 10:131-37 (1982).

20. F. Royal, "Homeopathy and EDT: Upheld by modern science — with case histories," American Journal of Acupuncture 20(1):55-65 (1992).

21. "Drug R & D costs doubled in decade," American Medical News (May 18, 1990), pages 3, 53.

22. The Third International Congress of Electro Dermal Screening Health Practitioners met in Utah in November of 1996. An organization called the International Society of Electrodermal Testers, Inc., has been formed for the purpose of uniting practitioners, technicians and manufacturers into a coalition that will establish standards, policies and programs for performance and use, and for certification and registration in accordance with federal and state laws and regulations.

23. D. Eggleston, D.D.S., "Electro-acupuncture according to Voll (Dermatron), T-cells, etc." (lecture), quoted in B. Russell Manning, How Safe Are Silver (Mercury) Fillings? (Calistoga, California: 1983), page 36.

Chapter 4

1. G. Hindes, et al., "Dentistry," Colliers Encyclopedia CD-ROM (February 28, 1996).

2. W. Hoffmann-Axthelm, History of Dentistry (Chicago: Quintessence Publishing Co., Inc., 1981), pages 60-63, 194-95, 250, 287-93, 334-35.

3. "What can be done about dental quackery?", JADA 115:679-85 (1987).

Chapter 5

1. R. Siblerud, "A comparison of mental health of multiple sclerosis patients with silver/mercury dental fillings and those with fillings removed," Psychological Reports 70:1139-51 (1992).
2. M. Lee, "Two studies suggest risk from silver fillings," Chicago Tribune (August 15, 1990), pages 1-2.
3. H. Casdorph, M. Walker, Toxic Metal Syndrome Garden City Park, New York: Avery Publishing Group, 1995), page 160.
4. J. Pleva, "Mercury poisoning from dental amalgam," Journal of Orthomolecular Psychiatry 12:184-93 (1983); M. Vimy, et al., "Serial measurements of intra-oral air mercury: Estimation of daily dose from dental amalgams," Journal of Dental Research 64(8):1072-75 (1985); R. Siblerud, "The relationship between mercury from dental amalgam and the cardiovascular system," Science of the Total Environment 99:23-35 (1990).
5. M. Lee, op. cit.
6. H. Casdorph, et al., op. cit., page 156, citing D. Wenstrup, et al., "Trace element imbalances in isolated subcellular fractions of Alzheimer's disease brains," Brain Research 553:125-31 (1990).
7. E. Duhr, et al., "Hg2 + induces GTP-tubulin interactions in rat brain similar to those observed in Alzheimer's disease," FASEB 75th Annual Meeting in Atlanta, Georgia, April 21-25, 1991, Abstract #493.
8. D. Eggleston, et al., "Correlation of dental amalgam with mercury in brain tissue," Journal of Prosthetic Dentistry 58:704-07 (1987); M. Nylander, et al., "Mercury concentrations in the human brain and kidneys in relation to exposure from dental amalgam fillings," Swedish Dental Journal 11:179-87 (1987).
9. See "Media events, August-October, 1990," Dental & Health Facts 3(4):1 (November 1990); S. Begley, et al., "Return of the toxic teeth," Newsweek (January 14, 1991), page 45.
10. K. Sehnert, M.D., et al., "Is mercury toxicity an autoimmune disorder?", Townsend Letter for Doctors and Patients (October 1995), pages 134-37.
11. T. Friend, "Alzheimer's deaths 'underestimated,'" USA Today (March 4, 1996); H. Casdorph, et al., op. cit.
12. T. Levy, M.D., "Teeth — the root of most disease?", Extraordinary Science (Apr/May/Jun 1994), citing B. Choi, "Methylmercury poisoning of the developing nervous system," Neurotoxicology 7(2):591-600 (1986); M. Marlowe, et al., "Main and interaction effects of metal pollutants in emotionally disturbed children," in R. Rutherford, ed., Monograph in Behavioral Disorders, vol. 7 (Reston, Virginia: Council for Children with Behavioral Disorders, 1984), pages 67-79.
13. V. Valerian, "Deadly mercury: How it became your dentist's darling," Perceptions (March/April 1996), pages 32-35.
14. A free copy of the Fact Sheet may be obtained by sending a large stamped self-addressed envelope to EDA, 9974 Scripps Ranch Blvd. #36, San Diego, California 92131.
15. K. Sehnert, et al., op. cit.
16. V. Valerian, op. cit.
17. S. Saxe, "Dental amalgam and cognitive functions in older women: Findings from the nun study," Journal of the American Dental Association 126:1495-1501 (1995).
18. J. Vimy, et al., "Maternal-fetal distribution of mercury released from dental amalgam fillings," American Journal of Physiology 258:939-45 (1990).
19. G. Drasch, et al., "Mercury burden of human fetal and infant tissues," European Journal of Pediatrics 153:607-10 (1994).
20. T. Levy, op. cit.; K. Sehnert, et al., op. cit.
21. R. Siblerud, et al., "Evidence that mercury from silver dental fillings may be an etiological factor in multiple sclerosis," Science of the Total Environment 142:191-205 (1994).
22. T. Levy, op. cit.
23. R. Siblerud, "A comparison of mental health of multiple sclerosis patients with silver/mercury dental fillings and those with fillings removed," Psychological Reports 70:1139-51 (1992).

24. W. Craelius, "Comparative epidemiology of multiple sclerosis and dental caries," Journal of Epidemiology and Community Health 32:155-65 (1978).
25. T. Ingalls, "Epidemiology, etiology, and prevention of multiple sclerosis," American Journal for Medicine and Pathology 4(1):55-61 (1983).
26. B. Aholrot-Westerlund, "Multiple sclerosis and mercury in cerebrospinal fluid," paper given at Second Nordic symposium on trace elements in human health and disease, Odense, Denmark, cited in R. Siblerud, "A comparison of mental health of multiple sclerosis patients . . .," op. cit.
27. R. Casdorph, et al., op. cit., page 149, citing U. Ahlrot, et al., Nutrition Research, supplement of 1985, page 403: Second Nordic Symposium on Trace Elements in Human Health & Disease, Odense, Denmark, August 1987.
28. K. Sehnert, op. cit.
29. D. Swartzendruber, "The possible relationship between mercury from dental amalgam and diseases I: Effects within the oral cavity," Medical Hypotheses 41:31-34 (1993).
30. R. Siblerud, "A comparison of mental health of multiple sclerosis patients . . .," op. cit. A 1969 study comparing MS patients to patients with muscular dystrophy found that twice as many MS as muscular dystrophy patients suffered from depression, countering the argument that MS patients are depressed just because they have a crippling disease. See D. Surridge, "Investigation into some psychiatric aspects of multiple sclerosis," British Journal of Psychiatry 115:749-64 (1969).
31. R. Siblerud, ibid.
32. P. Bennett, N.D., "Toxic teeth," Townsend Letter for Doctors and Patients (August/September 1997), pages 144-48.
33. R. Siblerud, "Evidence that mercury from silver dental fillings may be an etiological factor in smoking," Toxicology Letters 68:307-10 (1993).
34. R. Siblerud, et al., "Psychometric evidence that mercury from silver dental fillings may be an etiological factor in depression, excessive anger, and anxiety," Psychological Reports 74:67-80 (1994).
35. Y. Omura, et al., Acupuncture Electrotherapy Research 21(2):133-60 (1996).

Chapter 6

1. T. Warren, "Beating the diagnosis: The case for unlocking brain disease," Townsend Letter for Doctors and Patients (April 1997), pages 50-60.
2. H. Huggins, D.D.S., Proper Amalgam Removal: Avoiding the "Frying Pan Into the Fire" Syndrome (Colorado Springs: Huggins Diagnostic Center, 1993), pages 19-34.
3. S. Ziff, "Letters to the editor," Townsend Letter for Doctors (August/September 1995), page 91.
4. J. Klotter, "Chemical contributors to Gulf War Syndrome," Townsend Letter for Doctors & Patients (June 1997), page 27; A. Gaby, "Toxic chemicals: The effect of cumulative exposure," ibid., page 31.
5. Dr. H. Casdorph, Dr. M. Walker, Toxic Metal Syndrome (Garden City Park, New York: Avery Publishing Group, 1995), page 126, citing G. Wenk, et al., Neurotoxicology 3:93-99 (1982); and J. Bjorksten, "Dietary aluminum and Alzheimer's disease," Science of the Total Environment 25:81-84 (1982).
6. B. Russell Manning, How Safe Are Silver (Mercury) Fillings? (Calistoga, California: 1983), page 38.
7. H. Casdorph, et al., op. cit., pages 140, 162.
8. R. Siblerud, "The relationship between mercury from dental amalgam and the cardiovascular system," Science of the Total Environment 99:23-35 (1990), citing M. Hanson, "Amalgam: Hazards in your teeth," Journal of Orthomolecular Psychiatry 12:194-201 (1983). [Emphasis added.]
9. D. Eggleston, D.D.S., "Electro-Acupuncture According to Voll (Dermatron), T-Cells, Etc." [1983 Wholistic Dental Convention lecture], quoted in B. Russell Manning, op. cit., pages 41-42.

Chapter 7

1. In re George A. Guess, 393 S.E.2d 833 (1990).
2. See, e.g., "Mercury-free dentistry," Townsend Letter for Doctors & Patients (April 1996), page 9.
3. "Colorado dentist denies charges: Claims he's victim of vendetta to silence criticism," ADA News (September 18, 1995), page 4.
4. "Is this happening to me? Could this happen to you? Of course," Townsend Letter for Doctors & Patients (April 1996), pages 103-06.
5. Tolhurst v. Johnson & Johnson, et al., Case #718228, Superior Court of the State of California at Santa Clara, filed October 22, 1992.
6. See "Dentistry," Encyclopedia Britannica.

Chapter 8

1. E. Adler, M.D., Neural Focal Dentistry (Houston: Multi-Discipline Research Foundation, 1984), page 17.
2. G. Meinig, D.D.S., Root Canal Cover-up Exposed (Ojai, California: Bion Publishing, 1993), pages 7-19, 25-28, 57-61.
3. L. Tronstad, et al., Endo. Dent. Traumatol. 3:86-90 (1987); L. Tronstad, et al., "Periapical bacterial plaque in teeth refractory to endodontic treatment," Journal of Dental Research, vol. 69 (special issue), page 300, abstract #1529 (March 1990).
4. P. Bennett, N.D., P. Brawn, D.D.S., "Toxic teeth," Townsend Letter for Doctors (August/September 1997), pages 144-48.
5. D. Williams, "The dangers of root canal therapy," Alternatives 5(8):57-61 (February, 1994).
6. W. Price, D.D.S., Dental Infections—Oral and Systemic [vol. 1] and Dental Infections and the Degenerative Diseases [vol. 2] (Cleveland, Ohio: Penton Publishing Co., 1923).
7. G. Meinig, op. cit., page 144.
8. These refinements in scientific understanding throw new light on a study relied on conventionally as demonstrating the safety of the root canal procedure, in which rabbits injected with streptococcus bacteria suffered no ill effects. Dr. Meinig observes that the bacteria used were the ordinary, harmless, unmutated strep bacteria found in every mouth. The protected, oxygen-lacking environment provided in the root tips by root canal therapy allows otherwise-benign, oxygen-using mouth bacteria to undergo a toxic transformation, becoming virulent, mutated, anaerobic bacteria capable of producing by-products that are quite toxic to the body. The immune system is capable of handling bacteria in organs like the heart, which it can bathe in blood; but it is unable to rout out the protected mutants hiding in the teeth. That insight also helps explain Dr. Price's empirical observation that infection typically disappears from the diseased organ after the offending tooth has been removed. Ibid., pages 28, 79-80.
9. D. McCann, "Avoid overprescribing of antibiotics: CSA," ADA News (October 21, 1996), page 13.
10. G. Kolata, "New suspect in bacterial resistance: Amalgam; the mercury in dental fillings may spur resistance to antibiotics," New York Times (Science Times Pages), page B5 (April 27, 1993).
11. E. Adler, M.D., Neural Focal Dentistry (Houston: Multi-Discipline Research Foundation, 1984), pages 5, 31-33.
12. F. Shull, M.D., "Neural therapy," Townsend Letter for Doctors (April 1988), page 121.
13. Available from Medicina Biologica, 4830 NE 32nd Avenue, Portland, OR 97211.
14. Personal interview with Dr. Huggins' former nutritionist, Mary Buckley, who supplied the photo.
15. Personal interview with George Schuchard, D.D.S., of Chino, California.
16. B. Russell Manning, How Safe Are Silver (Mercury) Fillings? (Calistoga, California: 1983), pages 37, 44; W. Klotzer, "Metals and alloys — corrosion, toxicity, sensitivity reactions I" [German language], Zwr 100(5):300-04, 307 (1991).

17. P. Bennett, N.D., "Toxic Teeth," <u>Townsend Letter for Doctors</u> (August/September 1997), pages 144-48.

Chapter 9

1. D. Eggleston, D.D.S., "Electro-Acupuncture According to Voll (Dermatron), T-Cells, Etc." (lecture), quoted in B. Russell Manning, <u>How Safe Are Silver (Mercury) Fillings?</u> (Calistoga, California: 1983), page 44.
2. M. Vimy, D.D.S., <u>Toxic Teeth</u> (University of Calgary, Alberta, Canada, 1993).
3. E. Blaurock-Busch, Ph.D., "Dental health or dental illness?", <u>Townsend Letter for Doctors</u> (August/September 1996), page 108.
4. M. Vimy, <u>op. cit.</u>, pages 19-20.
5. H. Savolainen, "Biochemical and clinical aspects of nickel toxicity," <u>Rev. Environ. Health</u> 11(4):167-73 (1996); D. Gawkrodger, "Nickel dermatitis: How much nickel is safe?", <u>Contact Dermatitis</u> 35(5):267-71 (1996); J. Wataha, et al., "Correlation between cytotoxicity and the elements released by dental casing alloys," <u>International Journal of Prosthodontics</u> 8(1):9-14 (1995); M. Grimsdottir, et al., "Cytotoxic and antibacterial effects of orthodontic appliances," <u>Scandinavian Journal of Dental Research</u> 101(4):229-31 (1993); Y. Teraki, et al., "Inorganic elements in the tooth and bone tissues of rats bearing nickel acetate- and lead-acetate-induced tumors," <u>Odontology</u> 78(2):269-73 (1990); S. Sahmali, et al., "Systemic effects of nickel-containing dental alloys," <u>Quintessence International</u> 22(12):961-96 (1991).

Chapter 10

1. "Developments to watch," <u>Business Week</u> (September 16, 1996), page 111.
2. P. Bennett, N.D., "Toxic teeth," <u>Townsend Letter for Doctors</u> (August/September 1997), pages 144-48.

Chapter 11

1. D. Williams, "The dangers of root canal therapy," <u>Alternatives</u> 5(8):57-61 (February 1994).
2. Cavalleri, et al., "Comparison of calcium hydroxide and calcium oxide for intercanal medication," <u>G-Ital-Endodonzia</u> 4(3):8-13 (1990). See also M. Georgopoulou, et al., "In vitro evaluation of the effectiveness of calcium hydroxide and paramonochlorophenol on anaerobic bacteria from the root canal," <u>Endo. Dent. Traumatol.</u> 9(6):249-253 (December 1993).
3. N. Gutknecht, D.M.D., "The bactericidal effects of the diode laser in root canals," research abstract of report presented during the ALD's Fourth Annual Conference, January 15-18, 1997, in Koloa, Kauai, Hawaii.
4. A. Das, M.D., "Helium-neon (HN) laser to treat dental root canals and Meniere's disease," <u>Townsend Letter for Doctors</u> 130:488-89 (May 1994).

Chapter 12

1. R. Peterson, "Laser dental drill has FDA approval: New technique causes less pain," <u>USA Today</u> (May 8, 1997).
2. L. Joseph, "The new world of dental care," <u>Consumers Digest</u> (May 1, 1996).

Chapter 13

1. I. Shapiro, et al., "Neurophysiological and neuropsychological function in mercury exposed dentists," <u>Lancet</u> 1147-50 (May 22, 1982).
2. B. Russell Manning, <u>How Safe Are Silver (Mercury) Fillings?</u> (Calistoga, California: 1983).

3. H. Huggins, D.D.S., Proper Amalgam Removal: Avoiding the "Frying Pan Into the Fire" Syndrome (Colorado Springs: Huggins Diagnostic Center, 1993), pages 19-34.
4. See T. Levy, M.D., "Teeth — the root of most disease?", Extraordinary Science (spring 1994); "Is there poison in your mouth?", 60 Minutes [TV news clip], December 16, 1990.
5. See, e.g., S. Ziff, M. Ziff, D.D.S., Dentistry Without Mercury (Orlando, Florida: Bio-Probe, Inc., 1995), page 46.
6. T. Levy, op. cit.; H. Huggins, D.D.S., Proper Amalgam Removal, op. cit.; H. Huggins, It's All in Your Head (Boulder, Colorado: Life Sciences Press, 1989).

Chapter 14

1. N. Hallaway, R.N., Z. Strauts, M.D., Turning Lead into Gold: How Heavy Metal Poisoning Can Affect Your Child and How to Prevent It (Vancouver: New Star Books, 1995), page 57.
2. E. Adler, M.D., Neural Focal Dentistry (Houston: Multi-Discipline Research Foundation, 1984), page 4.
3. See Chapter 5.
4. T. Levy, M.D., "Teeth — the root of most disease?", Extraordinary Science (Apr/May/Jun 1994); D. Williams, "The dangers of root canal therapy," Alternatives 5(8):57-61 (February, 1994).
5. M. Vimy, D.D.S., Toxic Teeth (University of Calgary, Alberta, Canada, 1993), pages 36-37.
6. Medical Hypotheses 82(9):265-82.
7. D. Williams, "Cleaning house," Alternatives 4(12):97-100 (1992).
8. M. Vimy, op. cit., pages 31-37.
9. V. Bradshaw, "Mercury poisoning from amalgam fillings," Townsend Letter for Doctors (May 1997), pages 104-08.
10. F. Batmanghelidj, M.D., Your Body's Many Cries for Water (Falls Church, Virginia: Global Health Solutions, 1995).
11. See N. Clarke, et al., "Treatment of occlusive vascular disease with disodium ethylene diamine tetra-acetic acid (EDTA)," American Journal of Medical Science 239:732 (1960); N. Clarke, et al., "Treatment of angina pectoris with disodium ethylene diamine tetra-acetic acid," ibid. 232:645 (1956); C. Lamar, "Chelation therapy of occlusive arteriosclerosis in diabetic patients," Angiology 15:379 (1964).
12. R. Evers, M.D., "A successful therapy for the relief of chronic degenerative diseases" (200 Beta St., Belle Chasse, LA 70037; undated).
13. S. Ziff, et al., Dental Mercury Detox (Orlando, Florida: Bio Probe, Inc., Publisher), pages 37-40.
14. R. Keith, et al., "Utilization of renal slices to evaluate the efficacy of chelating agents for removing mercury from the kidney," Toxicology 116:67-75 (January 1997).
15. Y. Omura, et al., Acupuncture Electrotherapy Research 21(2):133-60 (1996).
16. S. Ziff, op. cit., page 40.
17. See D. Ullman, The Consumer's Guide to Homeopathy (New York: G. P. Putnam's Sons, 1995), pages 44-46.
18. Ibid., page 56.
19. T. Warren, Beating Alzheimer's (Garden City Park, New York: Avery Publishing Group, Inc., 1991), pages 47-48.

Chapter 15

1. M. Muir, "Current controversies in the diagnosis and treatment of heavy metal toxicity," Alternative and Complementary Therapies (June 1997), pages 170-78.
2. Research summarized in J. Heimlich, What Your Doctor Won't Tell You, page 156.
3. B. Russell Manning, How Safe are Silver (Mercury) Fillings? (Calistoga, California: 1983), page 27.
4. See A. Lockie, N. Geddes, The Complete Guide to Homeopathy (New York: Dorling Kindersley, 1995).

5. T. Warren, "Beating the diagnosis: The case for unlocking brain disease," <u>Townsend Letter for Doctors and Patients</u> (April 1997), pages 50-60, quoting Norwegian researcher Dr. Harald J. Hamre.

Chapter 16

1. R. Gerber, <u>Vibrational Medicine</u> (Santa Fe, New Mexico: Bear & Co., 1988), page 200.
2. See D. Kennedy, D.D.S., <u>How to Save Your Teeth: Toxic-Free Preventive Dentistry</u> (Delaware, Ohio: Health Action Press, 1993), pages 17-19.
3. J. Gofman, <u>Preventing Breast Cancer: The Story of a Major, Proven, Preventable Cause of This Disease</u> (San Francisco: Committee for Nuclear Responsibility, 1995); see P. Radetsky, "The mad-as-hell scientist," <u>Longevity</u> (February 1995), pages 58 ff.; "The x-ray link to cancer: Officials scorn new findings," <u>CornerStones</u> (October 1995), pages 1-2.
4. R. Bertell, "Effects of radiation on health," <u>Health and Environment Task Force International Panel Discussion</u>, United Nations Chapel, New York City, March 9, 1994, citing R. Bertell, <u>Handbook for Estimating Health Effects of Ionizing Radiation</u> (1986); R. Bertell, <u>Breast Cancer and Mammography</u> (1992); and the U.S. National Academy of Sciences, "The Biologicial Effect of Ionizing Radiation" (1990).
5. D. Kennedy, <u>op. cit.</u>
6. L. Joseph, "The new world of dental care," <u>Consumers Digest</u> (May 1, 1996).
7. B. Inglis, et al., <u>The Alternative Health Guide</u> (New York: Alfred A. Knopf, 1983), pages 116-18.
8. J. Diamond, M.D., <u>Your Body Doesn't Lie: How to Increase Your Life Energy Through Behavioral Kinesiology</u> (New York: Warner Books, 1997), page 32.

Chapter 17

1. Quoted by W. Price, D.D.S., in <u>Nutrition and Physical Degeneration</u> (republished by Keats Publishing, Inc., New Canaan, Connecticut, 1989), page 504.
2. <u>Ibid.</u>
3. H. Hawkins, <u>Applied Nutrition</u> (La Habra, California: International College of Applied Nutrition, 1947). See also W. Price, <u>op. cit.</u>, pages 377-78.
4. W. Price, <u>op. cit.</u>, pages 288, 444-49.
5. <u>Ibid.</u>; see, e.g., pages 408-09, 500.
6. <u>Ibid.</u>, pages 379, 405-09, 411-12, 500.
7. <u>Ibid.</u>, pages 288, 438, 444-49.
8. G. Meinig, D.D.S., <u>Root Canal Cover-up Exposed</u> (Ojai, California: Bion Publishing, 1993), page 23.
9. F. Pottenger, "The effect of heat-processed foods and metabolized vitamin D milk on the dentofacial structures of experimental animals," <u>American Journal of Orthodontics and Oral Surgery</u> 32(7):467-85 (1946).
10. An over-the-counter product promoted at a health fair a number of years ago for preserving the teeth was one called "Xero-Lube." Its advertised use was as a remedy for dry mouth, but proponents maintained it could also prevent cavities by balancing the mineral levels in the saliva and augmenting the body's production of saliva. The product needed only to be sprayed in the mouth before bed. Whether this remedy actually works remains to be proven, but the concept is intriguing.
11. H. Hawkins, <u>op. cit.</u>, pages 66-67.
12. See A. Colbin, <u>Food and Healing</u> (New York: Ballantine Books, 1986), page 162.
13. <u>Ibid.</u>, page 160.
14. E. Mazariegos-Ramos, "Consumption of soft drinks with phosphoric acid as a risk factor for the development of hypocalcemia in children," <u>Journal of Pediatrics</u> 126:940-42 (1995).
15. A. Colbin, <u>op. cit.</u>, pages 161-62.
16. E. Barrett-Connor, et al., <u>JAMA</u> 271:280-83 (1994).

Chapter 18

1. J. Collin, "Center for Stupidity in the Public Interest," Townsend Letter for Doctors (June 1995), page 124.
2. H. Hawkins, Applied Nutrition (La Habra, California: International College of Applied Nutrition, 1947), page 156.
3. Reprinted as Food Enzymes for Health and Longevity (Woodstock Valley, Connecticut: Omangod Press, 1980), pages 84-85.
4. J. Annand, "Hypothesis: Heated milk protein and thrombosis," Journal of Atherosclerosis Research 7:797-801 (1967); J. Annand, "The case against heated animal protein," Journal of Atherosclerosis Research 3:153-56 (1963).
5. "Enzyme in homogenized milk said to damage arteries," Vegetarian Times (March 1984), page 14.
6. A. Colbin, Food and Healing (New York: Ballantine Books, 1986), page 155.
7. C. Sugarman, "The impact of the raw milk ban," Washington Post (August 26, 1987). An option in Europe is milk and cheese products preserved with hydrogen peroxide, a system that greatly reduces pathogenic organisms without overheating the milk and without leaving toxic residue in the food chain.
8. J. Sheehan, et al., "Interactions of magnesium and potassium in the pathogenesis of cardiovascular disease," Magnesium 3:301-14 (1984); R. Peat, Nutrition for Women (Eugene, Oregon: Kenogen, 1981), page 16.
9. Interview with George Schuchard, D.D.S., of Chino, California.
10. J. Campbell, "The answer to better health is not through consuming more milk," Townsend Letter for Doctors (February/March 1994), page 230.
11. Chart compiled by Stephane Turner, R.D., reprinted in J. Lee, "Osteoporosis reversal: The role of progesterone," International Clinical Nutrition Review 10(3):384-91 (1990).

Chapter 19

1. Quoted in W. Price, Nutrition and Physical Degeneration (republished by Keats Publishing, Inc., New Canaan, Connecticut, 1989), page 461.
2. See "Food irradiation: A hot issue," Harvard Health Letter 17(10):1-3 (August 1992).
3. U.S. Senate Document No. 264, 74th Congress, 2nd Session, 1936.
4. See G. Anderson, et al., "Effect of dietary phosphorus on calcium metabolism . . . ," Journal of Nutrition 102:1123-32 (1972); J. Froom, "Selections from current literature: Hormone therapy in postmenopausal women," Family Practice 8(3):288-92 (1991); E. Brown, L. Walker, The Informed Consumer's Pharmacy (New York: Carroll & Graf, 1990), pages 342-43.
5. B. Dawson-Hughes, et al., "A controlled trial of the effect of calcium supplementation on bone density in postmenopausal women," New England Journal of Medicine 323:878-83 (1990).
6. O. Epstein, et al., "Vitamin D, hydroxyapatite, and calcium gluconate in treatment of cortical bone thinning in postmenopausal women with primary biliary cirrhosis," American Journal of Clinical Nutrition 35:426-30 (1982); "Microcrystalline hydroxyapatite versus calcium gluconate," Meta Update 90(3):4 (March 1990); Townsend Letter for Doctors (December 1990), page 863.
7. A. Schauss, Ph.D., "An analysis of colloidal mineral claims," Health Counselor (1997).
8. N. Fuchs, "Calcium controversy," Townsend Letter for Doctors (August/September 1993), pp. 906-08.
9. J. Lieberman, Light: Medicine of the Future (Santa Fe, New Mexico: Bear & Company Publishing, 1991), page 70.
10. J. Ott, "Color and light: Their effects on plants, animals, and people," Journal of Biosocial Research, vol. 7, part I (1985).
11. R. Neer, et al., "Stimulation by artificial lighting of calcium absorption in elderly human subjects," Nature 229:255 (1971).
12. D. Lawson, et al., "Relative contributions of diet and sunlight to vitamin D state in the elderly," British Medical Journal 2:303-05 (1979); M. Poskitt, et al., "Diet, sunlight,

and 25-hydroxy vitamin D in healthy children and adults," British Medical Journal 1:221-23 (1979); D. Fraser, "The physiological economy of vitamin D," Lancet (April 30, 1983), pages 969-72; D. Corless, et al., "Response of plasma-25-hydroxyvitamin D to ultraviolet irradiation in long-stay geriatric patients," Lancet (September 23, 1978), pages 649-51.
13. J. Lieberman, op. cit., pages 70-71; D. Fraser, op. cit.
14. M. Holick, "Photosynthesis of vitamin D in the skin: Effect of environmental and life-style variables," Federation Proceedings 46:1876-82 (1987).
15. Ibid.
16. S. Berne, Creating Your Own Personal Vision (Santa Fe, New Mexico: Color Stone Press, 1994).
17. See V. Beral, et al., "Malignant melanoma and exposure to fluorescent light at work," Lancet 2:290-92 (1982); B. Pasternak, et al., ibid. 1:704 (1983); D. Rigel, et al, ibid. 1:704 (1983).
18. Z. Kime, M.D., Sunlight (Penryn, California: World Health Publications, 1980).
19. J. Lieberman, op. cit., pages 141-43.
20. R. Peat, "Preserving the tissues: Osteoporosis and the skin," Townsend Letter for Doctors & Patients (April 1996), pages 68-70.

Chapter 20

1. Quoted in M. Marble, "Oral health also effected by disease," Women's Health Weekly (December 25, 1995), page 13.
2. Ibid.
3. J. Lee, M.D., Natural Progesterone (Sebastopol, California: BLL Publishing, 1993), pages 56-58.
4. R. Peat, "Preserving the tissues: Osteoporosis and the skin," Townsend Letter for Doctors (April 1996), pages 68-70.
5. J. Lee, "Osteoporosis reversal: The role of progesterone," International Clinical Nutrition Review 10(3):384-91 (1990); J. Lee, "Is natural progesterone the missing link in osteoporosis prevention and treatment?", Medical Hypotheses 35:314-16 (1991).
6. J. Lee, ibid. (both articles). See E. Brown, L. Walker, Menopause and Estrogen (Berkeley, California: Frog, Ltd., 1996).
7. H. Huggins, D.D.S., Proper Amalgam Removal: Avoiding the "Frying Pan Into the Fire" Syndrome (Colorado Springs: Huggins Diagnostic Center, 1993).
8. D. Swartzendruber, "The possible relationship between mercury from dental amalgam and diseases I: Effects within the oral cavity," Medical Hypotheses 41:31-34 (1993).
9. See G. Kennedy, D.D.S., How to Save Your Teeth (Delaware, Ohio: Health Action Press, 1993), pages 189, 190.

Chapter 21

1. J. Yiamouyiannis, Fluoride: The Aging Factor (Delaware, Ohio: Health Action Press, 1986), page 63.
2. "What can be done about dental quackery?", JADA 115:679-85 (November 1987).
3. Quoted in J. Yiamouyiannis, op. cit., page 138.
4. See J. Crimmins, "Fluoride blamed in dialysis deaths," Chicago Tribune (July 31, 1993), Sec. I, page 15; and cancer and hip fracture studies cited later in this chapter.
5. C. Steelink, "Fluoridation controversy," Chemical & Engineering News (July 27, 1992), page 2.
6. Imai, Y., "Study of the relationship between fluoride ions in drinking water and dental caries in Japan," Japanese Journal of Dental Health 22:144-96 (1972); J. Colquhoun, "Child dental health differences in New Zealand," Community Health Studies 11:85-90 (1987); S. Teotia, et al., "Dental caries: A disorder of high fluoride and low dietary calcium interations," Fluoride 27:61 (1994).
7. "EPA scientists take stand against fluoridation!", Bio-Probe Newsletter (September 1997), page 4.

8. R. Foulkes, M.D., "Celebration or shame? Fifty years of fluoridation," <u>Townsend Letter for Doctors & Patients</u> (November 1995), pages 52-63.

9. <u>Ibid.</u>

10. F. Sowers, <u>American Journal of Clinical Nutrition</u> 44:889-98 (1986); F. Sowers, et al., <u>American Journal of Epidemiology</u> 133:649-60 (1991); S. Jacobsen, et al., <u>JAMA</u> 264:500-02 (1990); C. Cooper, et al., <u>JAMA</u> 266:513 (1991); C. Danielson, et al., <u>JAMA</u> 268:746-48 (1992). See also Dr. Cooper's British study in <u>JAMA</u> (July 24, 1991), and Dr. J. Colquhoun's New Zealand study in <u>New Zealand Medical Journal</u> (August 1991).

11. U.S. National Research Council, <u>Diet and Health</u> (Washington, D.C.: National Academy Press, 1989), page 121.

12. J. Lee, M.D., <u>Natural Progesterone</u> (Sebastopol, California: BLL Publishing, 1993), page 68.

13. "Neurotoxicology of sodium fluoride in rats," <u>Neurotoxicology and Teratology</u> 17(2):169-77 (1995).

14. R. Foulkes, <u>op. cit.</u>

15. M. Cimons, "Fluoridation: A shining public health success," <u>Los Angeles Times</u>, Home Edition, Part A, page 5, January 26, 1995.

16. <u>Journal of the Canadian Dental Association</u> 10:763-64 (1987); <u>Journal of Dental Research</u>, "Special Issue," vol. 69, February 1990.

17. J. Yiamouyiannis, "Water fluoridation and tooth decay: Results from the 1986-1987 National Survey of U.S. Schoolchildren," <u>Fluoride</u> 23(2):55-67 (1990).

18. M. Gold, "Fluoridated water does not prevent tooth decay" [Internet article].

19. R. Zeigelbecker, "Fluoridated water and teeth," <u>Fluoride</u> 14:123-28 (1981).

20. R. Zeigelbecker, "WHO data on dental caries and natural water fluoride levels," <u>Fluoride</u> 26(4):263-66 (1993).

21. R. Foulkes, <u>op. cit.</u>; E. Jerard, et al., "The summing of fluoride exposures," <u>International Journal of Environmental Studies</u> 3:143 (1973); R. Berk, et al., <u>Aluminum: Profile of the Industry</u> (New York: McGraw-Hill, 1985), page 148.

22. J. Griffiths, "Fluoride: Commie plot or capitalist ploy," <u>Covert Action</u> 42:26 (1992).

23. J. Yiamouyiannis, <u>op. cit.</u>, pages 140-41.

24. <u>Ibid.</u>

25. E. Bernays, <u>Propaganda</u> (New York: H. Liveright, 1928), page 18.

26. J. Griffiths, <u>op. cit.</u>

27. J. Yiamouyiannis, <u>op. cit.</u>

28. <u>Ibid.</u>, pages 63-67, 141, citing <u>Aitkenhead v. Borough of West View, Pennsylvania</u>, GD 78-4585 (1978), and <u>Illinois Pure Water Committee v. Director of Public Health, State of Illinois</u>, No. 68-E-128, Third Judicial Circuit, Madison County, Ill. (1982).

29. Quoted in E. McCabe, <u>Oxygen Therapies</u> (Morrisville, New York: Energy Publications, 1988), page 162.

30. J. Yiamouyiannis, <u>op. cit.</u>, pages 140-41.

31. <u>San Francisco Examiner</u> (October 6, 1983), quoted in E. McCabe, <u>op. cit.</u>, page 163.

32. S. Begley, "Don't drink the water?", <u>Newsweek</u> (February 5, 1990), pages 60-61.

33. U.S. Public Health Service, <u>Review of Fluoride Benefits and Risks</u> (Washington, D.C.: Department of Health and Human Services, 1991), pages iii, F-3.

34. J. Griffiths, <u>op. cit.</u>

35. <u>Ibid.</u>; J. Raloff, "The St. Regis syndrome," <u>Science News</u> (July 19, 1980), pages 42-43.

36. <u>Air Pollutants Affecting the Performance of Domestic Animals</u>, U.S. Department of Agriculture Handbook No. 380, August 1970, page 46.

37. Legislative Assembly for the Australian Capital Territory, Standing Committee on Social Policy, "Inquiry into water fluoridation in the Act," January 1991, pages 183-84.

38. C. Steelink, <u>op. cit.</u>

39. Lee Foundation for Nutritional Research, <u>The Real American Tragedy</u> (1960), discussed in B. Russell Manning, <u>How Safe Are Silver (Mercury) Fillings?</u> (Calistoga, California: 1983), page 143.

40. W. Price, D.D.S., <u>Nutrition and Physical Degeneration</u> (republished by Keats Publishing, Inc., New Canaan, Connecticut, 1989), pages 302-25.

41. G. Kennedy, D.D.S., How to Save Your Teeth (Delaware, Ohio: Health Action Press, 1993), pages 145, 148.

Chapter 22

1. W. Price, D.D.S., Nutrition and Physical Degeneration (republished by Keats Publishing, Inc., New Canaan, Connecticut, 1989), page 378.
2. J. Phillips, Acquiring and Maintaining Oral Health (Osseo, Wisconsin: PHB, Inc., 1985), page 17.
3. Ibid.
4. W. Price, op. cit., pages 377-78.
5. D. Swartzendruber, "The possible relationship between mercury from dental amalgam and diseases I: Effects within the oral cavity," Medical Hypotheses 41:31-34 (1993).
6. R. Pearson, Fasting and Man's Correct Diet (Mokelumne Hill, California: Health Research, 1921), pages 16-17.
7. P. Airola, N.D., Are You Confused? (Phoenix, Arizona: Health Plus, Publishers, 1971), pages 112-13, 137.
8. B. Jensen, D.C., Tissue Cleansing Through Bowel Management (Escondido, California: Bernard Jensen, D.C., 1981).
9. M. Garten, D.C., The Health Secrets of a Naturopathic Doctor (West Nyack, New York: Parker Publishing Co., Inc., 1967), page 59.

Chapter 23

1. Dr. M. T. Morter Jr., Dynamic Health (Rogers, Arkansas: Best Research, Inc., 1995), page 22.

ALSO BY ELLEN BROWN

The Alternative Pharmacy: Break the Drug Cycle with Safe Natural Treatments for 200 Everyday Ailments, co-authored with Dr. Lynne Walker (Paramus, New Jersey: Prentice Hall, 1998).

Forbidden Medicine: Is Safe, Non-toxic Cancer Treatment Being Suppressed? (Murrieta, California: Third Millennium Press, 1998)

Menopause and Estrogen: Natural Alternatives to Hormone Replacement Therapy (formerly Breezing Through the Change: Managing Menopause Naturally), co-authored with Dr. Lynne Walker (Berkeley, California: Frog, Ltd., 1994, 1996).

The Informed Consumer's Pharmacy co-authored with Dr. Lynne Walker (New York: Carroll&Graf, 1990).

With the Grain: Eat More, Weigh Less, Live Longer (New York: Carroll&Graf, 1990).

To order by mail, telephone 1-800-891-0390

CENTER FOR ADVANCED DENTISTRY
1031 Rosecrans Ave., Suite 104
Fullerton, CA 92833

Richard T. Hansen, D.M.D., F.A.C.A.D.
Director

Alternative Dentistry at its Finest
Providing the Ultimate in Patient Comfort and Care

Dr. Hansen lectures extensively, has helped pioneer many new techniques, and provides ongoing research in advanced dentistry. He was the principle investigator responsible for FDA approval of the Erbium laser for cavity preparation and is the director of the Pacific Institute for Advanced Dental Studies - a training center located in Fullerton, California, dedicated to educating and training dentists, staff and other health professionals on advanced dentistry as it relates to total patient care.

Dear Dr. Hansen, please add my dentist to your mailing list.

Name: _____

Address: _____

State: _____ City: _____ Zip: _____

Phone: _____